Revelation

INTERPRETATION
A Bible Commentary for Teaching and Preaching

INTERPRETATION

A BIBLE COMMENTARY FOR TEACHING AND PREACHING

James Luther Mays, *Editor*
Patrick D. Miller, Jr., *Old Testament Editor*
Paul J. Achtemeier, *New Testament Editor*

M. EUGENE BORING

Revelation

INTERPRETATION

A Bible Commentary
for Teaching and Preaching

John Knox Press
LOUISVILLE

Library of Congress Cataloging-in-Publication Data

Boring, M. Eugene.
   Revelation / M. Eugene Boring.
      p.   cm. — (Interpretation, a Bible commentary for teaching and preaching)
   Bibliography: p.
   ISBN 0-8042-3150-8

   1. Bible. N.T. Revelation—Commentaries. I. Series.
BS2825.3.B574 1989
228'.07—dc19
                              89-1829
                              CIP

© Copyright John Knox Press 1989
10 9 8 7
Printed in the United States of America
John Knox Press
Louisville, Kentucky 40202-1396

SERIES PREFACE

This series of commentaries offers an interpretation of the books of the Bible. It is designed to meet the need of students, teachers, ministers, and priests for a contemporary expository commentary. These volumes will not replace the historical critical commentary or homiletical aids to preaching. The purpose of this series is rather to provide a third kind of resource, a commentary which presents the integrated result of historical and theological work with the biblical text.

An interpretation in the full sense of the term involves a text, an interpreter, and someone for whom the interpretation is made. Here, the text is what stands written in the Bible in its full identity as literature from the time of "the prophets and apostles," the literature which is read to inform, inspire, and guide the life of faith. The interpreters are scholars who seek to create an interpretation which is both faithful to the text and useful to the church. The series is written for those who teach, preach, and study the Bible in the community of faith.

The comment generally takes the form of expository essays. It is planned and written in the light of the needs and questions which arise in the use of the Bible as Holy Scripture. The insights and results of contemporary scholarly research are used for the sake of the exposition. The commentators write as exegetes and theologians. The task which they undertake is both to deal with what the texts say and to discern their meaning for faith and life. The exposition is the unified work of one interpreter.

The text on which the comment is based is the Revised Standard Version of the Bible. The general availability of this translation makes the printing of a translation unnecessary and saves the space for comment. The text is divided into sections appropriate to the particular book; comment deals with passages as a whole, rather than proceeding word by word, or verse by verse.

Writers have planned their volumes in light of the requirements set by the exposition of the book assigned to them. Biblical books differ in character, content, and arrangement. They also differ in the way they have been and are used in the liturgy, thought, and devotion of the church. The distinctiveness and use of particular books have been taken into account in decisions about the approach, emphasis, and use of space in the commentaries. The goal has been to allow writers to develop the format which provides for the best presentation of their interpretation.

The result, writers and editors hope, is a commentary which both explains and applies, an interpretation which deals with both the meaning and the significance of biblical texts. Each commentary reflects, of course, the writer's own approach and perception of the church and world. It could and should not be otherwise. Every interpretation of any kind is individual in that sense; it is one reading of the text. But all who work at the interpretation of Scripture in the church need the help and stimulation of a colleague's reading and understanding of the text. If these volumes serve and encourage interpretation in that way, their preparation and publication will realize their purpose.

The Editors

PREFACE

Revelation was designed to be read aloud and heard all at once, in the context of worship (see on 1:3). This is not optional; the Apocalypse must be grasped as a whole, for it simply cannot be understood verse by verse. It is a narrative, a drama with action and movement that conveys the message of each part within the context of the story in its totality.

Like Revelation, this commentary is written to be read and understood as a single document. Just as one cannot understand Revelation by examining isolated verses, this commentary cannot be used as a reference book in which individual items are "looked up" without reference to the whole. In responsible preaching and teaching from the Bible, there can be no quick homiletical fixes, no Saturday night specials, no raiding of either the Bible or books about it for valuable but loosely attached items that may be converted into a quick profit.

This is the reason for the extensive introduction, and for the lengthy excursuses ("Reflections"). This is why sizable sections of Revelation that deal with similar materials, such as the seven messages of chapters 2—3 and the series of plagues portrayed by the seals, trumpets, and bowls, are dealt with as whole units rather than piecemeal. Sermons and lessons may certainly deal with smaller units, but preaching and teaching from any text in these larger units must be aware of how the unit as a whole is composed and functions theologically.

Revelation is so written that its major themes are interwoven, each appearing numerous times. A commentary cannot discuss each theme each time it appears. Some themes are gathered into "Reflections," others are dealt with extensively the first or major time they appear. Thus the treatment of the earlier chapters requires proportionately more space. Preaching and teaching on other texts in which these themes appear cannot ignore the discussion of the same themes earlier in the commentary.

Inclusive language is an important issue that must neither be treated cavalierly nor be subjected to an ideology. After much soul-searching and discussion with colleagues of varying, mostly opposed, points of view, I have decided in this book to continue my present practice of being as "inclusive" as possible when dealing with human beings, but to retain the traditional biblical language for God, masculine-dominated as it is. I do not believe God is a male (or female) being; I believe that all our language about God is metaphorical. I believe that the language we use can create, express, and reinforce a mind-set that is damaging to persons; I wish in no way to perpetuate the oppression of women, linguistic or otherwise, that is communicated by the tradition of a patriarchal society. It is theologically important to preserve personal language for God. It is important to preserve traditional language for God, particularly in a document such as Revelation which functions by evocatively alluding to the language of the Hebrew Scriptures. These allusions must be recognizable in order to understand what is going on in Revelation. "Child," for instance, often fails to communicate the richness of biblical meaning associated with "son." This is a subject on which I am still working, but have not yet found a way to eliminate the predominantly male orientation of biblical language about God and preserve the meaning of biblical texts, and this is the chief business of a commentary—as it is of preaching and teaching from the Bible.

I complete this book with gratitude to the colleagues and students at the Graduate Seminary of Phillips University and at Texas Christian University with whom I have studied Revelation in numerous classes during the last twenty years. In particular, I am grateful to my colleagues Ronald B. Flowers of the Department of Religion-Studies and Joseph R. Jeter Jr. of Brite Divinity School for their careful reading of and responses to previous drafts of this book, to Editors of this series Paul J. Achtemeier and James Luther Mays for their encouragement and help along the way, as well as for finally accepting a manuscript considerably longer than they anticipated, and to Edward J. McMahon and Lana N. Byrd, whose competent and cheerful assistance in completing this project has been far beyond the line of duty. The volume is dedicated to Fred B. Craddock, W. Clark Gilpin, Leo G. Perdue, and Kenneth T. Lawrence, colleagues whose comradeship, personal and professional, has embodied that rare combination of wisdom expressed in Proverbs 18:24 and 27:17.

M. Eugene Boring

CONTENTS

INTERPRETATION

Abbreviations used in citations

Apoc. Abram.	Apocalypse of Abraham
Apoc. Bar.	Apocalypse of Baruch
Apoc. Elijah	Apocalypse of Elijah
As. Mos.	Ascension of Moses
Baba B.	Baba Batra, Talmud
Bar.	Baruch
Ber.	Berakot
Esdr.	Esdras
Gos. Bart.	Gospel of Bartemaeus
JB	Jerusalem Bible
Jub.	Jubilees
KJV	King James Version
LXX	Septuagint
Mart. Isa.	Martyrdom of Isaiah
NEB	New English Bible
Ps. Sol.	Psalms of Solomon
RSV	Revised Standard Version
Sanh.	Sanhedrin
Sib. Or.	Sibylline Oracles
Sir.	Sirach
T. Sanh.	Babylonian Talmud, Sanhedrin
Test. Asher	Testament of Asher
Test. Benj.	Testament of Benjamin
Test. Dan.	Testament of Daniel
Test. Gad	Testament of Gad
Test. Jos.	Testament of Joseph
Test. Judah	Testament of Judah
Test. Levi	Testament of Levi
Test. Mos.	Testament of Moses
Test. Reub.	Testament of Reuben
Test. Sim.	Testament of Simeon
Test. Sol.	Testament of Solomon
TEV	Today's English Version
Tob.	Tobit
Wis. Sol.	Wisdom of Solomon
1QM	War Scroll
1QH	Hymns of Thanksgiving
4QpIs	4Q Isaiah Pesher

To
Fred
Clark
Leo
Ken

Introduction

How can thinking Christians who want to live faithfully and responsibly in our contemporary world hear the word of God in Revelation? The basic information one needs in order to read the Apocalypse with insight and appreciation can be concentrated into two simple sentences which represent the thesis of this commentary:

1. *The last "book" of the Bible is a pastoral letter to Christians in Asia in the late first century who were confronted with a critical religiopolitical situation, from a Christian prophet who wrote in apocalyptic language and imagery.*

2. *Like the Bible in general, there is some difficulty in understanding Revelation, but it can and should be understood, for it has had enormous influence in religion, history, and culture and has an urgently needed message for the contemporary church.*

These two sentences contain ten theses on understanding Revelation which we may now explore one at a time.

The Last "Book" of the Bible

Although the Bible is a "library" of "books" with a variety of theologies, the Bible as a whole is also and primarily one book with one story. In a helpful oversimplification, it can be seen as a narrative drama in five acts, with God as author, producer, director, and main character:

1. **Creation** (Genesis): God created all that is.

2. **Covenant** (Exodus—Malachi): When creation was spoiled by rebellious humanity, God created a people, Israel, to be his agents and witnesses and bearers of the promise of God's salvation to come.

3. **Christ** (Matthew—John): God came himself, in the person

1

of his Son the Messiah, to accomplish salvation and mediate reconciliation.

4. Church (Acts—Jude): God has continued Israel's mission in the church by creating an inclusive community from all nations to be witnesses and agents of his saving act already accomplished for all people.

5. Consummation (Revelation): God will bring history to a worthy conclusion when the creation which *de jure* belongs to God's kingdom will *de facto* "become the kingdom of our Lord and of his Christ, and he shall reign for ever and ever" (11:15).

In vivid, sometimes grotesque pictures of the future establishment of God's just rule throughout the creation, including scenes of the last battle and the last judgment, the "book" of Revelation portrays the triumphant finale of this drama, and thus was appropriately placed by the church at the end of the canon as the last "book" of the Bible.

The inclusion of Revelation in the Christian Bible did not happen without a struggle. From the moment of its composition, Revelation has been a controversial writing. We should not suppose that everyone in the seven churches to which it was originally addressed accepted it as authentic Christian teaching, for these churches contained rival prophets and teachers who opposed John and his message (2:2, 6, 14–15, 20–23). The letter was, however, accepted by many Christians and within a few decades had achieved such a wide circulation that it was cited as authoritative Christian teaching by bishops and other Christian leaders, not only in its native Asia (Melito, Bishop of Sardis, 160–190, who wrote a commentary on it) but in Egypt (Clement of Alexandria, d. 215), North Africa (Tertullian, d. 220), Rome (Muratorian Canon), and South Gaul (Irenaeus, 177–202).

Yet questions and disputes arose. A second-century Christian leader named Montanus caused much excitement by teaching that the church had entered into the final age of the Spirit, and predicted that the End was near and the new Jerusalem would descend at the nearby town of Pepuza, in what is now Turkey. Since he and the sect that followed him drew support from Revelation for their views, Revelation fell into disrepute among "mainline" Christians—not the last time in church history that Revelation would be rejected because of its misuse by its false friends. The "Alogi," an anti-Montanist group, refused to use Revelation on the basis that it contained errors in fact and had not been written by an apostle. Gaius, an influential presbyter of the Roman church, wrote (ca. 210) a manifesto declaring that Revelation had been written by the gnostic heretic Cerinthus. About 250 the Bishop of Alexandria, Dionysius, made a careful study of the language and grammar of Revelation and concluded that it could not have been written by the same author as the Gospel of John and that it was therefore not apostolic. His conclusion provided helpful support for those Alexandrian Christians who wanted to oppose the use of Revelation in the churches, on the basis that its literal interpretation, especially of the "millennium," was a distortion of the spiritual nature of Christianity. Thus as late as the fourth century, when Eusebius (d. 340) classified the Christian literature purported to be Scripture into "accepted," "rejected," and "disputed," Revelation was still classified as "disputed." Cyril of Jerusalem (315–386) was even more negative, omitting it from the list of canonical books and forbidding its use publicly or privately.

Even after its official acceptance into the canon, many Christians have been hesitant to regard Revelation as a part of *their* Bible. Although Martin Luther included Revelation in his Bible, he denied it functional canonical status because, in his view, it was not theologically adequate. The Swiss reformer Ulrich Zwingli likewise refused to base Christian teaching on Revelation, pronouncing it "no biblical book." John Calvin passed over it in silence in his biblical exposition, writing commentaries on twenty-*six* New Testament books. Rudolf Bultmann is only one example of those modern theologians who, even though they regard the New Testament as the normative witness to the meaning of the gospel for the church's faith and life, relegate Revelation to the margin. To this day, Catholic and Protestant lectionaries have only minimal readings from Revelation, and the Greek Orthodox lectionary omits it altogether. On the other hand, Christian thinkers from Irenaeus and Augustine in the early centuries through Walter Rauschenbusch and Paul Minear in America and Bishops Hans Lilje and Eduard Lohse in Germany are among those who have found Revelation to measure up to its canonical role of providing direction and sustenance for the church's life and mission, especially in extraordinary times.

INTERPRETATION

This brief historical sketch documents two aspects of Revelation that are still very much with us and call for immediate attention.

1. Revelation was one of the relatively few documents from among the vast literary output of early Christianity that survived the canonical process and became Holy Scripture for the Christian community. This slow and deliberate process, from the point of view of faith, was a process in which the Spirit of God was effectively at work. This process placed Revelation among the small list of documents through which the Christian community expects to hear the word of God, and to which it listens for authentic Christian declarations of the meaning of salvation through Jesus Christ, for teaching on how to live according to the will of God, and for assurances regarding the fate of the earth and of ourselves.

2. Many Christians have, from the earliest days, been uncomfortable with this decision, or have simply rejected it in practice. These hesitations have not been based on petty or superficial objections; they represent serious and deep questioning as to whether Revelation can function in the church as a Christian book. The reservations of some have been based on the real dangers that have emerged when Revelation has been interpreted in foolish, sub-Christian or anti-Christian ways. Although every biblical book is subject to misinterpretation, no other part of the Bible has provided such a happy hunting ground for all sorts of bizarre and dangerous interpretations. Some people in practically every generation from John's own to the present have understood Revelation to be predicting the last days of the world in their own time.

Yet it is not only how the book has been understood that has raised reservations about its acceptance and use as a Christian book. The thoughtful reader of the book also finds things that are difficult to integrate into faith in and discipleship to the Man for Others who taught and lived love, forgiveness, and reconciliation. In Revelation the evil city Babylon receives not forgiveness but double for all her sins (18:6). Martyrs cry out for vengeance (6:10). Those who receive the mark of the beast "shall be tormented with fire and sulphur in the presence of the holy angels and in the presence of the Lamb" (14:10). This is in contrast to Jesus' own response to his persecutors (Luke 23:34), and to that of his followers (e.g., Acts 7:60). In Revelation violent scene after violent scene is perpetrated by God, the heavenly armies, and by Christ himself—not only against their enemies but against the cosmos (6:1–8; 8:7—9:21; 16:1–20). In contrast, the Jesus of the Gospels teaches people to turn the other cheek, to love their enemies, and to pray for their persecutors (Matt. 5:38–39, 44); and he embodied this teaching in his own life and death. In Revelation salvation sometimes seems to be on the basis of one's own deeds rather than on the grace of God (the word "grace" does not occur in Revelation except in letter formulae).

These objections are real. Should not a book that is beset within and without with such dangers simply be left alone? No, it should not. Other reasons will be given below, but here it is sufficient to call attention to the fact of the canonical status of Revelation. Part of what it means to have a canon is that the Bible is not treated as a cafeteria from which we choose what appeals to our individualistic tastes; we accept it as a whole as the collective wisdom of the Spirit-guided community of faith.

A Pastoral Letter

We study Revelation because it is in our Bible. However, John did not write it as the "last book of the Bible"; it was a letter to Christians he knew and for whom he felt a pastoral responsibility. However, by "letter" we do not mean a private communication. The letter was not intended for private, silent reading but was written to be read aloud in the worship services of the churches of Asia (1:3). We should not picture the original readers as poring over the pages of the document in silent, individualistic contemplation or puzzlement but gathered in the community of praise and prayer, hearing the letter read forth by the worship leader. The imagery of Revelation, which sometimes seems bizarre to modern readers, is mostly taken from the tradition of images familiar to those who were accustomed to hearing the Bible read in the worship services of the ongoing People of God. In order to capture something of the original experience of the readers (who are more properly called "hearer-readers"), a contemporary congregation, class, or study group might be well advised to gather in a church sanctuary or other worship setting, sing a hymn of praise, join in prayer, and then listen to the Revelation as it is read forth in its entirety by a good reader. (It is not too long for this; it was written for precisely such a hearing!) Much that is contained in the Apocalypse is best perceived by the ear and the imagination, as the

5

visions of Revelation unfold in the mind's eye. Those who remember the great days of radio drama will immediately appreciate this, and others of our eye-oriented age dominated by television may be pleasantly surprised at the richness of their latent aural-imaginative perception.

Those who accepted the prophetic authority of John would have considered the message of the letter as something to be taken seriously, but they did not yet hear it as "the last book of the Bible." They did not hear it as a "book" at all. (The Greek word translated "book" in 22:18 is *biblion,* which means simply "document"; we have specific instances of its use as a synonym for "letter.") Although I have followed the convention of referring to Revelation as a "book," this is generically a misleading designation, not only for Revelation but for all the real letters of the New Testament. Revelation is a "book" only in the same sense that the *Letter* to the Romans is a "book" of the Bible. Recognizing the correct genre of a document is vital for understanding it, so it is important to make a clear distinction between a book and a letter. The author of a book writes for a general readership, a "public," which he or she does not know personally. A book is thus a public document. In a book the author is a particular person, but the readership is vague and unknown to the author and the other readers. A book may be addressed to a particular reading public, such as football fans or medical students, but it is not addressed to particular persons. The distinctive thing about the real letter as a communication form is that, in contrast to a book, both the author and the readers are particular persons. A real letter presupposes the particular features of the situation of the readers and addresses them specifically.

Why did the prophet John choose the letter form, so atypical for prophets, as the medium for communicating his message? John stands in the tradition of the Pauline churches and is influenced by the Pauline letter form and its use in worship. John expects his letter to be read forth to the assembled congregations (1:3), after which the worshipers will celebrate the Eucharist. There is thus a very specific connotation to the imagery of the messianic banquet throughout the book (cf. e.g., 3:20; 19:9). The concluding lines (22:6–21) form something of a transition to the eucharistic celebration, as does the conclusion of some of Paul's letters (cf. I Cor. 16:21). John is affected by this traditional use of the letter form in the churches of Asia, but he chooses the letter form not so much in imitation of Paul as for the same reason as Paul: He has something important to say which he cannot say personally to the congregations because he is absent. As in the case of Paul, the letter is a substitute for the personal presence of the prophet. His voice is made present and real even though he is absent.

The fact that Revelation is a letter has important consequences for understanding it. It is the nature of a letter to have a particular address. As a letter, Revelation was not written to the public at large. It was not even a general circular letter, addressing typical situations in first-century Christianity; it was written to specific Christians in a specific place, time, and situation. And it was *not* written to *us*. Just as the first letter of Paul to the Corinthians was not written to us, so the letter of John to the seven churches of Asia was not written to us. Just as we will certainly misunderstand Paul if we ignore the particularities of the situation in first-century Corinth, so we will misunderstand Revelation if we read it as though it were written directly to us. If we want to understand Revelation, the first principle is to read it in terms of its original hearer-readers and their situation.

The original hearer-readers needed no explanation of the situation, since they experienced it directly. Indeed, explaining the obvious to the original hearer-readers would have robbed the letter of its power. Later readers will have to be informed of the situation in order to understand it. Passing along the historical tradition that allows later generations to understand its canonical documents is part of the task of the ongoing Christian community, the church.

As a letter, Revelation is not a collection of "ideas" or "general principles" but a particular message to a particular situation. There is something of basic theological importance here. The historical particularity of the message of Revelation, like that of the Bible in general, corresponds to the fundamental Christian affirmation of the incarnation. The gospel's basic declaration is not that God is revealed in general, not even in humanity in general, but that he has definitively revealed himself in Jesus: a particular Aramaic-speaking Jew who conducted his ministry in a particular time and place and died on a particular Roman cross. In the incarnation the Absolute is made manifest in the relative, the Word was made flesh (John 1:14). In the biblical documents the word of God is still mediated to us

7

through the relativities of history—through the stories and laws of a particular people, through the stories and sayings of a particular Man, through the letters of particular Christian leaders to specific Christians living in particular historical situations. In the canonizing process by which the church selected from the variety of early Christian writings those documents that bore authentic witness to the meaning of the Christ event, only those literary genres were included that were appropriate vehicles of a time-bound, historically conditioned revelation, namely gospels and epistles. It is no accident that our New Testament canon is composed of Gospels (including Acts as the second volume of a Gospel), which contain the continuing voice of Jesus within the historical form of a narrative, and letters, which mediate the church's message about God's act in Jesus within the historical particularity of a letter. In biblical interpretation, teaching and preaching through which the word of the Bible becomes contemporary, all interpretations share in the hypothetical, relative, "iffiness" of historical study and the word of God still comes through the relativity of finite historical judgments. The relative and inconclusive nature of historical biblical study, in which there is never absolute certainty, is no liability. To long for the Absolute, uncontaminated by the finitude of historical existence, is to disregard the incarnation and to make the Bible into something it is not. This "scandal of particularity" of a God who acts in history is part of the scandal of the cross itself (I Cor. 1:23; Gal. 5:11) and is inherent in the Christian faith.

Bible interpretation must be historically oriented, because the Bible is oriented to the mighty acts of God in history. This means that the task of understanding Revelation includes attempting to understand something about the historical situation of those to whom it was originally addressed. What was that historical situation?

Written to First-century Christians in Asia in Crisis

"Asia" is the name of the Roman province located on the western coast of what is now Turkey. Christian churches had been established there by Paul and his co-workers during the fifties of the first century, with the result that a tradition of Pauline Christianity extended into John's own time in the nineties. Ephesus (Rev. 1:11; 2:1–7) had been a center of Paul's own work (cf. Acts 19). The letter form continued to be used by Paul's disciples. Ephesians is addressed to the leading church in the area; Colossians mentions the church at Laodicea (Col. 4:16; cf. Rev. 1:11; 3:14–22). All of this shows that Pauline Christianity, interpreted in various ways, continued to be an important influence in the churches of Asia.

In the period after the catastrophic war in Palestine between the Romans and the Jewish rebels (or freedom fighters, depending on one's perspective) in 66–70, there was a large influx of Jewish and Jewish-Christian immigrants and refugees into Asia, where there had already been an established Jewish community for generations. Partly as a result of this conflict, Judaism was undergoing a clarification of its own identity and a restructuring of its institutions. Previously, Jewish Christians had often understood themselves, and had been understood by both the secular and religious authorities, as members of the Jewish community. After 70, the restructuring of Judaism led to conflicting claims about who was really a Jew. Christians in Asia were sometimes caught in these conflicts, which are reflected in Revelation.

During this period increasing social and political pressures were brought to bear by government policies and there were tensions between the Christian community and other social groups, particularly the Jews, as well as tensions and conflicts within the church itself. The church was in a transitional and vulnerable situation, trying to find its way forward in the generation between the death of its apostolic leaders and the emergence of a firm structure and sense of self-identity. What did it mean to be Christian, to try to follow Jesus as Lord, in such a place and time? Revelation addresses this implicit question of all John's hearer-readers. An appreciation of both the readers' question and John's response will be enhanced by a more careful look at the times when the letter was written.

Since a letter is a historically conditioned form, knowing the date of a letter is important to the process of understanding it. Ancient letters identified their writers and addressees, but not their dates, as a glance at the opening words of Paul's letters and the letters contained in Acts will make clear (Acts 15:23; 23:26). This is another instance of the historical particularity of the letter form. Like all writers of real letters, John could presuppose that the readers to whom he directed his letter would know when it was written—their own time—and the situation it presupposed—their own situation. Later readers of a letter,

9

however, need to know its date as precisely as possible if they are to understand it correctly.

Our earliest tradition dates Revelation "near the end of Domitian's reign" (Irenaeus, *Against Heresies* V.30.3). The emperor Domitian reigned from 81 to 96, so Irenaeus' comment places Revelation in 95 or 96. Since such traditions are not always accurate, however, modern scholars have argued for a variety of other dates from as early as the time of Claudius (41–54) to as late as the reign of Trajan (98–117). Most scholars have decided for the time of either Nero (54–68) or Domitian (81–96), with the great majority opting for the latter. Jewish and Christian literature written after the 66–70 war used "Babylon" as a transparent symbol for Rome, since Rome had besieged and destroyed Jerusalem just as the Babylonians had done centuries before (II Kings 25; cf. II Esdras 3:1–2, 28–31; II Apoc. Bar. 10:1–3; 11:1, 67:7; Sib. Or. 5:143, 159; I Peter 5:13). Revelation likewise uses "Babylon" as a transparent symbol for Rome (14:8; chaps. 17—18, cf. esp. 17:18). This practice did not become common until after the destruction of the city and would not have been appropriate before. It is thus among the strongest items of evidence for dating Revelation some time after 70. The commentary will indicate that the internal evidence of the book seems to fit best the time advocated by the earliest external tradition, the reign of Domitian. Revelation is thus best understood as a letter written in 96 by John, a Christian prophet, to churches in Asia that he expected would be facing a terrible persecution.

The people to whom John wrote had lived through tumultuous times, and many of them perceived their own time as being fraught with crisis. The empire was troubled with wars. Roman troops had actually suffered a traumatic defeat on the eastern boundary of the empire by the Parthians (62). Major wars had been fought against rebellions in Gaul (68), Germania (69), and Judea (66–70). The tyranny and death of Nero in 68 had not been followed by stability but by further wars and by three "emperors" in two years. Famines in the early nineties had taken their toll. The earth itself seemed unstable. Earthquakes devastated Asia in the sixties. In 79, Vesuvius erupted, burying Pompeii and neighboring towns and creating a widespread cloud of darkness, which caused foreboding and consternation throughout the empire. While the pagan population sought to come to terms with such disasters through philosophy, religion, and superstition, Christians wondered what it meant in such a cataclysmic world to claim that God was sovereign and that Jesus was his anointed king.

Christians in Asia at the end of the first century had problems to face which the population at large did not. They were considered to be adherents of a sect that primarily appealed to the lower classes, a sect that had no long history or glorious institutions, a suspect group which met for its cultic practices in private homes on a day which was not a public holiday, a sect that was widely suspect of being unpatriotic, a group about which wild stories were told. After all, did they not speak of eating flesh and drinking blood (cannibalism!); did they not meet for private "love feasts" (incest! orgies!); had not their leader been crucified by the government as a rebel and enemy of the public welfare (unpatriotic!)? In the first few generations Christianity won its converts mainly, though not exclusively, from the lower economic classes, including slaves (see e.g., I Cor. 1:26). Although the nineties was a time of general prosperity in Asia, the poor did not share in it. So their perceived poverty was even greater by virtue of the wealth that surrounded them, and this contributed to their feeling of social deprivation. Even Christians who were of a social status that permitted them to participate in the social and political life of the Roman Empire were often hesitant to do so, because of the association of such participation with the Roman gods. Christians were thus considered to be unpatriotic and irreligious, sometimes being called "atheists" because they had no "gods." Thus, they were likely candidates to become scapegoats for disasters, such as the fire which destroyed much of Rome in 64. Nero could accuse Christians of arson and arrest and kill many of them without public outcry only because the public already considered them to be outsiders within the social structure and because the Christians thus tended to look upon themselves as outsiders.

Christians in John's time and place were thus often subject to social and economic discrimination, to more or less constant tensions and harassment (resulting from trying to be Christians in a pagan culture), and sometimes subject to the kind of unofficial mob violence and plundering of property described in Hebrews 10:34; 12:4; I Peter 4:14, 16; 5:9. Such an outsider position in a society is difficult to endure without a strong sense of group and personal identity. And here too John's readers were beset with something of an identity crisis. The pressures of their situation forced the question on them: "Who are we?"

Christians and Jews

Since Revelation makes statements that have later been understood as anti-Semitic (2:9; 3:9), it is important to explore the relations between Jews and Christians in the context of the seven churches addressed in Revelation. Jews also did not fit into the pagan culture and were often maligned and discriminated against by their gentile neighbors. In Asia in the nineties, however, the Jewish community had the advantages of a long and admirable history. They enjoyed a close-knit community with established and respected institutions, with a sense of community self-identity. They had already shed their martyrs' blood as a testimony to the reality of their faith. Despite the dislike and suspicion with which they still had to deal in their pagan environment, they were known as an old and stable element in the empire and in its local communities. After the fire in Rome in 64, Nero did not succeed in his attempt to convince the public that the Jews were responsible. (He blamed it on the Christians only after his first effort against the Jews failed.) The Roman government officially excused Jews from some responsibilities that violated their religious faith, such as serving in the army and participating in the worship of Roman gods. The Jews had worked out an agreement which convinced the Romans of their loyalty to the empire, an agreement which included the obligation of Jews to pray *for* the emperor but not *to* him. It was in fact the cessation of sacrifices for the emperor in the Jerusalem temple in 66 that signaled the beginning of the Jewish revolt.

How did Christians fit into Judaism, from the Jewish, from the Roman, and from their own perspective? At first, of course, all Christians were Jews, as was Jesus, and rightly were seen by the Romans and themselves as a variety of Judaism. As such, they were entitled to the protection from Roman demands to which all Jews were entitled. John himself was a Jewish Christian (see below), and it is likely that significant elements in his congregations were themselves of Jewish background, especially since many Jews and Jewish Christians had immigrated to Asia in the wake of the disastrous war in Palestine in 66–70. John considers the name "Jew" to be a worthy name for the true People of God—and is thus to be denied to the Jews in the

12

synagogue who have rejected Jesus as the Messiah. Yet this fundamental difference in faith is not the only reason for the evident hostility that exists between Jews and Christians in Asia, a hostility so deep from John's side that he can call the Jews of Smyrna and Philadelphia "synagogues of Satan" (2:9; 3:9). By John's time Christianity was already predominantly a gentile religion, even though Christians still understood themselves to be the true "Israel of God" (Gal. 6:16; Phil: 3:3; I Peter 1:1, 17; see the commentary on 1:5 and chaps. 7 and 12), since Abraham was the father of all who believed (Rom. 4:16–17). This, of course, was a perspective not shared by the Jews themselves. Jewish leaders would thus be inclined to dispute the identification and clarify the situation with the Roman authorities, in order to preserve the synagogue from the troubles with the government in which the Christians were involved. Further, after the crisis of 70, Judaism itself underwent a kind of restructuring and purging in which elements considered to be extraneous or heretical were excluded. This meant that at the very time when Christians might want to be included in the protection offered by the synagogue, they found that they were no longer considered Jews by their Jewish neighbors. Rejected by Jew and Gentile alike, Christians faced a serious crisis of community and personal identity, and John's letter addresses this crisis among others. "Who are the People of God?" and "What is the meaning of belonging to the church?" were not abstract theological questions but burning personal issues for John's readers, questions which helped shape the agenda of John's prophetic response.

A Religiopolitical Crisis

Except for Revelation itself, we unfortunately have nothing from Asia during Domitian's reign which might throw light on the relations between Christians and the Roman government. The nearest such documentation we have is the following interchange of official letters between Pliny, the governor of Bithynia (the province just north of Asia) and the Emperor Trajan. The letters were written about 112, within twenty years of the writing of Revelation, and constitute the earliest pagan evidence we have about the attitude of the Roman government to Christians. Since these letters offer such valuable insight into the letter of Revelation, they are printed here in their entirety.

13

INTERPRETATION

I have made it a rule, Lord [Latin *domine,* equivalent of Greek *kurios,* used by Christians only of God and Jesus as Lord, but claimed as a title by the emperors and especially important to Domitian in John's time], to refer everything to you about which I am in doubt. For who could better provide direction for my hesitations or instruction for my lack of knowledge?

I have never been present at the interrogation of Christians. Therefore, I do not know how far such investigations should be pushed, and what sort of punishments are appropriate. I have also been uncertain as to whether age makes any difference, or whether the very young are dealt with in the same way as adults, whether repentance [Latin *paenitentiae*] and renunciation of Christianity is sufficient, or whether the accused are still considered criminals because they were once Christians even if they later renounced it, and whether persons are to be punished simply for the name "Christian" even if no criminal act has been committed, or whether only crimes associated with the name are to be punished.

In the meantime, I have handled those who have been denounced to me as Christians as follows: I asked them whether they were Christians. Those who responded affirmatively I have asked a second and third time, under threat of the death penalty. If they persisted [Latin *perseverantes,* related to "endurance," Greek *hypomone,* the central virtue for Christians in Revelation] in their confession, I had them executed. For whatever it is that they are actually advocating, it seems to me that obstinacy and stubbornness must be punished in any case. Others who labor under the same delusion, but who were Roman citizens, I have designated to be sent to Rome.

In the course of the investigations, as it usually happens, charges are brought against wider circles of people, and the following special cases have emerged:

An unsigned placard was posted, accusing a large number of people by name. Those who denied being Christians now or in the past, I thought necessary to release, since they invoked our gods according to the formula I gave them and since they offered sacrifices of wine and incense before your image which I had brought in for this purpose along with the statues of our gods. I also had them curse Christ. It is said that real Christians cannot be forced to do any of these things.

Others charged by this accusation at first admitted that they had once been Christians, but had already renounced it; they had in fact been Christians, but had given it up, some of them three years ago, some even earlier, some as long as twenty-five years ago [Note that this would be in the time of Domitian]. All of these worshipped your image and the statues of the gods, and cursed Christ. They verified, however, that their entire guilt or error consisted in the fact that on a specified day before sunrise they were accustomed to gather and sing an antiphonal hymn to Christ as their god and to pledge themselves by an oath not to engage in any crime, but to abstain from all thievery, assault, and adultery, not to

14

break their word once they had given it, and not to refuse to pay their legal debts. They then went their separate ways, and came together later to eat a common meal, but it was ordinary, harmless food. They discontinued even this practice in accordance with my edict by which I had forbidden political associations, in accord with your instructions. I considered it all the more necessary to obtain by torture a confession of the truth from two female slaves, whom they called "deaconesses." I found nothing more than a vulgar, excessive superstition.

I thus adjourned further hearings, in order to seek counsel from you. The matter seems to me in need of good counsel, especially in view of the large number of accused. For many of every age and class, of both sexes, are in danger of prosecution both now and in the future. The plague of this superstition has spread not only in the cities, but through villages and the countryside. But I believe a stop can be made and a remedy provided. In any case it is now quite clear that the temples, almost deserted previously, are gradually gaining more and more visitors, the long neglected sacred festivals are again regularly observed, and the sacrificial meat, for which buyers have been hard to find, is again being purchased. From this one can easily see what an improvement can be made in the masses, when one gives room for repentance.

The Emperor's Response:

My Secundus! You have chosen the right way with regard to the cases of those who have been accused before you as Christians. Nothing exists that can be considered a universal norm for such cases. Christians should not be sought out. But if they are accused and handed over, they are to be punished, but only if they do not deny being Christians and demonstrate it by the appropriate act, i.e., the worship of our gods. Even if one is suspect because of past conduct, he or she is to be acquitted in view of repentance *(paenitentia).*

Anonymous accusations may not be considered in any trial, for that would be a dangerous precedent, and does not fit our times.
(Pliny the Younger, *Letters* X.96–97 translation by MEB)

Here is no full-scale persecution of Christians by the state, but there is much more than neighborhood resentment against the sect of Christians. These letters deal with official government responses to the Christian community, and portray the whole range of Christian response from renunciation of the faith to martyrdom.

In John's time Rome had not singled out Christians for oppression and persecution. Christianity was included among those cults, sects, and movements which seemed damaging to the public welfare for which the Romans were responsible. Roman leaders and the Roman public generally believed that the safety and welfare of their states depended on the proper observance of the civic gods. If the official religion was respected, local residents could also worship whatever other local gods they chose and participate in as many local cults as they desired, so long as such participation did not constitute a threat to public order and decency. This was a rather tolerant policy, with which only the exclusive monotheism of Jews and Christians had problems. Jewish and Christian faith in the one God made any acknowledgment of the Roman gods impossible for them. As we have seen, the Jews had worked out a satisfactory arrangement with the government; and so long as Christianity could be regarded as a variety of Judaism, Christians managed to stay on officially good terms with the government, except for sporadic attacks against them, as in Nero's time. (And even then, arson was the crime of which they were accused, not their religion as such.) But as Christianity grew and it became apparent that it was not just a sect of the Jewish religion, collisions with the Roman authorities were sure to occur, especially as they were encouraged by the unpopularity of Christians for the reasons given above. Christianity as such was finally declared illegal, and later emperors made a systematic, concerted effort to root it out.

Precisely what sort of opposition between the empire and the Christians is the historical context for understanding Revelation? Already in early Christianity it was believed that there was a widespread and official persecution of Christians by the Roman government in John's day (e.g., by Tertullian [*Apology* 5] in the second century and by Eusebius in the fourth [*Ecclesiastical History* III.17–20]), and that Revelation was written to strengthen and console Christians who were enduring such persecution for their faith. It was supposed that the government had actively forced Christians to engage in the official worship of the Roman gods, including the emperor, or face capital punishment and that every Christian had to renounce the faith or become a martyr.

There is considerable evidence in Revelation itself that John believed the Roman Empire was about to engage in such a systematic persecution of all Christians. Three of the seven churches to which John writes already have had a time of persecution: Ephesus (2:2–3), Pergamum (2:13), and Philadelphia (3:8–10). In 2:10 John indicates that the church in Smyrna is about to suffer and some will be cast into prison, and 3:10 de-

16

clares that this "hour of trial is coming on the whole world." The vision of 6:9 portrays the souls of (presumably Christian) martyrs under the heavenly altar, and 6:11 indicates that yet more martyrdoms are to occur. In 7:14 there are great multitudes in heaven who had come out of the great tribulation (via martyrdom). Such scenes portray John and his churches already living in the dawn of the final tribulation. Chapters 12 and 13 are transparently a picture of the imperial persecuting power to which all Christians must yield or die, and 17:6 pictures Rome drunk with the blood of the martyrs.

Nevertheless there are problems with this traditional view. Recent research has made it increasingly clear that there was no universal, systematic persecution of Christians in Domitian's time. The situation pictured in Pliny's letter, above, is not that of Rome actively engaged in a persecution but of a local official trying to decide what to do when Christians are accused before the local court. Christians may occasionally be brought before Roman governors and be condemned because of their Christian faith, but Rome is not yet taking the initiative. There is no evidence for widespread martyrdom in John's time. Approximately sixty years later, when Bishop Polycarp of Smyrna was burned alive, he was the twelfth in the combined list of martyrs for Smyrna and Philadelphia (Eusebius, *Ecclesiastical History* IV.15). John names only one martyr in the churches to which he writes, Antipas of Pergamum (2:13), and of course John himself has not been martyred, though he has encountered difficulties with the authorities and has been banned to the island of Patmos (see on 1:9 below).

John has already seen the beginnings of conflict between the church and the state, a conflict that was intensifying in Domitian's time, so he writes his pastoral letter in the glow of the expected persecution; but he has seen only the first stages of what he supposes will be a universal persecution. Though the kind of sporadic arrests that had resulted in his own banishment and Antipas' death made life precarious for any Christian in John's area, the systematic persecution he thought was about to break over the church never happened during his lifetime or the lifetime of his readers, probably because of Domitian's death and the relaxation of the demand for emperor worship.

None of this is to minimize the seriousness of the crisis which John and his fellow Christians did in fact face. Pliny's letter pictures the kind of event which we may well suppose

17

was already happening in John's time: A Christian or group of Christians is accused, from whatever motives, of engaging in illegal cultic practices and is brought before the Roman magistrate. Neither accuser nor judge understands very much about Christianity. The Christian(s) are told they must prove their loyalty by offering wine and incense before the images of the Roman gods, including the image of Caesar. According to a tradition which probably represents the actual situation, they were required to make the two-word acknowledgment of Roman sovereignty, *"Kurios Kaisaros"* ("Caesar is Lord"), an exact counterpart to the basic Christian confession "Jesus is Lord" (cf. Rom. 10:9; I Cor. 12:3). In addition, they were required to curse Christ. We have documentation that those in later periods who complied were given a certificate exempting them from persecution. Although we have no specific evidence, it is likely that even in John's day those who complied were given some kind of certification (cf. the discussion of 13:18 below). Those who did not comply could be tortured or executed.

Both Revelation and our external evidence reveals the vulnerability and helplessness of Christians in such a situation. Most were not citizens of the empire, who were treated with more respect in the courts (cf. the case of Paul, whom Luke, a contemporary of John, pictures as a Roman citizen [Acts 21: 27—28:31], and the different treatment of Roman citizens mentioned in Pliny's letter above). Christians had no defense against the arbitrary power of the Roman government officials who understood little about Christianity, even when they attempted to be decent and fair.

Christians and the Emperor Cult

For many Christians, including John, the Roman ideological threat was intensified because of its focus on the person of the emperor, who seemed to be a rival of Christ as Lord. Understanding some features of the emperor cult is very important for understanding Revelation as a whole.

In John's time the Emperor Domitian decreed that all government proclamations must begin "Our Lord and God Domitian commands. . . ." It was reported that he had many people executed for "atheism," failure to worship the gods of Rome, of whom he was one (Dio Cassius, *Roman History* 67.14). This was not simply an expression of egomania on his part. The emperor cult itself has a complex history. Domitian did not just suddenly decide that he wanted to be worshiped as a god.

The idea that the king was divine was not a native Roman idea; in fact it was quite alien in the West, and only gradually gained ground during the New Testament period. It had been a common idea in the East for centuries, however. In ancient Egypt the Pharaoh was considered divine by nature. In Babylon the ruler was regarded as divine by virtue of being the deity's son. Israelites came into contact with this idea in Canaan, but never accepted their neighbors' idea that rulers were actually divine; in Israel kings were only "adopted" as sons of God (Pss. 2:7; 89:26–27; II Sam. 7:14).

When Alexander the Great conquered the East, with his vision of "one world" under the domination of Greek government and culture (333–23 B.C.E.), he was pleasantly surprised to be hailed as a god. With the dissolution of the smaller city-states, the people needed a religion big enough to embrace the vastness of their newly discovered world. Historians of Greek religion speak of a "failure of nerve" during this period which helped to generate a longing for a universal religion. Worship of the universal ruler and unifier of the world seemed to many to be the answer. As the local gods appeared to be less and less capable of providing assurance in the vast new world, the emperor became the symbol of the all-embracing god. Few drew a distinction between what the emperor symbolized and the person of the emperor himself. Alexander found the worship of the emperor a helpful political tool by which to shift the loyalty of his subjects to his larger empire.

At Alexander's death, his successors in the East continued to accept, even to promote, the idea of their own divinity. The claims of Antiochus Epiphanes IV to divinity (the name itself means [god] "manifest") are reflected in Daniel 8:9–11, 25; 11: 36. When world empire passed from Greece to Rome the idea of the deified ruler already had a long history. The concept continued to be foreign in the West, but the provinces of the eastern part of the empire vied with one another for permission to build temples to the divine Caesar. Augustus (Octavian, 27– 14) tolerated emperor worship in that he allowed Roman citizens to worship his dead predecessor, the deified Julius Caesar, and even granted permission for non-citizens in the East to worship himself during his lifetime. Of Revelation's seven churches, at least three had temples to Caesar in John's day

19

(Ephesus, Smyrna, and Pergamum). An inscription from Asia (Revelation's territory) *circa* 9 C.E. extols Augustus as savior and son of God. Worship of the emperor was promoted sporadically during the first century. Nero (54–68), Vespasian (69–79), and Titus (79–81) did nothing to encourage it, and Tiberius (14–37) and Claudius (41–54) actively discouraged it.

Some emperors, however, were personally attracted to the idea of their own divinity, and/or saw its value as a political tool. Gaius (Caligula) (37–41) was both physically sick and a mentally deranged egomaniac. He was the first emperor to take his own divinity seriously. In 39 he insisted that his image be placed in the Jerusalem temple, a stupid event politically that would have caused a terrible war if the Roman officials in Palestine had attempted to carry it out, but fortunately Caligula died before this occurred. Although it was only a dangerous episode, the picture of a Caesar who could insist on being worshiped made an indelible impression on the consciousness of Jews and Christians alike and is probably reflected in the New Testament (Mark 13; II Thess. 2).

Nero continued to use such expressions of himself as "Nero, Lord [*kurios*] of all the earth," and accepted divine accolades from his subjects. Dio Cassius reports that the Armenian king Tiridates said to Nero: "I am the descendent of Arsaces . . . and thy slave. And I have come to thee, my god, to worship thee as I do Mithras" (63.5.2). Even though Nero seems to have done nothing personally to promote emperor worship, neither did he discourage it. Two events in his career are extremely important for understanding how the Caesars are pictured in the imagery of Revelation:

1. He was the first emperor to persecute the Christians. After his dream of Roman urban renewal resulted in a disastrous fire, for which the people held him responsible, he at first attempted unsuccessfully to blame it on the Jews. He then accused the Christians of Rome, rounded them up, and executed them in inhumanly cruel ways. The image of Nero as beast was burned deeply into the Christian consciousness.

2. Nero committed suicide in 68, but the circumstances of his death helped generate the Nero myth, which had two versions. Immediately after his death, which seemed to much of the population too good to be true, rumors spread that Nero had not really died but had fled beyond the eastern boundary of the empire to the Parthians, of whom the Romans had an almost

pathological fear. The expectation spread that he would return at the head of conquering armies. In later versions of the myth, current in John's time and reflected for example in the Sibylline Oracles, Nero's death was accepted as a reality; but in the popular imagination his image became mixed with that of the Antichrist, a demonic figure from the underworld, identified with Beliar, who would return in the last days and wreak terror on the earth's inhabitants.

The idea of the divine emperor took on new life in the reign of Domitian (81–96). He insisted on divine honors, and had even leading citizens executed or banished who refused to comply. When he appeared in public, the crowds were urged to shout: "All hail to our Lord [*kurios,* the same word used for Jesus in the New Testament] and to his Lady." Everyone who addressed him in speech or in writing must begin "Lord and God." Some spectators at the games who booed his team were put to death for despising his divine nature. Domitian put police power behind the state's claim to absolute loyalty and religious veneration.

In John's time, to refuse to accord divine honors to Domitian could be considered an act of political disloyalty or even treason. And it was an act of ingratitude. Caesar represented Rome. Alongside—in fact prior to—the deified emperor was the goddess Roma, the deified state. Emperor worship was a grass roots movement among the people, not only imposed from the top down. The act of "emperor worship" would be considered an important formality like "pledging allegiance" to the flag, an expression of one's solidarity with the empire and genuine gratitude for what it had done. Since most were polytheists, there was no religious problem. Not only the government, the population as a whole, was unable to understand the Christians' hesitation.

The Options

Christians in Asia during the nineties of the first century were under tremendous political, economic, and social pressure to go through the "formality" of veneration of the image of the Caesar or face the fearful consequences. What options were available to one who confessed Jesus as Lord in A.D. 96? Christians in John's churches passionately discussed the possibilities before them. These may be briefly listed:

1. Quit. Some Christians chose this option. When they became Christians they had not expected it to cost them their reputation, job, freedom, or life; and so they cursed Christ and bowed before Rome. John is not easy on those who took this option.

2. Lie. A good "situation ethics" case can be made (and most probably was made by sincere and thoughtful people) for doing this. Their reasoning was that the Romans did not understand the Christian faith and that it was not God's will for anyone to actually die for a misunderstanding. Veneration of the emperor was only a formality not to be taken seriously in any case. It was the lesser of two evils or what love (for children, parents, neighbors) required in this situation. Therefore Christians should go through the ceremony that showed they were loyal and grateful subjects of the empire, but with mental reservations, keeping their real religious faith to themselves. "True religion is a matter of the heart, not the formalities of public life." John's word for such people is "liars," and he reserves places in the lake of fire for them (21:8).

3. Fight. Although active resistance was hardly a real possibility for Christians in John's situation, it was at least a theoretical option. Only a few years before, the Zealots of Palestine had initiated a disastrous armed rebellion against the Romans under the slogan that only God can be worshiped as God. John may have been in contact with the Zealot movement during his earlier period in Palestine, but he had rejected the Zealot option of violence.

4. Change the "law." This too was a theoretical possibility, but hardly a real one. Government in the Roman Empire did not work by democratic process, and in any case the members of John's churches were without political and economic power. "Working within the system" through a lobby in Rome to change an unjust law was not a real option.

5. Adjust. Many Christians in John's churches were tempted to think as follows: "The ideas and practices of Christianity had been developed by earlier generations, in another time and place. In the light of the modern situation, perhaps there is a good way to preserve the essential elements of Christianity and combine them with the good features of Roman culture and religion. Christian theology should be rethought in such a way that it could incorporate the ways God is revealed in other religions, including the emperor cult. In any case, intolerance and exclusiveness must be avoided, so that Christians

22

should do nothing that would indicate disrespect for the religion of other people." It is likely that many of John's readers had already adjusted to the cultural "civil religion" and thus did not see themselves as living in a situation of crisis as Adela Yarbro Collins has pointed out (*Crisis and Catharsis,* p. 77). In this case John's letter was written to them not so much to encourage or console them in their experienced crisis but to make clear to them the crisis they had not yet perceived.

6. Die. The present situation was an opportunity to bear witness to the reality and meaning of Christian faith in the one God and Jesus as the only Lord, even if it meant dying at the hands of the Romans as had Jesus himself. John affirms this as the only Christian response.

What was the will of Christ the Lord for his people in this situation? All of these solutions were likely advocated in John's churches as "right," some of them as the way of Christian discipleship (cf. the discussion of the Nicolaitans, Balaam, and Jezebel in the commentary to 2:6, 14, and 20). The churches of Asia were now in a situation far different from that of Jesus and his disciples in Palestine. How could one who wanted to be an obedient disciple of Jesus know his will in this new situation? It is at this point that an understanding of the meaning of Christian prophecy becomes crucial for interpreting Revelation.

By a Christian Prophet

The author of Revelation claims that the content of his letter to the seven churches is "prophecy" (1:3; 19:10; 22:7–10, 18–19) and numbers himself among the "prophets" (22:9). But what is "prophecy"?

In our modern culture "prophecy" is often understood as "prediction of the future," and this is a valid understanding of the word in many modern contexts. A fundamental misunderstanding of biblical prophecy occurs, however, when it is equated with "predicting the future." This misunderstanding is furthered when modern readers observe the way in which early Christians expressed their belief that they were living in the time of fulfillment promised by Old Testament prophets (e.g., Luke 24:44; Acts 2:14–36; Rom. 15:4), which sometimes encouraged them to understand their Scripture, our Old Testament, as a book of predictions (e.g., Acts 3:18; and cf. the use of the O.T. in Matt. 1:18—2:23). The prophets of the Old Testament did in fact sometimes make predictions, both of this-worldly

23

historical events (e.g., Isa. 7:1—8:15, the Syro-Ephraimite war) and of the final victory of God at the end of history (e.g., Isa. 2:2–4; 9:2–7; 11:1–9). Their predictions of historical events were not of the long-range future, however, as though they were writing for later generations of readers. They sometimes announced impending events which affected the present of their hearers. When they predicted historical events, they were sometimes right (e.g., Isa. 7:1—8:15, cf. II Kings 16:5–9) and sometimes wrong (e.g., Amos 7:11, cf. II Kings 14:29; Ezek. 26:7–14, cf. Ezek. 29:7–20; Jonah 3:4, cf. v. 10), but it is a fundamental misunderstanding of Old Testament prophecy to regard it as essentially "prediction."

The current pop-eschatology misunderstanding of Revelation as a book of long-range predictions forecasting events in our own time is encouraged not only by the cultural misunderstanding of prophecy as prediction but by the fact that John does announce events in the future. The future John announces, however, is always either the immediate future of his first-century readers (e.g., 2:10) or the ultimate future of the victory of God at the end of history (e.g., 21:1—22:5), which John perceived as near at hand. On this point we can readily understand how important it is to regard Revelation as a *letter*, written to first-century readers who were expected to understand it, and they *did*. If Revelation were "really" a book of predictions of later events, such as the oil crisis in the Middle East, Russian and American militarism, it would have been meaningless to its first readers and would not have been a letter to *them* at all. An additional important factor is that John expected the End to come soon, in his own generation, and has no long-range predictions of the historical future (see "Reflection: Interpreting the 'Near End' in Revelation"). When interpreted responsibly, Revelation has a message *to* our time, but it does not make predictions *about* it.

If we derive our understanding of prophecy from the Hebrew Scriptures, as John did, the essential nature of prophecy is clear. Israel believed that God communicated with his people directly by choosing certain individuals who were given their message by divine revelation and charged to deliver it to the people. The authority behind the prophet's message is not empirical observation, common sense, human experience, religious tradition, or interpretation of Scripture, as is the case with scribes, rabbis, and teachers. The prophet is one who speaks because he or she has been given his or her message directly from God. The prophet speaks on the basis of revelation. The message thus received may or may not contain predictions; it is prophecy because it comes as a revelation from God.

It was a common belief in first-century Judaism that prophecy had ended with the biblical prophets and that God no longer communicated with his people directly. It was believed that God's will is now made known by the interpretation of Scripture and tradition. Yet it was expected that in the last days the gift of prophecy would be renewed, and prophets would again allow the word of God to be heard directly. One aspect of the faith of John the Baptist, Jesus, and the early Christians that they were living in the eschatological days of the time of fulfillment was that the gift of prophecy was renewed among them. John the Baptist and Jesus understood themselves as prophets, and were so understood by their followers. After the death and resurrection of Jesus, prophets appeared in the Christian community (Matt. 23:34; Acts 2:14–21; 13:1; 15:32; 20:23; 21:4, 10; Rom. 12:6; I Cor. 12:10, 28; 13:2, 8; 14:1–40; Eph. 2:20; 3:5). The prophet was still understood on the biblical model of the spokesperson for the Lord, but in the Christian context "the Lord" meant the risen and exalted Lord of the church's faith, the Lord Jesus. Christian prophets were thus those who spoke the message of the risen Lord directly to the Christian community.

The Prophet as Interpreter of History

This is exactly what John's churches needed! Perplexed as they faced new critical situations for which their Bible and traditional teachings of Jesus gave little direct guidance, those who wanted to be faithful Christians in this new situation needed a word from the Lord to direct them. They needed to understand their present situation and what Christian faithfulness required of them in it. Prophets were not predictors of historical events of the distant future but were inspired interpreters of the historical events through which their hearers were living. This is already clear from a reading of the biblical prophets.

The prophets of the Old Testament are typically interpreters of the historical deeds of Yahweh, who does nothing without revealing his "secret" to "his servants the prophets" (Amos 3:7).

Amos declared Yahweh's judgment on the historical acts of nations, including his own, not on the basis of an ahistorical, individualistic, mystical experience but on the basis of the claim of divinely given insight into the meaning of contemporary history: the illusory prosperity occasioned by the advance of Assyria, which would soon bring destruction to Israel. Isaiah has a similar hermeneutical function in relation to the same historical crisis for Judah, Jeremiah to the advance of Nebuchadnezzar, II Isaiah to the rise of Cyrus with its accompanying events, Joel to the locust plague, Haggai to the drought, Daniel to the persecution instigated by Antiochus IV. The prophet is that figure in the community who is enabled by the Spirit to recognize the otherwise mute, surd-like events of history as acts of God, to interpret their meaning and to proclaim them to the community. The word of the prophet is never a purely vertical word from heaven directed at a point in human life; the prophetic word always operates by engagement with the horizontal line of that history which forms the essential context, and often the content, of the prophet's message.

John served as prophetic interpreter of events for his congregations in two ways: (1) He declared the meaning of the historical events through which they were living and Christian responsibility within it: The pressures experienced by Christians and the great persecution which John saw on the horizon were not meaningless tragedy but part of God's plan for the consummation of history; and Christian responsibility was to remain faithful in this crisis, even to the point of dying (2:10). (2) John continued to interpret the meaning of the event of the initial appearance of Jesus, giving it new interpretations and giving to Jesus new christological titles which were meaningful ways to understand the significance of the Christ event in John's time, but these interpretations would have been meaningless earlier, for example, "the faithful witness, the first-born of the dead, and the ruler of kings on earth" (1:5). Here is illustrated the creative role of Christian prophets in the post-Easter formation of Christology as the church continued to develop its understanding of the meaning of Jesus through the inspired insights of its prophets. In the new post-Easter situations, Christian prophets go beyond what Jesus had said about himself, but they do it with the authority of the risen Jesus as the self-interpretation of the exalted Lord, and with his voice.

26

Inspiration and Tradition

Did John "really" have visions or are his reports of visions "only" a literary device? This question poses a false alternative. On the one hand, there is no reason to doubt that John had real visions. Ecstatic experience of various kinds is an aspect of human religion generally. It occurred in John's day and it occurs in ours, among Christians and people of other religions. "Visions and revelations" were not uncommon among the prophetic figures in the early church, as Paul and Acts document (I Cor. 14; II Cor. 12:1–10; Acts 10:1–23; 22:17; 27:21–26). John was one of those early Christian prophets who experienced visions and revelations as an authentic aspect of his religious experience and who considered what he wrote to be prophecy.

On the other hand, this does not mean that what we have in Revelation is simply the "reporting" of what John "saw" in his visions. The images from the Scripture and John's religious tradition that resided in his imagination were already active in the revelatory experience itself, providing the raw materials which were reshaped by his visionary experience. In later reflection and composition he used all the resources of his tradition and his creative literary imagination to express the visions to his hearer-readers, painting them in colors drawn from the rich palate already prepared in the Bible and other prophetic and apocalyptic tradition. In their present form the visions are literary compositions based on John's visionary experience, not merely descriptive reports of what he "actually" saw and heard. This becomes clear when one attempts to picture, or even imagine in one's mind, what John portrays. Many of the scenes in his visions are literally unimaginable, they cannot be imaged (see below).

The use of sources and traditional materials is not incompatible with authentic visionary experience. What sources and traditions did John actually use? First and foremost, his Bible: Revelation is saturated with allusions to the Old Testament, showing that the author's mind was itself steeped in Scripture, the words and images of which were available to provide the raw material for his visions, and the literary means by which to later express them. In the forty-eight pages of text in the standard edition of the Greek New Testament (Nestle[26]), there are approximately five hundred allusions to the Scriptures. Yet, though John uses the words and images of Scripture in almost

27

every line of his letter, he never once formally cites an Old Testament passage. The text of Scripture becomes in his hand the vehicle for communicating the present word of the risen Lord. Scripture is represented in new forms and combinations which break down the distance between the "past" of Scripture and the "present" of the hearer-readers in John's churches.

Just as the content of John's letter is not merely the reporting of what he saw in his visions, neither is it the result of his own free, creative composition. Just as the Old Testament prophets adapted material from their tradition of Israelite prophecy (cf. e.g., Isa. 4:1-4; Micah 4:1-4; and Joel throughout), and Paul adapted material from previous Christian prophets (cf. e.g., I Thess. 4:15-18), John too takes over and adapts materials from his prophetic predecessors in the church. Comparison with other apocalyptic literature reveals many similarities of imagery, which indicates that John also knows and uses a common stock of apocalyptic materials in order to express his visionary experience. This does not necessarily mean that John incorporates written sources. A previous generation of scholars posited extensive literary sources behind John's composition and attempted to identify them. The present tendency is to see the whole as John's composition, though making use of traditional materials. Since John's ministry is carried out in the territory where a generation earlier Paul and his disciples had founded churches, Pauline traditions continued to be used and reinterpreted by both John and his churches, although not always in the same way.

On the other hand, John seems to use only minimally the traditional words of Jesus that were circulating in the church and seems not to have known any of the written Gospels. As was also the case with Paul, it is not the traditional sayings of Jesus of Nazareth but the word of the exalted Lord that is authoritative for him. In the few places where he may be reflecting a traditional saying of the historical Jesus (2:7 and seven times in chaps. 2 and 3), these are incorporated into his message from the risen Christ, not cited as the words of a past authority.

Structure

To appreciate John's literary achievement, we must get the content and structure of Revelation as a whole in mind. The content of Revelation may be briefly stated: The risen Christ appears to John on the island of Patmos and gives him messages

28

to be sent to seven churches in Asia. John is then caught up into the heavenly throneroom, where he sees Christ open the sealed book. The seventh seal, rather than being the end, opens into seven trumpet scenes, the last of which again calls forth not the end but announces seven bowls of the wrath of God. John beholds the plagues and devastation that result from the seals, trumpets, and bowls, climaxing in the destruction of Babylon. Then come the visions of the final triumph of God as Christ returns: the dead are raised, the final judgment is held, and the new Jerusalem is established as the capital of the redeemed creation.

This content is not the mere report of a spectator to heavenly scenes who then transcribed them as a random accumulation of what he had seen. What we have here is the composition of an author and artist who exercised his own literary and theological creativity to communicate in a compelling way the meaning of life and the world in the light of the Christ event, as mediated through his revelatory experience. One aspect of this literary craftsmanship is the structuring of his composition into a coherent whole. We thus need to inquire into the outline of Revelation.

The general compositional scheme followed by John is clear, for it is a narrative presentation of the broad apocalyptic pattern found in many other documents (see the next section on "apocalyptic"). This pattern begins with the present troubles, portrays them as intensifying just before the End, and then pictures the ultimate victory of God in the End itself. The author and his readers stand at the beginning of the time of the last troubles. This means that things will get worse before they get better, and must do so, for these eschatological troubles represent the final intensification of evil just before the End, when evil is finally destroyed forever. John's and his readers' own situation is represented in chapters 1—3, the vision of the exalted Christ who communicates a message from God to the Christians in seven cities of Asia. The time of eschatological distress is portrayed in chapters 4—18, the vision of the heavenly throneroom in which Christ opens the seven seals, which open in turn to seven trumpets and then to seven bowls of wrath, climaxed by the destruction of the "Great City," "Babylon." The final victory is depicted in chapters 19—22, climaxed by the appearance of the "Holy City," the heavenly new Jerusalem. The issue posed and addressed by this structure is, "Will the Christians who must decide how to live their lives in the mundane cities of Asia (Part I) orient themselves to the 'Great City' that will receive God's judgment (Part II) or to the 'Holy City' that will be redeemed by God (Part III)?" Each of these three major sections is preceded by a scene portraying the heavenly glory of God and/or Christ. Introductory and concluding sections in which John communicates with his readers on the earthly plane surround these transcendent visions, resulting in the following broad outline of the structure of the letter.

OUTLINE OF REVELATION

Letter Opening	1:1–8
Part One: God Speaks to the Church in the City	1:9—3:22
Actor: God-defined-by-Christ	
Action: God/Christ speaks	
Location: Actual cities of Asia where Christians live in 96	
Time: The hearer-readers' present, 96	
A. Transcendent Christ	1:9–20
B. Seven Messages	2:1—3:22
Message to Church in Ephesus	2:1–7
Message to Church in Smyrna	2:8–11
Message to Church in Pergamum	2:12–17
Message to Church in Thyatira	2:18–29
Message to Church in Sardis	3:1–6
Message to Church in Philadelphia	3:7–13
Message to Church in Laodicea	3:14–22
Part Two: God Judges the "Great City"	4:1—18:24
Actor: God-defined-by-Christ	
Action: God/Christ judges	
Location: "Babylon"—the rebellious world seen in transcendent perspective	
Time: The immediate future of John's hearer-readers	
A. Transcendent God/Christ	4:1—5:14
B. Seven Seals, Trumpets, and Bowls of God's Judgment	6:1—18:24
Opening the Seven Seals	6:1—8:1

John structures his book in a more refined, detailed fashion than indicated by this broad outline. It is clear, for example, that many items are structured in sevens, as had already become traditional in apocalyptic literature. Second Esdras, a Jewish apocalypse written about the same time as Revelation, is a series of seven revelations, has seven ways the evil are punished, and seven ways the righteous rejoice. John adopts this apocalyptic convention and structures much of his composition by septets. He enumerates some of them (letters, churches, seals, trumpets, bowls), but also structures items in septets even when he does not highlight it for the reader. There are, for examples, exactly seven beatitudes (1:3; 14:13; 16:15; 19:9; 20:6; 22:7, 14), seven ascriptions of praise (5:12), seven categories of people (6:15), seven references to the altar (6:9; 8:3, 5; 9:13; 11:1; 14:18; 16:7), seven prophetic affirmations of the eschatological coming of Jesus (2:16; 3:11; 16:15; 22:7, 12, 17, 20). Since there are obviously too many of these to be coincidental, some scholars

31

have thought that all of Revelation is structured in series of sevens, seven acts of seven scenes each (e.g., Lohmeyer; Bowman [pp. 64–65]), but it requires too much force to fit John's material into so neat a pattern, and no two of these efforts agree.

Similarly, in looking at the broad outline, one might expect that John's pictorial narrative of the future would begin with his own time and then proceed chronologically through the series of plagues and disasters represented by the seals, trumpets, and bowls to the time of eschatological salvation. This linear, chronological understanding of the sequence of visions has been advocated by several scholars, above all by R. H. Charles' classic commentary. Yet Charles was able to make the visions of Revelation fit this linear, chronological scheme only by arbitrary rearrangements of the text, the "original" order of which he thought had been damaged by a dishonest and unintelligent editor. Current scholarship is unanimous in rejecting this theory.

The content of the visions presents two problems in holding the view that they represent a chronological series. First, the End seems to come at the conclusion of each series of seven. The sixth seal (6:12–17), for instance, portrays the dissolution of the cosmos, which makes it difficult, to say the least, for history to continue through two more series of plagues and disasters. Second, the announcement of salvation is not withheld until the final scene but is already declared during the time of troubles (e.g., 7:9–17; 14:1–5; 15:1–4). These aspects of the text have led some scholars to pose, instead of a straightforward linear progression, a theory of recapitulation according to which the same series of historical woes leading to final salvation is told repeatedly in the form of seals, trumpets, and bowls. While, as we shall note in the commentary below, there is some considerable parallelism between the series of events represented by the seals, trumpets, and bowls, the material must again be forced to make it fit a neat scheme of recapitulation. The series of visions is not a chaos of disorder, but neither is it architectonically precise. It moves forward as a kind of impressionistic, interrelated spiral, bringing previous scenes before the imagination in new and intensified light, but never in some predictable, diagrammable way. John's style of communication is allusive and evocative, imaginative and pictorial, rather than rigidly logical and consistent.

32

This lack of neatness and predictability in the structure of the Apocalypse is not the result of the author's lack of literary competence. In fact, the carefully structured composition shows both John's skill as a communicator and his theological concern. John is not writing a "book" to be admired or analyzed. He has a message to communicate to a particular group of hearer-readers. His message is embodied in a large corpus of materials, some of them traditional, including at least three series of seven visions of the troubles that must precede the promised eschatological salvation. Yet John's own intuitive knowledge of the psychology of communication prohibits his simply leading the hearer-reader through a series of twenty-one plagues before the End comes. Such a series is too much to ask of the hearer. So he incorporates some of his sevens into other sevens, presenting them to the hearer-readers one at a time in familiar apocalyptic style. As a skilled oral communicator addressing congregations who lived in an oral/aural culture rather than a culture like ours, oriented to visual media, John has facilitated his message's making a lasting impression on the imagination of his hearer-readers by building into it many aids to their memory (see Barr, pp. 243–56). Likewise, it is too much to ask for the patient, even suffering, hearer-reader to wait until the coming disasters are all described before hearing a word of hope. Thus anticipatory announcements of the coming salvation are sprinkled throughout the woes. This is not only good psychology, it is also Christian theology. The Christian confession is not only that Christ is to come at the end of history but that Christ has already come; not only that salvation awaits the believer in the eschatological future but that salvation is already experienced, in an anticipatory but real way, in the here and now, in the midst of troubles and not only at their end. The theology on which this structure is based affirms the reality of the future. The future is in the sovereign hand of God and already affects the present. The present is thus not simply the automatic accumulation of the past—if this were so, every present would be predetermined by the past and would be predictable and unescapable. The present is shaped not just by the past but by God's future. John affirms that by being given a future we are given a present, and he has incorporated this conviction into the structure of his message.

33

Authorship

Unlike other writers of apocalyptic books, John gives his own
name and writes in his own person, rather than under the
assumed name of some figure of the past (cf. discussion of apocalyptic literature below). Such an assumption of another name
was not necessary, for John and his churches no longer believed
that the prophetic gift of the Holy Spirit was only a remembered aspect of the revered past. It was a matter of their own
experience that the Spirit spoke again to the churches through
Christian prophets (see 1:10; 2:7, 11, 17, 29; 3:6, 13, 22; 4:2;
22:17). While John claims to be a prophet, he makes no claim
to being an apostle, and in fact distinguishes himself from the
apostles (21:14). He recounts no stories or sayings from the
ministry of Jesus, though some would have been appropriate for
the message he advocates (e.g., Mark 12:13–17), nor does he
give any other indication that he had known Jesus during his
earthly life. This John is therefore not the John numbered
among the disciples in the Gospels. Nor is he the same as the
author of the Gospel and Letters of John, as the differences in
language, theology, and general point of view make clear. Although John writes in Greek to Greek-speaking churches, his
Greek is peculiar and full of grammatical irregularities. The
nature of his peculiar Greek suggests that his native language
was Hebrew or Aramaic. Since John is also acquainted with
Palestinian prophetic traditional material, it is likely that he was
originally a Palestinian Christian prophet who had immigrated
to Asia, probably as a refugee during or just after the war of
66–70 (cf. Satake).

The oldest manuscripts of Revelation have as the title simply "The Apocalypse of John." A few later manuscripts add "the
Evangelist," and most of the later ones add "the Theologian,"
both additional titles intended to identify John with the author
of the Fourth Gospel, whom later Christian tradition assumed
to be the Apostle John. John's own "title" for his composition is,
of course, 1:1–3. All the titles are additions made by the church
editors, mainly reflecting their theological interest in indicating
that the book was apostolic, that it contained authoritative
Christian interpretation. Their claim that the book is an authentic witness to the truth of the Christian faith is in no way com-
promised by the historical-critical conclusion, in agreement

34

with Revelation's own claim, that it was written not by an apostle but by the prophet John.

This particular prophet communicated his message by means of a letter filled with apocalyptic language and ideas. Revelation is a letter in form, but apocalyptic in content. To grasp the message of Revelation, it is therefore important to consider the nature of apocalyptic thought.

In Apocalyptic Language and Imagery

"Apocalypse" (Eng. trans., "revelation") is the first word of 1:1. "Apocalypse," then, is not only a technical word used by Bible scholars, but is John's own designation of his writing. What is an apocalypse? What is "apocalyptic" language and thought? Not all scholars use the terminology in the same way, but it has proven helpful to separate the answer to the question "What is apocalyptic" into three sub-categories: apocalyptic as a literary genre, apocalyptic as a social movement, and apocalyptic as a particular kind of thought.

Since understanding the message of Revelation is our primary concern, I will concentrate on apocalyptic as the kind of thought represented in Revelation. What I present here is something of an oversimplification, since there are apocalypses which do not contain the kind of eschatological thought found here. Yet, oversimplifications are sometimes useful in grasping the essence of the matter. We may thus first express an approach to understanding apocalyptic thought that has proven helpful in the study of Revelation: *Apocalyptic is a particular kind of eschatology, which in turn is a particular understanding of the doctrine of providence.* We will now "unpack" this concentrated sentence one element at a time and elaborate the meaning of "apocalyptic."

Providence, Eschatology, and Apocalyptic

Providence is the overarching biblical category within which eschatological and apocalyptic thought can best be understood. Our word "providence" comes to us from Greek by way of two Latin words, "pro," which means "before," and "video," which means "see." "Providence," therefore, has to do with seeing what is before one, looking out ahead. To believe in the providence of God is to believe that not only our individual lives but history as a whole is under the sovereignty of One who is "looking out ahead," that Someone is in the driver's seat of history. The faith expressed in the doctrine of providence might be summed up in the words "God is guiding history."

"Eschatology" can be thought of as a particular kind of thought within the doctrine of providence. All eschatological thinking is providential, but not all providential thinking is eschatological. *Eschaton* is simply the Greek word for "end." It can be used for the last in a series, temporal or otherwise. In a narrative it is the conclusion, not simply the end. A damaged book from which the last chapter is missing has a last page, but still has no conclusion. In a story, a person's life, or the history of the world, the eschaton is the last scene, the conclusion of the story.

In theological terms the eschaton can be thought of individually (the meaning of a person's death, what happens to the individual at death), nationally (e.g., the "golden age" of the nation that is its destiny to come), or historically and cosmically. Since biblical theology is concerned with God as the Creator of the universe and the Lord of history as a whole (not merely of individual souls or particular nations), most biblical eschatological thought is expressed within this cosmic framework.

Eschatological thought goes beyond the general affirmation of the doctrine of providence, "God is guiding history," to a more specific statement: "God is guiding history to a final goal." The doctrine of providence, as such, affirms that history has a Lord, but not that history has an end. Providential thinking has no necessary place for thought about the "end of the world." It is concerned with the process, not the goal, of history. Eschatological thought, on the other hand, is the counterpart to the doctrine of creation: Just as the world and history have not always existed, but came into being by the act of the Creator, so this world and its history are not eternal, but will be brought to their goal by the God who declares not only that he is the Alpha but also the Omega of all that is (Rev. 1:8; these are the first and last letters of the Greek alphabet). Although "end of the world" thinking is often thought of as gloomy and pessimistic, we shall see that in the Bible generally and in Revelation in particular the doctrine of the end of this world is a joyous hope to be celebrated—and that not because of any negative view of this world and its values.

36

It may come as a surprise to learn that there is a considerable eschatological element in the Bible. Although there are exceptions in individual books, most biblical authors in both the Old and New Testaments operate with the presupposition that God has a plan for the world and history which he will carry to fulfillment. In a vast variety of imagery and forms of thought, many passages in the Old Testament indicate that the present state of the world is not God's final will for it. Rather he will bring the world into a fulfilled state which does represent his own will for his creation. The law and narrative books contain passages which express this eschatological hope (e.g., Gen. 12:1–3 [a foundational passage]; 49:9–12; Num. 24:17–19). Many of the psalms were written to be used in the worship of Israel which longed for or already celebrated in advance the coming age of salvation, especially as this was linked to the idea that the final age of fulfillment would be brought to realization through the new or coming king God would raise up for this purpose (e.g., Pss. 2; 21; 45; 72; 74; 104; 110). The prophets, especially the post-exilic ones, frequently portray the eschatological hopes of Israel in terms of both judgment and salvation (e.g., Amos 1—2; 5:4, 6, 14, 15, 18–20; 7:4; 8:1–2, 9–10; 9:11–15; Isa. 2:2–4, 6–20; 4:2–6; 7:1–25; 9:1–7; 11:1–9; 14:24–27; 19:16–25; 35; 40—66; Ezek. 32—37; 38—39; 40—48; Joel 2—3; Hos. 1:10–11; Jer. 31:31–33; Micah 5; Mal. 4:1–6; Zech. 9—14; Zeph. 1:1–18).

Just as eschatology is a certain kind of thinking about God's providence, so for our purposes in understanding Revelation, apocalyptic may be thought of as a certain kind of thinking about eschatology. Apocalyptic thought, as represented in Revelation, affirms that God is guiding history to a final goal *which God himself will bring about in the near future, in a particular way that is already revealed.*

The understanding of apocalyptic thought here proposed accords with the definition of apocalyptic developed by a team of scholars within the Society of Biblical Literature led by John J. Collins of the University of Notre Dame:

> "Apocalypse" is a genre of revelatory literature with a narrative framework, in which a revelation is mediated by an otherworldly being to a human recipient, disclosing a transcendent reality which is both temporal, insofar as it envisages eschatological salvation, and spatial insofar as it involves another, supernatural world.
>
> (J. J. Collins, ed., *Apocalypse*, p. 9)

37

The group based its definition on the analysis of a large number of Jewish, Christian, and Greco-Roman apocalypses.

INTERPRETATION

Revelation is not a unique literary or theological work but belongs within a broad stream of Jewish and Christian apocalyptic writings, with some elements closely related to Hellenistic writings resembling apocalyptic. The following documents, some of which are only partly apocalyptic, would be included on most lists as more or less representative of Jewish apocalyptic:

Daniel	165 B.C.E.
First Enoch or Ethiopic Enoch (a collection of apocalyptic books) from ca. 164	B.C.E. onward
Jubilees	ca. 150 B.C.E.
Sibylline Oracles, Book III	from ca. 150 B.C.E. onward
Testaments of the Twelve Patriarchs	latter part of second century B.C.E.
Psalms of Solomon	48 B.C.E.
Assumption of Moses	6–30 C.E.
Life of Adam and Eve or Apocalypse of Moses	shortly before 70 C.E.
Testament of Abraham 9—32	ca. C.E. 70–100
Second Enoch or the Book of the Secrets of Enoch	first century C.E.
Sibylline Oracles, Book IV	ca. 80 C.E.
Second Esdras (IV Ezra) 3—14	ca. 90 C.E.
Second Baruch or Apocalypse of Baruch, or Syriac	after 90 C.E.
Third Baruch	second century C.E.
Sibylline Oracles, Book V	second century C.E.
From the Qumran literature (Dead Sea Scrolls):	second century B.C.E. to first part of first century C.E.

Commentaries on Isaiah, Hosea, Micah, Nahum, Habakkuk, Zephaniah, and Psalm 37

The War of the Sons of Light Against the Sons of Darkness

A Midrash on the Last Days

Description of the New Jerusalem

An Angelic Liturgy

The Prayer of Nabonidus and a Pseudo-Daniel Apocalypse

A Genesis Apocryphon

(Cf. Russell, pp. 36–69. The texts themselves may be read in Charlesworth; the dates given are Russell's.)

Not only were Jewish apocalypses circulating in the first century, the early Christians also produced other apocalyptic books which were not included in the canon, such as the Shepherd of Hermas, the Apocalypse of Peter, and the Book of Elchasai. (The texts themselves may be read in M. R. James or Hennecke and Schneemelcher.)

For many who attempt to interpret Revelation for our day, Revelation and Daniel may represent the only apocalyptic material they have seen. The point of having such a list here is to make clear that this was not the case for the first readers of Revelation. They had the advantage of recognizing that the communication from their prophet John was expressed in a language and thought with which they were already familiar. An excellent exercise for the modern interpreter is to read at least one of the above works; Second Esdras (also called IV Ezra) is readily available in editions of the Bible which include the Apocrypha or Deutero-Canonical books. Revelation will never look the same once one has seen even a small sample of the category of thought to which it belongs.

Some elements of this definition of apocalyptic thought may now be elaborated, in order to apply them more directly to our study of Revelation.

The Final Goal

As understood here, God's bringing the world and history to an end is a fundamental aspect of apocalyptic thought. Even the casual reader of Revelation must notice that the ending of this world and the beginning of the new world in which God's rule is a reality is a constituent part of John's message (e.g., 6:12–17; 21:1–4). It is important to understand that this is not a morbid or speculative interest of the apocalyptists in general or of John in particular. Their question was not the speculative "Will there be an end of the world?" but "Is God faithful?" Their concern for the ultimate goal of history, that is, whether this world in its present status is ultimate or not, is the theological concern of faith as it responds to a crisis of faith/theology. The apocalyptists lived in impossible situations, when mothers saw their babies killed because they had circumcised them in faithfulness to the Law (Daniel), or when children saw their parents imprisoned or killed because their faithfulness to their confession of Jesus as the only Lord made it impossible for them to yield to the imperial religion (Revelation). In an impossible situation, how can one still believe in the faithfulness of God? It was the honor and integrity of God as God that was at stake, not just human selfish longing for golden streets and pearly gates.

The problem was a problem for both faith and theology, which are inseparable in any case. The problem was not just a conceptual, intellectual crisis, though this element is not to be minimized for faith. Theology is thinking about faith, faith's expression of itself in thought. Theology and faith are not the same, but there can be no faith without theology. Thus the apocalyptists' efforts to make theological sense of their crisis situation was not only an intellectual struggle but a struggle of faith. The problem to which apocalyptic is the response may be generally stated as follows:

1. God has made promises to bless his people (e.g., Deut. 28:1–14) and through his people, the world (e.g., Gen. 12:1–3; Isa. 42:1–4).

2. The people had been unfaithful by not keeping the Law (often the case, especially in the pre-exilic situation); then, when disaster came, there was no conceptual problem; the prophets could declare that the disaster was God's judgment on the people because of their sins. (This, of course, is the burden of most of the prophets of the O.T.; cf. Amos; Isaiah 1—8; Jeremiah.)

3. When, however, the people experienced disaster and persecution *because* they were faithful (and it was precisely those who were most faithful to Yahweh and the Law who experienced terror and tragedy), what conceptual options were

available? One could logically decide that God was unfaithful; he was able to avert tragedy, but he had broken his promise. This was not acceptable to the apocalyptists. Alternatively, one could decide that God was faithful, wanted to reward his people, but was incapable of doing so. For the apocalyptists, to believe in a God who was himself somehow victim of circumstances, who wanted to help his suffering people but was unable, was a denial of faith in God as the Creator and the Almighty; it was a denial that God was God. (Note how often the themes of God as the Creator and God as the Almighty occur in Revelation!)

The apocalyptists' answer represents faith's conceptual effort to hold on to the faithfulness of a God who is the Almighty, who is not himself the victim of the evil in the world. "Apocalyptic preserved the faith" (Napier, p. 332). For apocalyptic thinkers, eschatology was not a separate or optional subject of theology but an aspect of the doctrine of God. The conviction that despite the experienced evil of their situation God was both the almighty creator and was faithful to his covenant promises generated, from the materials available in the eastern Mediterranean, the major themes of apocalyptic thought.

God Himself Will Act

God is the Almighty and the sole ruler of the world. Otherwise he is unworthy of the name "God." Yet the terrible evil which continued unabated in the apocalyptists' present meant to them that God could not be *directly* in control and could not be charged with direct responsibility for the world's evil. Rather, the apocalyptists inferred, on the basis of ideas already present in the biblical and Jewish traditions, that God had delegated aspects of the rulership of the world to angelic beings, who have misused their power, have become demonic, and who will themselves be punished in the great judgment to come (cf. e.g., I Cor. 6:3, where Paul makes use of this apocalyptic idea). Thus apocalyptic thought is "dualistic" in that it typically deals with God and angels on the one hand and Satan and demons on the other. Human beings live their lives at the intersection of these two worlds. Human experience of, and responsibility for, good and evil is seen in the context of the cosmic struggle between God and the powers of evil. For the apocalyptists, the evil of the world is too big to be merely of human doing, and too big to be overcome by human effort

41

(see the "Reflection: Interpreting Revelation's Satan Language"). But the "dualism" is not ultimate, and the outcome of this struggle is not in doubt. The promises have not failed. God will still be faithful. If there is no way for God to fulfill his promises in this world, he will bring this world to an end—not as a gesture of cosmic frustration but as the means to the redemption of the whole creation. This is the reason for the emphasis on the future and the "otherworldliness" of apocalyptic thought. The present situation is so unjust, and the righteous so powerless to correct it, that humanity's only hope is in the intervention of God.

The apocalyptists are "pessimistic" about this world, but their "pessimism" is not ultimate. God's justice will prevail, even though there is no way in *this* world for it to prevail (except in relative and fragmentary ways that are not to be disdained). This is why apocalyptic thought emphasizes the resurrection and judgment in a transcendent world where the great balancing of books will take place, and why salvation is pictured as breaking into history from the transcendent world rather than arising from immanent good forces or our own efforts in this world. If there is to be redemption for the world, that is, if God is to be considered faithful, then it must come from God himself if it comes at all. The new Jerusalem is not built up from below but comes down out of heaven from God (Rev. 21:2). Those contemporary Christians who live in situations where they see manifestations of the good rule of God about them and have political and economic power which they can use to change some of the evil in this world can understand Revelation better if they remember that it, like apocalyptic in general, was written in and for a different situation. Apocalyptic is an expression of the faith of the politically powerless and oppressed in a situation where the empirical evidence of God's goodness is not to be seen. This is one reason why Revelation has continued to speak directly to the church in times and places where Christians with no political or economic power have experienced inhuman cruelty, such as the Nazi era in Europe or the church today in countries governed by oppressive dictatorships. Response to the message of Revelation is an expression of faith in the faithfulness of God in a situation which gives no indication of it in this world; it is faith's "nevertheless" when "therefore" makes no sense.

For Apocalyptic, the End Is Near

There is one God who is ultimately in control and who will bring all evil powers, human and otherwise, to account in the great judgment to come. In the meantime, however, these evil powers who know that their time is limited continue to perpetrate evil in this world. For apocalyptic thought, the intensification of evil experienced in the present world is itself an indication that eschatological salvation is near. For the apocalyptists, the suffering of their own times was no random accident or blind fate but part of the plan of God. The persecutions they experienced were part of the necessary struggles of the endtime and revealed that the End was near. Apocalyptists typically did not make speculative predictions of the end of the world at some date centuries hence, which would have been of interest only to futurologists among their contemporaries, but addressed their own generation with the urgency of those who cry out for meaning in their own struggle and suffering. Their question was not "When will the End come?" but "What is the meaning of our suffering?" It was not speculative calculation but the tenacity of faith which came to expression in their conviction that the End must be near. (See the "Reflection: Interpreting the 'Near End' in Revelation.")

Extent in Bible

This kind of apocalyptic thought is not a marginal note in the theology of the Bible. Although influenced to some degree by the religious ideas of Israel's neighbors during the Persian period and afterward, apocalyptic was not a late borrowing of foreign ideas but was basically the child of prophecy (Hanson), "prophecy in a new idiom" (Rowley). Already in the later prophetic books of the Old Testament there were transitional elements within which prophecy was fading into apocalyptic (Isa. 56—66; Zech. 9—14; Isa. 24–27), and the latest book in the Old Testament, Daniel (165 B.C.E.) was already a full-blown apocalypse. The appearance of embryonic apocalyptic ideas outside Israel, in such places as the Sibylline Oracles, the Egyptian Demotic Chronicle and Potter's Oracle, the Persian Oracle of Hystapes, and the Roman Fourth Eclogue of Vergil, shows that the development of Jewish apocalyptic was not an isolated phenomenon in its world but that it crystallized, in a way appropriate to Israel's faith, an intellectual phenomenon that was "in the air" (see J. J. Collins, "Sibylline Oracles," I, 322–23).

In the period "between the Testaments," however, apocalyptic flowered, so that when the New Testament opens apocalyptic ideas, such as the resurrection of the dead, are already presupposed. Apocalyptic thought was one of the major expressions of Jewish faith in the time of Jesus and the early church, and it formed the framework within which the earliest Christian faith was developed. *All* the authors of the New Testament were influenced by it in one way or another. The theology of Paul, the first and most prolific of New Testament authors, is thoroughly apocalyptic from the earliest letter (I Thess., cf. e.g., 1:10; 4:13–18) to the latest (whether this be considered Phil., cf. e.g., 1:6, 10; 3:20–21; 4:5, or Rom., cf. e.g., 8:18–25; 13:11). The fundamentally apocalyptic character of Paul's thought comes to expression not only in specific passages such as those mentioned above; it forms the background and framework of his thought as a whole, and thus appears in his greetings and thanksgivings (e.g., I Cor. 1:7–8) and in his premarital counseling (I Cor. 7:25–31). Even I Corinthians 13, the familiar "love chapter," presupposes the apocalyptic framework (cf. vv. 2, 8–10!). The Gospels and Acts were also written within the framework of apocalyptic thought and have many specific apocalyptic passages (e.g., Mark 13; Matt. 24; Luke 17:20–37; 21:5–36; John 5:25–29; Acts 17:30–31).

Early Christianity's adoption of apocalyptic categories of thought did not mean that Christian authors simply repeated traditional apocalyptic ideas. The fundamental difference was that Christians no longer simply looked forward to some saving event in the eschatological future. God was understood as the one who had already acted decisively in the Christ event. This means that Revelation cannot be reduced to an example of "millenarian piety" that can be adequately grasped by sociological categories used in the study of sectarian movements. Apocalyptic thought was commandeered and used by the early Christians as the vehicle for the expression of a radically new message: The Christ has come and made everything different.

Since the Gospels, Acts, and Paul offer other kinds of thought besides apocalyptic, in interpreting them it is possible for the preacher or teacher to ignore the apocalyptic element and read his or her presuppositions into the text—what Paul Minear aptly calls an "exercise in ventriloquism" (*New Testa-*

44

ment Apocalyptic, p. 96). Not so with Revelation. Here the interpreter has no place to hide, unless he or she is content to draw a few moralisms from the "seven letters." One must learn to interpret apocalyptic, or ignore Revelation. But since Revelation and apocalyptic belong not to one of the side eddies of New Testament thought but to the main channel, what one learns from interpreting the apocalyptic message of Revelation opens doors to the New Testament as a whole. While this is simply part of the assignment of being a preacher or teacher of the Bible and is an extremely rewarding task, it is not an easy one.

Difficult to Understand

Preachers and teachers should be hesitant to encourage people to read the Bible on the basis that it is "easy," a view which pays less respect to the Bible than to other literature written in ancient times. The dimensions of the Bible which make it valuable also make it difficult to understand. It is historical literature, expressed in the languages and cultural assumptions of a particular age and part of the world, written from within a religious conceptuality often alien to us (e.g., animal sacrifice). Biblical truth is never general moralisms, or narratives that begin "once upon a time," but always presupposes the historical realities and particularities of human existence—and not "human existence" in the abstract but the particular human experience of the people addressed in a certain time and place. This particularity of the biblical message corresponds to the particularity of the incarnation and is an indispensable aspect of biblical truth. It is also what makes the Bible difficult for readers in other times and places to understand, for it requires historical study.

Preachers and teachers who approach the Bible in this way often meet a sincere objection: "Does this mean that only those who have learned a lot of historical information and are equipped with historical method can understand the Bible? Can the sincere believer not find an authentic word of God just by reading the Bible? Is it really necessary to know about Roman emperors and the situation of churches in ancient Turkey to understand Revelation?" The objection contains an important truth, just as it fails to make an important distinction. Quite apart from historical study, the sincere reader of the Bible open to God's word can be *addressed* by the Word of God through Bible reading. We might well be grateful that God does

45

not wait on our perfect understanding before addressing us with his Word. But this is different from *understanding*. We can be addressed, spoken to in a way that shapes our existence, even by that which we do not understand completely, as every traveler in a foreign country knows. But *understanding*, whether it be the language and customs of a foreign country or the message of a biblical text, is difficult and requires study. This is true of Revelation as it is true of biblical books as a whole.

There are, however, particular difficulties inherent in Revelation which make our efforts to understand it even more difficult than other parts of the Bible: Revelation is written in an apocalyptic conceptuality alien to us. It deals with angels, demons, dragons, and beasts in the heavens. It describes the end of the world. It presupposes a view of the cosmos that clashes with our ideas of the structure of the universe: heaven, for instance, is a place to which John can be "caught up" to receive his vision (4:1) and from which the new Jerusalem can "come down" at the end of history (21:2). It is written in a kind of symbolic (not code!) language unfamiliar to us. And another difficulty is presented to many modern western readers: It was written by deprived, oppressed people who had no political or economic power, and knew they were not "in control."

The chief difficulty in understanding Revelation, however, may be neither historical nor conceptual but a matter of the heart. Biblical prophets offer a vision of reality which conflicts with the natural inclinations of the human will and its values (I Cor. 2:6–16). This is powerfully illustrated by John's vision of self-sacrificing love, the slaughtered Lamb, as representing the ultimate power of the universe (5:1–14), which not only goes against the grain of our cultural and conceptual understanding but also conflicts with our commonsense will to power. John's claim that this vision of reality is not our own achievement, the result of our own calculation, but is *revealed*, intensifies a claim latent in all the Bible, a claim to address us with a word from Beyond, a word we naturally resist. Revelation not only claims something about itself, it makes a claim on the reader, a claim we may not want to hear. This native resistance to the call to discipleship may be the ultimate barrier to understanding the message of Revelation. True understanding of Revelation requires belonging to the community in which the same Spirit that inspired John's message continues to be active. This is not an alternative to historical understanding, but it does go beyond it.

46

Can Be Understood

John expected the ordinary men and women of the churches of Asia to understand the book, though they were not Bible scholars, historians, or theological experts. They did not find it necessary to have study groups to discuss its meaning. Nor did they seal up the book for later centuries, when it would be understood (22:10, and contrast Dan. 12:4, 9). The issue for them was not what the book meant, which was transparent in their situation, but whether or not they would respond to its call to the kind of faithfulness advocated by John, even to the point of dying for the faith (2:10!). In succeeding generations, as the original situation of the letter which made it understandable was forgotten, the church which continued to reverence Revelation as a part of its Bible developed other ways of interpreting it. It is instructive to read a thorough history of the interpretation of Revelation (e.g., Bousset, pp. 49–119, still the best through the nineteenth century; cf. also Beckwith, pp. 318–34).

Types of Interpretation

One of the many unhelpful myths that abound with regard to Revelation is that through the centuries everyone has arbitrarily interpreted the book in his or her own way, resulting in an endless variety of interpretations, a trackless jungle. The fact is, Revelation has been interpreted in basically four different ways and their combinations, depending on which historical period the individual interpreter supposed was represented by the visions.

1. The first view can be labeled **non-historical**. (It is also sometimes called "poetic," "spiritual," or "idealist.") It interprets Revelation assuming that the author directs his message to no particular historical period and that the visions reflect no particular historical situation. Prophecy is understood as the visionary expression of "timeless truths." There are two forms of this view, the allegorical and the idealist. After the memory of the historical situation of John's letter faded, the allegorical approach was applied to Revelation as it was to other books of the Bible. In allegory the details of biblical texts are not related to particular historical situations but refer to ideas or events that are universally human. Origen, for instance, interpreted the beast with seven heads of Revelation 13 as representing the awfulness of the power of evil and the seven deadly sins, whenever and wherever they appeared.

47

When the allegorical approach to biblical interpretation passed away, a few interpreters of Revelation continued to read it unhistorically in terms of the spiritual truths symbolized in its visions, the eternal struggle of the kingdom of God with the powers of evil and the ultimate triumph of God's kingdom (Minear, Ellul, Stringfellow). The value of this approach is that it allows Revelation to speak to people in every time and place in terms of universal human symbols. But it ignores or minimizes the specific historical references in Revelation to its first-century situation, robs it of anything specific to say to its first readers who were facing a particular crisis, reduces its message to generalities, and denies its character as a real letter.

2. The **church-historical** interpretation is also called the continuous-historical or the world-historical view. Prophecy is understood as prediction of the long-range future. To be sure, the messages to the seven churches of chapters 2—3 are regarded as addressed to churches of John's own time, but the visions of 4—22 are interpreted as predictions of all of history from John's time through many centuries to the end of the world. In practice this meant that each interpreter saw John as predicting the course of history down to his or her own time. Practitioners of this approach typically see themselves as living in the last period predicted by Revelation. The author of the oldest extant commentary on Revelation, Victorinus of Pettau (ca. 300), understood himself to be living in the time of the sixth seal, just before the End (Bousset, p. 53). A certain parochialism is inherent in this view: Since it flourished in Europe, John was seen as predicting the course of European history, primarily church history, from the first century to the interpreter's own time. Various seals and trumpets are supposed to represent various events and rulers in European history, and the disasters they brought about. Following Luther, Protestant exegetes often saw the Papacy symbolized by the beast. Roman Catholics, in turn, found ways to make the name "Martin Luther" equal 666 (cf. 13:18). Because there is no agreement among the exponents of this view, which has generated a bewildering variety of interpretations, Revelation has the reputation of being interpreted in many different ways. However, all these are variations of one interpretation.

48

The value of the church-historical view was that it allowed the reader to see Revelation as relevant to his or her own time, which it supposedly predicted, and it affirmed that all of history was under the sovereignty of God. The major problems, of course, are apparent: (a) The book would have meant nothing to its first readers, who would have to wait centuries before it could be properly understood; (b) it misunderstands prophecy by reducing it to prediction; (c) the variety of interpretations cancel each other out and invalidate the method. Although widely held by Protestant interpreters after the Reformation and into the twentieth century, no critical New Testament scholar today advocates this view.

3. The **end-historical,** also called the "futurist," "dispensationalist," and "pre-millennialist" interpretation, likewise considers the prophecy of Revelation to be prediction, but it differs from the preceding view in two important ways: (a) The seven churches of chapters two and three are no longer seven real churches in first-century Asia but represent seven periods of church history from the apostolic church (Ephesus) to the dead church of the last days (Laodicea)—typically understood as the apostate church in the interpreter's own time. This interpretation has always flourished outside the "mainline" churches, which are considered to be degenerate. (b) The remainder of the book (chaps. 4—22) predicts only the events that are to happen in the last few years of world history and the eschatological events themselves. This means that most of the book predicts events still in the future of the advocates of this interpretation, who unanimously see themselves as living in the time *just before* the final countdown. The beast of chapter 13, for instance, is a monstrous ruling power yet to appear, "the last form of Gentile world power," a confederation of ten nations which will be the revival of the old Roman Empire (Scofield Reference Bible note on Rev. 13:1). This interpretation is correct to the extent that it recognizes that Revelation deals with eschatology and foresees only a short time before the End. Among its major problems is that it locates this brief interval in the *interpreter's* lifetime, thus making the whole book meaningless to its first readers. It too misconstrues the nature of prophecy and the kind of language used in Revelation and usually supports a sectarian understanding of Christianity.

It is this interpretation that has become so pervasive among media "evangelists" and the purveyors of pop-eschatological literature. It is an insidiously dangerous interpretation of Revelation, since it often advocates the necessity of a nuclear war as part of God's plan for the eschaton "predicted" in Revelation.

The preacher or teacher might well be aware of the historical roots and rationale for this interpretation. This is the most recent of the four types of interpretation, its basic lineaments having been devised by a group of British and American fundamentalist ministers during the late nineteenth century's concern for the "apostasy" of the church. It was congealed into a doctrinal system by John Nelson Darby within the group of Plymouth Brethren in England, then popularized in America by Charles Ingersoll Scofield. Scofield was a St. Louis lawyer-turned-preacher without theological education who published an edition of the Bible, the Scofield Reference Bible, with his interpretative scheme embodied in the footnotes and incorporated into the outline headings of the biblical text itself. Scofield founded the Correspondence Bible School in Dallas, Texas, as his own personal enterprise, not representing any church. The Correspondence Bible School continued after Scofield's death as Dallas Theological Seminary and has been the major center for the dissemination of this dispensational view. (Further details of dispensationalism are found in Ahlstrom, pp. 808–12. On recent militarist use of Revelation to advocate nuclear war, see Halsell.)

4. In the **contemporary-historical** interpretation, "contemporary" refers to John and his contemporaries, not to the period contemporary with the reader. This view is also called "preterist" (a grammatical term equivalent to "past tense"), historical, and historical-critical. Except for the potential confusion with the "church-historical" view above, we could simply designate this view as the "historical" interpretation. That is, it is simply the application of historical method to the study of Revelation, attempting to determine the meaning of a text in its original historical context, to its original readers, before attempting to determine its meaning to us. This interpreation understands Revelation to be directed to a particular situation in the first century, just as were the other New Testament letters. This is the view detailed above and represented in this commentary, as it is the method followed by practically all critical Bible scholars of all theological persuasions today. Contrary to popular supposition, there is a broad consensus of agreement among such scholars on the interpretation of Revelation, more than for most New Testament books. This view assumes that John had a message to the churches to which he was writing which concerned their own situation, that they understood the message,

and that the modern interpreter cannot accept any interpretation of the book which its first readers would not have understood. Exactly as in the case of interpreting Paul's letter to Rome, the interpreter assumes that legitimate interpretation must be responsible to and derived from the meaning the text had for its original readers, even if it does not simply repeat it.

Interpreting Symbolic, Mythological Language

In interpreting Revelation two types of language need to be distinguished and contrasted. These are not simply "figurative" and "literal," for "figurative" language can be interpreted with a kind of pedestrian literal-mindedness (see Funk, pp. 111–38). The issue is not just "literal" or "figurative" but "propositional" or "pictorial." John of course uses both types of language, not only pictorial. Human life cannot function without the everyday use of propositional language. But the message of John's visions is expressed primarily in pictorial language, which can best be characterized in comparison and contrast to propositional language:

Propositional language is objectifying language. It supposes it is talking about objects, realities that can be grasped by our minds and described by our language. This style of discourse tends to suppose that all true language refers to something "out there" in the "real" world and that language is serving its proper truth function when it accurately describes this reality. It supposes that the only alternative to this kind of language is "subjective," to which the condescending adjective "merely" is often prefixed. Subjectivity is disdained; truth is best described "objectively," from the spectator, non-involved standpoint.

Propositional language may use "symbols," but only in a literalizing manner, as "signs" or "steno symbols." It understands "symbols" as codes for literal, objectifying meanings. The Greek letter "Pi" is a symbol in this sense for the relationship between the circumference and the radius of a circle, as are mathematical symbols in general. This type of symbol can readily be translated into propositional language, for which it is only a convenient shorthand designation.

Propositional language is logical. It operates within the canons of logic and inference, and thus makes consistency a criterion of truth.

Propositional language is diachronic. It deals with things one at a time, in a straightforward and chronological manner,

51

prizes this kind of clarity as an indication of truth, and considers the attempt to deal with "everything at once" to be a mark not of profundity but of confusion.

Propositional language contrasts "myth" with "truth." Propositional language tends to use "mythical" as a synonym for "false," and to contrast it with "fact," which is equated with "truth." At most, "myth," like "symbol," may be used in a decorative or illustrative manner for something which supposedly can be said more clearly in straightforward propositional language.

To a degree greater than other apocalyptic texts, the language of Revelation is visionary language that deals in pictures rather than propositions. Pictures themselves are important to John as the vehicle of his message. They are not mere illustrations of something that can be said more directly. A picture makes its own statement, is its own text. It does not communicate what it has to say by being reduced to discursive, propositional language. Just as is the case in visiting an art gallery, while commentary and explanation may help one to "get the picture," language about the picture can never replace the message communicated in and through the picture itself.

In preaching and teaching it may be helpful to point out that John gives us images by which to imagine the ultimate End of all things, just as Genesis gives us images by which to imagine ultimate beginnings. It is not only a matter of religious faith, but is the accepted scientific view, that there will be an end to our present cosmos, just as there was a beginning. How should we think of it? *Ultimates can best be expressed in pictures, especially word pictures, by artists, rather than in logical, propositional statements.* Most of those who struggle to interpret Revelation will already have worked out a way to interpret the pictures of Genesis 1—3 that does not take them literally but still takes them seriously as the vehicle of God's word and on this basis can appreciate that picture language is the best medium for dealing with ultimates. Just as the pictures in Genesis need not conflict with the pictures of the origins of the universe and human life given by scientific research but communicate the *meaning* of the origin of the universe as God's creation and the origins of humanity as God's creatures, so the pictures of Revelation communicate the *meaning* of the end and goal of history without claiming to give scientific descriptions of it. The honest question naturally arises, "Why should one take these

images more seriously than others" (bang, whimper)? The response of biblical faith: "The pictures of ultimate beginnings in
Genesis and the ultimate ending in Revelation are not arbitrarily devised pictures, but they represent the collection of canonical images filtered through generations of Israel's and the
church's faith, a process in which the Spirit of God was active."

We may now characterize Revelation's pictorial language
in contrast to the propositional language described above:

Revelation's pictorial language is non-objectifying. Revelation does not "teach" a "doctrine" of the "second coming," the
"millennium," and such, but holds vivid pictures before us,
pictures which point beyond themselves to ultimate reality.
The non-objectifying pictorial language of Revelation acknowledges that our language and concepts cannot grasp ultimate
reality as it is; it can only point toward ultimate reality. This
does not mean that pictorial language gives up its claim to talk
about it. The language of Revelation is not only expressive po-
etry, it is also referential language. It is glad to abandon any
claim to describe this reality in an objectifying manner, for the
reality to which it points transcends anything that can be objectively described by finite minds and language. But the content
of Revelation is not just the subjective poetic outpourings of
John's own religious experience. What John has to say does
indeed refer to something: God's transcendent world and the
ultimate goal of the creation. It points to these transcendent
realities in a language which knows the limitation of language
itself to express them (cf. 10:4 and the commentary *ad loc.*). It
cannot fully describe or communicate them. It points—but it
points to something.

The language of Revelation is not descriptive spectator language. In interpreting Revelation it must never be forgotten
that the letter was written to be read in worship. Its language
is the participatory, confessional language of the involved worshiper, not the cool abstractions of the observer. Its statements
are not to be taken as premises on which a chain of logical
inferences can be built in order to construct doctrine; its statements are confessions of prayer and praise. Profoundly theological as it is, its language is more akin to the Psalter than to a
volume of systematic theology. Although the surface form of
John's language is often that of a reporter describing what he
has seen in the heavenly world, it does not actually function that
way, and it is misunderstood if taken as descriptive spectator

language. Many of the scenes John describes simply cannot be imaged. Not only can they not be placed on a canvas or movie screen, they cannot be placed on the screen of the mind. The vision of the exalted Christ in 1:12–16, for example, simply becomes grotesque if one attempts to understand it as a reporter's account of what John actually saw in the objective world. If one understands it as a description in objectifying language, one must then ask such questions as how the risen Christ spoke at all, with a sharp two-edged sword coming from his mouth, and what happened to the sword when he closed his mouth? The picture does become meaningful when understood as John's literary composition, however, in which the sword had traditionally symbolized the sharpness and power of God's word (cf. Isa. 49:2; Heb. 4:12; Eph. 6:17). John's language is not discursive, propositional logic, but neither is it description of scenes that can be imaged. His language stands on the border between word and picture: carefully crafted literary words that function to evoke "images" in the imagination that cannot really be imaged—one "feels the impact" (J. J. Collins, "Introduction," p. 79), though one cannot quite portray, even to oneself, what the "images" convey.

Revelation's symbols are tensive, evocative, and polyvalent. Revelation's pictorial language is not to be understood as steno symbols, code or allegory (which can also be used in their literal sense by propositional language). All these are only alternate forms of propositional language.

Revelation is not code-language, which communicates what it has to say by being translated into propositional language. For code-language, all one needs is the key. Code-language intentionally does not say what it means, in order to conceal the meaning from those who do not know the code. Code-language represents one letter, word, concept by another in such a manner that the encoded language can be decoded into another language. Code is thus a kind of *literal* language. This is different from John's *symbolic* language, which is polyvalent. It has sometimes been suggested that in view of the political situation under which Revelation was written John wrote his message in code so the Christians but not the Roman authorities could understand it. This view is false on several counts: (a) Only a fraction of the visionary material deals with Rome, yet all the visions are expressed in symbolic language; (b) the references to

54

Rome are transparent (e.g., 17:9, 18), so that only a very dull Roman would be fooled; (c) there are many undisguised statements that could be taken as subversive by the Romans—the many references to God or Christ as a king (11:15), even the ruler of earthly kings and King of kings (1:5; 17:14; 19:16), titles claimed by the Roman emperors, as well as the references to Christians having a kingdom (1:6); (d) unlike a code, John's symbols are not arbitrarily devised but are traditional and widespread (The combat myth at the basis of the imagery in chapters 12 and 13, for instance, was shared in one version or another by every people in the Greco-Roman world); (e) John used symbols in order to *communicate* that which cannot be expressed in any other way, not to *conceal* something that could be said more straightforwardly. The question was not *who* was meant by the imagery—that it was the Roman power was transparent to all. The question was rather *what* the Roman power represented. With reference to the Roman government, John does not veil whom he really means; he writes to reveal the essential nature of the Roman power, which was not at all obvious to many members of John's churches (*apocalypse* means literally "removing the veil").

The open-ended, polyvalent nature of John's symbolism means that, although the particular referent of John's imagery in his situation can often be identified with some probability, the significance of his language is not exhausted when, for example, the beast is identified with Rome, Nero, or Domitian. It is this evocative, polyvalent potential that allows his imagery to speak powerfully in more than one set of historical circumstances. "Babylon" (17:1–14), for instance, is not a univocal code-word simply identical with "Rome"—though that was the meaning in John's situation. Later generations of Christians have rightly used John's imagery to expose the true nature of arrogant human empire. This is different, of course, from claiming that John "predicted" these later situations. Thus the purpose of this commentary is not to offer a "decoded" version of Revelation. The modern reader misses the richness and power of Revelation's "visionary rhetoric" (Fiorenza, *Book of Revelation,* p. 187) if he or she supposes that what John was "really" talking about is achieved merely by scratching "Babylon" and inserting "Rome." Such reductionistic interpretation, valid as it sometimes is at one level, may actually serve as a way of *insulat-*

ing the modern reader from what Revelation may speak to us. "Explanation" is still not understanding; treating John's symbols as code is still not interpretation.

Revelation was not written primarily in allegorical language, although the document does contain a few allegorical touches. In allegory each feature of the vision or narrative represents some other reality. An example of allegorical interpretation can be found in Matthew 13:36–43, which interprets the parable of 13:24–30. When Revelation's visions are interpreted allegorically, each feature in the vision represents some mundane reality. An allegorical interpretation of the dragon in 12:3–4, for instance, would attempt to determine the meaning of the seven heads, the ten horns, the color red, the tail, and the third of the stars. While John himself occasionally interprets such details in a somewhat allegorical fashion (e.g., 1:20; 5:8; 17:9–10; 19:8), in the main his visions convey their message by means of the evocative impression they make as a whole. The vivid details serve as stage-setting, round out the picture, and enliven the total vision, but each detail is not allegorically important in itself.

Revelation is not signs but symbolic vision. John's language is not the language of signs that may be translated unambiguously into propositional language. Paul Tillich's distinction between "sign" and "symbol" is helpful here (*Dynamics,* pp. 41–42). "Sign" language is represented, for example, by traffic signs, which may be translated unambiguously into another medium, while the Eucharist is a symbol that cannot be reduced to something else. A national flag may be perceived either as sign or symbol. When the American flag is "explained" on the level that the thirteen stripes represent the thirteen original states, while the fifty stars represent the fifty current states, it is being interpreted as a sign. But when it is proudly carried in a patriotic parade or burned in a protest, its symbolic nature is clear. Both levels can be present at once, as the flag illustration indicates, so that the same vision in Revelation can be read at more than one level at the same time.

Neither is John's symbolic language the language of steno symbols that, like signs, can be reduced to discursive, objectifying language. The distinction between steno symbols and tensive symbols, made popular by Philip Wheelwright, is helpful in obtaining an adequate interpretation of John's symbols. Wheelwright's "steno symbols" are like Tillich's "signs," in that they do not produce any tension in the mind and would defeat their purpose if they did. Again, traffic signs may serve as the illustration: In traffic lights "red" means "stop," period. The traffic sign or signal is straightforward and unambiguous and would make havoc of the intersection if it were otherwise. A tensive symbol, on the other hand, sets up a tension in the mind, evokes images and overtones of meaning, and by involving the hearer-reader in the act of communication conveys a surplus of meaning that cannot be reduced to propositional language, or even to one level of meaning. A Lamb that shepherds (7:17) is a tensive symbol, as is the Lion that is a Lamb (5:5–6). A tensive symbol does not convey a clear "concept" that may be stated in objective discursive language. Tensive symbols are not informational; John's symbolic language does not function to convey objective information about the heavenly world.

Revelation's pictorial language is non-logical and non-inferential. The language of Revelation is not logically consistent language. Since John's language attempts to communicate the reality of God's transcendent world, it cannot and does not adhere to the laws of logical propositional language. This does not mean that John is irrational but that the ultimate realities he attempts to communicate shatter such language. Interpreters of Revelation should not attempt to fit John's surrealistic pictures into the logical and chronological confines of a space-time world.

Pictorial language can communicate the message expressed by a certain picture, vision, or symbol without affirming all the implications of the message if it were reduced to propositional language. Such pictorial language says what it says, not what it implies; it does not function as part of a larger logical inferential system. The Genesis narrative gives the reader a picture of Cain marrying and begetting children (Gen. 4:17). If one reduces this picture to linear logic, Cain's wife can only have been his sister (cf. Gen. 1—3). Yet the picture of Cain's wife does not even raise the question of who she was or where she came from, let alone "answer" it. Such questions miscontrue the kind of pictorial language as objectifying propositional language from which inferences can legitimately be made. Likewise, the pictorial language of Revelation presents us with images, each of which conveys its message evocatively and impressionistically, not in an objectifying manner from which inferences can be made. To ask how the sea can give up the dead in 20:13 when it has

57

already passed away with "earth and heaven" (the universe of Gen. 1:1; cf. NEB, TEV) in 20:11 is to misconstrue John's language, the same kind of question as "Where did Cain get his wife?" The truth of each picture is what it says, not the points that can be inferred from it. If John's language is misconstrued as inferential language from which additional "points" can be inferred, the result is a conglomeration of conflicting points—indication enough that his pictures do not function in terms of linear logic.

Revelation's pictorial language is not diachronic but synchronic. It functions not in terms of linear logic but as a gestalt of simultaneous images. The coherence of the Apocalypse is not the unity of linear logic of the type that could be represented in a two-dimensional chart or list of propositional statements but "a web interlaced in different ways" (Thompson, p. 16). We thus find numerous instances where John has more than one picture of the same ultimate reality, pictures which if reduced to propositional language clash with each other logically (e.g., the two books in 20:12; cf. commentary). While picture language is a better vehicle for dealing with ultimates than discursive propositional language, no *one* picture can capture or convey the reality of its subject matter. Thus a plurality of pictures of the same reality are found in Revelation, pictures that cannot be logically harmonized if reduced to statements, and yet pictures that cannot be reduced to one picture. No one picture can comprehend the ultimate, nor can all the pictures be fitted together into one super-picture. More than one picture is necessary when attempting to communicate transcendent truth. Conflicting pictures should not be "harmonized" with a pseudoconciliatory "both/and" or "partly/partly." Each should carry its full message even when it cannot be logically harmonized with other pictures. For example, Revelation sometimes pictures Christ as in heaven, enthroned *above* the turmoil of earth. The "point": Christ has already suffered, died, and triumphed, and stands behind this as a model for suffering Christians. Yet Christ is also pictured as *present* with his community, sharing their suffering. As propositional, objectifying language, these statements can only compete with each other; as pictures, both communicate christological reality, and neither picture should be sacrificed to the other. This logical and chronological oddity of John's symbolic language is not a defect but of the essence of symbolic language that deals with the ultimate.

Revelation's pictorial language uses myth as the vehicle of truth. John regards the conflict that rages between the values of the Roman religion and culture and those of the Christian faith to be a clash of transcendent realities: God versus Satan, which can be adequately expressed only in mythological language. The word "myth" is used in many senses. Here it is used to designate that kind of metaphorical narrative language that expresses the reality of the transcendent world in this-worldly imagery (the only imagery we have or could understand). Mythical language is the vehicle for expressing what one wants to say about the transcendent world, the world of divine reality not subject to empirical, scientific language.

The preacher and teacher will need to be clear about the nature and value of mythological language. Those whom he or she is attempting to help understand Revelation will have different assessments of "myth." Some will have a "scientific" view of the world that is suspicious of all mythical language, has difficulty in taking it seriously, and/or is offended by it. Others may identify "believing the Bible" with understanding mythical pictorial language as objectifying language, even if they concede that it is "symbolic" in the sense that propositional language uses "symbols," which is still a kind of literalism ("literal non-literal," cf. Funk).

Worth the Effort to Understand

A realistic appraisal indicates that it will take considerable effort to understand Revelation. Why should anyone make the effort? There are at least five reasons: canonical, apologetic/defensive, political, cosmic/environmental, fitness.

1. Canonical. Revelation is a part of our Bible. We are concerned with knowing and understanding Revelation for the same reason we are concerned to hear and understand the Bible as such: to measure the message we set forth as the Christian faith by its normative documents, to avoid having this message become merely the echo of the religiosity of our culture or of our own psyches.

2. Apologetic/defensive. Revelation will not lie dormant; it will always be interpreted by someone for the church and for the population at large. If responsible interpreters within the mainstream of church tradition do not make the effort to set forth the message of Revelation in terms that are faithful both to the Scripture and to our own times, this task goes by default to others. Christian preachers and teachers have a responsi-

59

bility inherent in the task of ministry to offer a viable alternative to irresponsible and sensationalist interpreters.

3. Political. We are political beings who live our lives in social, political structures. Revelation is a political book. It was not written for the individualist oriented to the other world who is concerned only with getting his or her own soul to heaven. Revelation was written to people in Christian communities who had to come to terms with hard political and social decisions. A clash of loyalties occupies the book, which has among its primary images "throne," "kingdom," "power"; it concludes with the vision of a redeemed city, not a picture of isolated individuals on solitary clouds.

4. Cosmic/environmental. Revelation is concerned with the fate of the earth and the cosmos. In our generation talk of "the end of the world" is heard not only among Bible scholars, theologians, and church people but also among physicists, geologists, astronomers, politicians. *Cosmos* (Sagan) and *The Fate of the Earth* (Schell), two widely read serious and thoughtful books, are concerned with human responsibility for the earth in a context where the "end of the world" is a real possibility. Study of Revelation lets such discussions be heard in an illuminating Christian theological context.

5. Fitness. "Fitness" means "appropriateness." Revelation is appropriate for our time because, despite the fact that in many ways its times were unlike our own, there are fundamental ways in which John's time and ours are much alike. John lived in a pre-Christendom situation, before there was a Christian culture with momentum to transmit Christian perspectives and values as part of the cultural heritage. The Christian communities to which he wrote were minorities, in a pluralistic world, without legality, respectability, impressive size, or institutions, who could not depend on the culture to present the Christian option. They were not a reflection of the religiosity of the culture, but within the culture offered a different option for the meaning of life and its values. To be a Christian meant to be a witness to this Christian message. This is why the language of witness and testimony plays such a large role in Revelation. We too live in a situation without Christendom, in which the church is once again a minority in a pluralistic world. Even in western countries, where the remnants of Christendom persist, the church is but one voice in a competing pluralistic society. Revelation has an appropriate message for such a church. "Fit-

60

ness" also means disciplined, "being in shape." Study of Revelation can help to equip Christians to be disciples of Christ in a pluralistic world.

Its Influence in Religion, History, and Culture

We may be grateful that Revelation has provided more than a morbid fascination for the religious quacks and cranks of history—it has attracted and inspired the great minds who have shaped the images that have influenced our culture and history. In the history of art one thinks, for example, of Albrecht Dürer's series of woodcuts (e.g., the *Four Horsemen of the Apocalypse, Saint Michael Fighting the Dragon*), and *The Prophet John and Christ*, of Michelangelo's *Last Judgment* in the Sistine Chapel, of Hubert and Jan van Eyck's *Adoration of the Lamb* in the Ghent altarpiece. Recent studies have shown that the form of the medieval cathedral, down to the smallest details, was influenced by the pattern of the heavenly city of Revelation 21:1—22:6. In accord with Augustine's exposition of Revelation, which interpreted the church as the city of God in a perpetual state of "descending to earth" (*City of God* 20.17), artists and architects were much influenced by John's vision of the beauty of the new Jerusalem, which they attempted to reflect in their majestic creations of stone and glass, light and color (cf. Rissi, *The Future of the World*, p. 39). In music oratorios such as Handel's *Messiah* come to mind and popular hymns such as Matthew Bridges' "Crown Him with Many Crowns" and language and imagery from many other hymns ("Holy, holy, holy! . . . casting down their golden crowns around the glassy sea . . ."). Scholars such as Joseph Priestly *(The Present State of Europe, Compared with Ancient Prophecies)* and Sir Isaac Newton *(Observations on the Prophecies of Daniel and the Apocalypse of John)* have been students of Revelation. In literature one could mention George Eliot's *Romola*, Edmund Spenser's *Faerie Queene*, D. H. Lawrence's *Apocalypse*, Dante's *Divine Comedy*, Thomas Hobbes' *Leviathan*, and John Milton's *Paradise Lost*. Revelation's vision of a redeemed social order has provided the stimulus for resistance to injustice and oppression in many settings, influencing, for example, Daniel Berrigan *(Beside the Sea of Glass)* and Martin Luther King, Jr. ("We Shall Overcome" was inspired by the vision of those who "conquer" by passive resistance in Revelation; "overcome" was the rendering of "conquer" in KJV).

61

INTERPRETATION

Its Message for the Contemporary Church

The preceding discussion has been written in the conviction that while Revelation does not speak *about* our time, it does speak *to* it. As important as Revelation has been for its inspiration for art, music, and literature, its significance for the church is not that of an aesthetic object to be enjoyed but the vehicle of a message to be heard and obeyed. It would be a violation of Revelation's mode of communication to attempt to summarize its message in a manner that would make the text itself unnecessary. The following commentary is not intended as a statement of the meaning of Revelation. It is intended as an aid to facilitate an encounter with the text in which Revelation will communicate its own message in the mind and imagination of the reader.

PART ONE

God Speaks
to the Church in the City

REVELATION 1:1—3:22

Jesus Christ is not dead, absent, hidden, or silent; he is present among his churches and speaks through his prophet to the distress and crisis of their particular situations in a revelation that comes ultimately from God (1:1–3). This message from the risen Christ is conveyed in letter form (1:4–8) which begins with John on the island of Patmos, where he receives a vision of the exalted Christ (1:9–20), whose word is communicated to the churches in seven messages (2:1—3:22).

The first three chapters of Revelation form one indivisible unit that must be interpreted together. The vision of Christ in 1:9–20 cannot be considered by itself, for the only act of Christ in this vision is to dictate the messages to the seven churches. Nor can the "letters to the seven churches" be interpreted apart from the vision of Christ in chapter 1, to which they are integrally related in vocabulary and form. As the Christophany of chapter 1 looks ahead to the messages of chapters 2—3 as its goal, so the seven messages look back to the appearance of Christ in chapter 1 as their basis. On the other hand, there is a clear break in form and content between chapter 3 and chapter 4. The scene in chapters 1—3 is an earthly scene with this-worldly relationships. At 4:1 the scene changes as John is caught up into the heavenly world and communication is on the transcendent plane. When one is preaching or teaching from any of the smaller subunits discussed below, their context in the larger unit of chapters 1—3 should be kept in mind.

Revelation 1:1-3
Titular Summary

The title in our Bibles, "The Revelation to John," and its variations in the manuscripts, is not from John but was added by church editors during the process of canonization. John's "title," which is really a titular summary of the document, is found in verses 1–3. John's title is similar to the titles of Old Testament prophetic books and thus identifies John's letter in the minds of the hearer-readers with the prophetic books of the Scripture they were accustomed to hearing read in worship (cf. Isa. 1:1; Jer. 1:1; Ezek. 1:2–3; Hos. 1:1; Joel 1:1; Amos 1:1; Obad. 1:1; Micah 1:1; Nahum 1:1; Hab. 1:1; Zeph. 1:1; Hag. 1:1; Zech. 1:1; Mal. 1:1). John's letter is by no means yet "Bible" for his hearer-readers; their Scripture was the "Old Testament." Yet John places his writing in continuity with the biblical revelation. The God who speaks here is not a different God from the one heard in the words of the biblical prophets.

In his first words John indicates that the revelation is *signified* (1:1; RSV "made known"). The word John uses as the main verb for the revelatory act is *esemanen,* the verb form of the noun *semeion,* usually translated "sign" elsewhere in the New Testament (e.g., John 20:30) and meaning "symbol" in the sense discussed above ("Interpreting Symbolic, Mythological Language"). The revelation from heaven is not simply a straightforward report, for heavenly things cannot be so simply spoken about, but neither does it conceal the transcendent realities; it points to them in a series of evocative images which involve the hearer-reader in the interpretative process.

The title added later by the church identifies the book as the "Revelation of John." John himself identified it as the revelation of Jesus Christ (1:1). As is also the case in English, the "of" here is ambiguous in John's Greek text. It could be taken in the objective genitive sense (a revelation about Jesus Christ) or the subjective genitive sense (a revelation from Jesus Christ), or a combination of the two. The grammar (the connection with the relative clause) as well as the theology (the setting of Jesus

64

Christ within the revelatory chain) and the nature of Christian prophecy (which comes directly to the prophet from the risen Christ but is not necessarily about him) all indicate that John intends the expression in the subjective genitive sense. What the hearer-reader is about to receive is a revelation from Jesus, the exalted Lord of the church who is present with his congregations in worship and addresses them in the prophetic word.

The revelation does not originate with Jesus, however. It is the revelation he receives from God. Thus the content of Revelation can be called, as a whole, "word of God" (1:2; 19:9). Nor does it come directly from Jesus to the churches; it proceeds through the angel and especially through the prophet John, so that the book as a whole can also be called "all that he [John] saw" (1:2). Designating the book in its totality as word of God, revelation from Christ and Christ's own testimony, and at the same time word of the human being John is important for us theologically. John conceived this simultaneity of the divine word and the human word as one inseparable revelatory event.

God is the ultimate source of the revelation. The word that is heard in Revelation is ultimately the Word of God (v. 2; cf. 19:9, 13). John's theology is thoroughly theocentric. As in Genesis 1:1, so also in Revelation 1:1, the first active verb in the first sentence has God for its subject, the God who is the hidden actor throughout. For John, Christ is not a competitor or alternative to the one God. But who is God for John? How should we think of this One with whom we ultimately have to do?

Christ is the definitive member of the revelatory "chain." John does not call his document "God's revelation through Jesus," which would make Jesus only another member of the chain. Jesus is not merely one member among several; he is mentioned first as the constituting member of the revelatory chain. For John, God is not someone we already know on some other basis than his self-revelation in Jesus, about whom Jesus then gives further increments of information. What God has to say to the churches and through them to the world is mediated through Christ. For John, as for Christian faith generally, "God" is "the one definitively revealed through Jesus Christ." The christological affirmations of Revelation are not a response to the question "Who is Jesus?" but "Who is God?" (cf. Ogden). As "God" is defined by "Christ," so "Christ" is defined by "Jesus." "Jesus" for John is not the teacher or miracle worker; primarily he is the one who died at the hands of the Romans, not as a

65

tragic victim but as the act of God for our salvation. As "Christ" is defined by "Jesus," so "Jesus" is defined by "dying-for-us" (1:5*b*; 5:9). In Jesus, God has defined himself as the one who suffers for others, whose suffering love is the instrument of the creation's redemption.

The angel is a typical figure in apocalypses (cf. e.g., Dan. 9:20–23; II Esdr. 4:1), appearing frequently in the revelatory and visionary scenes of early Christianity (cf. e.g., Luke 1:11–23, 26–38; Acts 10:3; 27:23). Such revelatory angels play a prominent role in the visions of John's apocalypse as well (chaps. 14—17; 20—22), but John is concerned that not too much be made of them. Like Paul, John's worldview includes the reality of angelic beings (cf. Gal. 1:8–9; Rom. 8:38–39), but he wants the hearer-readers to understand that angels are only creatures of God like the Christians themselves and are not to be accorded transcendent honors (19:9–10; 22:8–9; and contrast Col. 2:18). The angel thus plays only a stereotypical role in the revelatory event, in accord with the first-century worldview.

John is himself an indispensable link in the revelatory chain which mediates God's word to the world. Every word of the prophecy is the prophet's own word, bearing the impress of his own personal history, written in his language and thought patterns for his situation. This is not an alternative to seeing the whole book as the "word of God and the testimony of Jesus Christ" (v. 2). The way the revelatory event is thought of here is analogous to (but not identical with) what happens in the act of preaching, in which word of the preacher repeatedly becomes word of God without ceasing to be the human word of the preacher; this is analogous to the incarnation itself, in which once for all Jesus became the presence and definitive revelation of God without ceasing to be the truly human Jesus.

His (God's/Jesus') servants are the recipients of the revelation, and not John alone. John's revelatory experiences were not intended as private religious experiences to be treasured for his own personal benefit. Christian prophecy generally had its setting and function in the worship life of the community, not in the private life of the individual prophet. John is a link in a chain, an agent of a mission.

The world is not explicitly mentioned in this chain. This corresponds to the view that the prophetic message is directed to the community of faith, that community with a tradition of prophetic speech that is equipped to accept, understand, and critique the revelatory word (I Cor. 14:29). But the prophetic message is not restricted to insiders; it is also intended for outsiders (I Cor. 14:23–25). "The world" is always implicitly included in the prophetic message. This corresponds to the "testimony" nature of prophecy twice mentioned here (John "bore witness" to the "testimony" of Jesus Christ) and is important throughout the book (1:9; 6:9; 12:17; 19:10; 22:16, 20). The revelatory message is directed to the church, but not for its private enjoyment. On the basis of the prophetic message, the church is to bear witness to the world, the ultimate object of the love and care of the God who speaks in this book. The revelatory chain is also a chain of command: God, Christ, angel, prophet, church.

The titular summary closes with a beatitude (1:3), a pronouncement of blessing on the lector who reads forth John's letter in the worship services of the Asian churches and on those who hear and obey the prophetic message it contains. That John has exactly seven beatitudes (1:3; 14:13; 16:15; 19:9; 20:6; 22:7, 14) is an indication that he considers the form itself important. The beatitude was one of the powerful linguistic forms used by the prophets of Israel (Isa. 19:25; 30:18; 56:2; Jer. 17:7), adopted by Jesus (Matt. 5:3–12; Luke 6:20–23), and continued in the apocalyptic tradition by Christian prophets. As used by Jesus and the prophets, it was not an expression of commonsense conventional wisdom (cf. e.g., Prov. 3:13; Sir. 25:8) but a declaration of the way things really are in the face of empirical evidence. A beatitude is performative language, in the indicative mood. As indicative language, it declares something to be a fact, rather than exhorting. As performative language (like "I do" in a wedding ceremony, or "I forgive you" in personal relations), it does not merely describe something that happens—it makes it happen. The saying of it makes it happen; the pronouncement of blessing conveys the blessing. In preaching and teaching such language should not be perverted too quickly into the language of exhortation. In this text the blessing pronounced on the lector and the hearers of this book should not become a homily along the lines of "we really should read the Bible." Rather, this text assumes that there will be Christian congregations that assemble to worship and that within their worship services this book will be read forth as a message from the risen Christ, and it therefore pronounces such congregations blessed.

67

INTERPRETATION

The blessing embraces those who hear in the full biblical sense, those who respond in obedience to the prophetic word mediated by the book. Again, this is not to be understood individualistically. In its context it means those who live as part of the faithful community, participating in its confession of Christ as Lord despite the cultural and political pressures to the contrary, in solidarity with other Christian communities, with its life oriented by the word of God spoken definitively in Christ. However it may appear empirically, John pronounces this community to be blessed. When the pronouncement is accepted in faith, the indicative is heard to contain an imperative; the gift becomes an assignment.

REFLECTION

Interpreting the "Near End" in Revelation

Twice in these opening words, before John gives us a glimpse of the content of his message, he tells us that the book reveals what must "soon" take place (v. 1) and that "the time is near" (v. 3). These comments are more than incidental; they are integral to his message: the first one is a word he has intentionally added to the scriptural expression borrowed from Daniel 2:28; the second instance comes as the emphatic conclusion of this unit, giving the basis for the obedient response to which it calls the hearer-readers.

Like John, we must face this issue of the expectation of the nearness of the End squarely and early on, for it is fundamental to interpreting not only the Apocalypse but much of the New Testament. The interpreter who learns how to deal faithfully with this issue here learns something that will be helpful in understanding the New Testament as a whole.

We may first note that this motif of the nearness of the End is woven throughout into the fabric of the Apocalypse. In addition to 1:1 and 1:3 just noted, the following references in Revelation affirm the nearness of the End:

2:16. The risen Jesus warns those in Pergamum to repent, because he is coming soon.

2:25. The risen Jesus encourages the faithful at Thyatira to hold fast what they have "until I come." While no interval is specified before this "coming" is to occur, the word loses its function of encouragement to steadfast endurance if a long period is intended; and it becomes utterly meaningless if a span of centuries is what is meant.

3:11. Similarly to the church at Philadelphia, "I am coming soon" functions as encouragement to faithfulness.

3:20. "Behold, I stand at the door and knock" is not only a spatial image for the church at Laodicea but a temporal image often found in apocalyptic which reflects the shortness of time before the coming of Christ: He is already at the door (cf. Mark 13:29; Luke 12:36; James 5:9).

6:11. The souls of the martyrs already in heaven who cry out for God's eschatological judgment of the world and ask "How long?" receive the response that they must wait only "a little longer."

10:6. The "mighty angel" in the vision swears by the Creator that there is to be "no more delay," but that the "mystery of God, as he announced to his servants the prophets," the divine plan for the establishment of God's just rule at the end of history, is about to be fulfilled.

11:2–3; 12:6. The longest period mentioned in Revelation is this span of time described variously as forty-two months, or 1260 days, derived from the period of three and a half years prophesied in Daniel 7:25; 8:14; 9:27; 12:7; 11, 12. This period became a traditional apocalyptic time frame (cf. Luke 4:25 and James 5:17 vs. I Kings 17:1; 18:1). While there is no reason to think John took the period as a literally exact definition of how much time remained before the End, there is also no reason to interpret it in terms of generations or centuries, as the context in each instance makes clear.

12:12. The evil that John's churches are suffering will intensify, in John's view, because the devil "knows that his time is short."

17:10. There are to be seven "kings" altogether, and John and his hearer-readers live in the time of the sixth. While this passage is difficult to interpret precisely (see commentary below), it is clear that in John's view only one more "king" (emperor) is to reign before the eschatological events begin.

22:6. The angel declares that the preceding visions reveal "what must soon take place."

22:7. The risen Christ declares "I am coming soon."

22:10. In contrast to Daniel, which was composed in the

literary form of a document written centuries before the events with which it deals were to take place and then "sealed" until the appropriate time, Revelation is not to be sealed, "for the time is near"; it deals with events of the time in which it is written.

22:12. The risen Christ declares (again!) he is coming soon.

22:20. "Surely I am coming soon" are the last words from heaven John hears, as "soon" was his own first word in 1:1.

This emphasis on the nearness of the End is not a peculiarity of Revelation. That the end of history is near in the writer's own time is a constituent part of apocalyptic thought (see the Introduction); thus it appears not only in Revelation but in other apocalypses, in and out of the Bible.

Major elements of earliest Christianity understood and expressed their new faith in apocalyptic terms, thus supposing that they were the last generation. The resurrection of Jesus was interpreted as the beginning of the eschatological event of the resurrection of all. Jesus was the "first fruits" (I Cor. 15:20); the remainder of the eschatological harvest was soon to follow. This apocalyptic stream of thought was incorporated into the message of many New Testament documents. (See, e.g., Matt. 4:17; 10:23; 16:28; 24:34, 44; Mark 1:15; 9:1; 13:28–30; Luke 9:27; 12:40; 18:8; 21:25–32; Rom. 13:11–12; 16:20; I Cor. 7:25–31; 15:52; Phil. 3:20–21; 4:5; I Thess. 1:9–10; 4:13–18; James 5:7–9; I Peter 4:7; I John 2:18.)

During the first Christian generation, there were several crises that convinced some early Christians that they were indeed experiencing the final events of history and the End was now upon them. There was widespread apocalyptic excitement among both Jews and Christians when Caligula attempted to place a statue of himself in the Jerusalem temple in 39, as there was during the terrible Neronian persecution of Christians in Rome in 64, during the catastrophic war in Palestine 66–70, and in the wake of the famines, earthquakes, and eruption of Vesuvius in the following decades. Yet these crises came and went, and the End did not come. How could Christians respond to this apparent disappointment of their eschatological hopes?

1. Rejection. Some decided that apocalyptic expectation as such was an error and simply rejected it. Gnostic streams of Christianity abandoned the hope that God would redeem the horizontal line of history in a mighty eschatological act and retreated to a verticalism in which individual souls are saved

into the transcendent world and/or already enjoy the eschatological realities in their present religious experience. Such
views were apparently advocated by the opponents of Second
Peter (cf. chap. 3), and may have been shared by John's opponents among the Nicolaitans (Rev. 2:6, 15) and the followers of
"Jezebel" (2:20), who advocated the teaching of "Balaam"
(2:14).

Some contemporary interpreters have responded to Revelation's apocalyptic expectation of the near end of history by
simply rejecting apocalyptic as a viable mode of Christian theology. This is often done without having an awareness of how
deeply rooted apocalyptic ideas are in the New Testament as a
whole and in Christian faith as such.

2. Reinterpretation. Other Christians held on to the apocalyptic language of the first generation but reinterpreted it in the
light of the failure of the End to appear. There were basically
two varieties of such interpretation:

On the one hand, *"soon" did not mean "soon."* Some early
Christian theologians held on to the hope for the apocalyptic
victory of God at the end of history, but postponed it to an
indefinite future time. They reaffirmed the early Christian faith
that "the End is coming soon," but reinterpreted the meaning
of "soon" in a non-literal manner. The author of Second Peter
was glad to find a text in his Bible, Psalm 90:4, declaring that
a thousand years in God's sight is only a day, which helped him
to understand "soon" in a different way than had the first generation of Christians (II Peter 3:3-13). Luke rewrites the story of
Jesus and the church to allow for a period of generations of
church history, the time of the Christian mission. The Christ
comes not at the end but in the midst of history; the time of
Christ is followed by the time of the church, a time of mission,
which will last indefinitely before the End finally comes.

There have always been interpreters of Revelation who
have sought to explain its expectation of the near End as only
an apparent expectation. In this view, since the End did not in
fact come soon, John must have known it, so that Revelation in
fact envisions a long future. The "church-historical" and "end-
historical" (dispensationalist) interpretations (see Introduction)
regularly assert this view, regarding John as consciously intending to predict events centuries beyond his own future. Other
conservative contemporary interpreters, who understand the
doctrine of the "reliability of Scripture" in such a way that John

71

could not have been mistaken in his expectation of the nearness of the End, interpret "soon" to mean that "the imminence of the End is moral rather than chronological" (Bruce, p. 665).

On the other hand, *"End" did not mean the "End."* There were Christian theologians of the second and following generations who reaffirmed the earlier faith that "the End is coming soon" by redefining the meaning of "End": the promised "End" did in fact come "soon," with the outpouring of the Spirit and the beginning of the church. The eschatological realities were no longer understood in a literal manner; they were spiritualized and understood to be a part of the present experience of the Christian life. This kind of "realized eschatology," elements of which had also been a dimension of the faith of the first generation (Paul!), was developed especially by the authors of the Gospel and Letters of John. These authors reinterpret all the realities expected to come at the eschaton as already present: The Antichrist is reinterpreted as the presence of false teachers in the church (I John 2:18; 4:3); the second coming of Christ is reinterpreted as Christ's coming again as the Spirit, the Paraclete (John 14—16); the defeat of Satan happened in Jesus' ministry (John 12:31). Furthermore the resurrection happens in the new life of the Christian (John 11:21–26; cf. 8:51); the judgment happens in the present encounter with Christ the judge (John 3:18–19; 12:31, 48), and eternal life is already the present possession of the believer (John 3:36; 6:47; 17:3). Some contemporary interpreters of Revelation deal with the near expectation in this way (e.g., Caird, pp. 12, 32, 49, 90, 209, 236; Minear, *New Testament Apocalyptic*, pp. 48–63).

3. Reaffirmation. In times of threat and persecution, Christians of the second and third generations revived the older apocalyptic expectations with the conviction that even though earlier predictions were wrong, *now* the End has indeed come near. In their situation apocalyptic language once again made sense and supplied an urgently needed means of holding on to the faith, despite all the empirical evidence to the contrary (see the Introduction). Thus in First Peter, written in a similar situation to John's, the author revives the expectation of the nearness of the End as a motive for Christian steadfastness in the face of persecution and trial (4:7; cf. 4:16–17; 5:9–10).

Revelation is best understood as fitting into this category. When John said "the time is near" (1:3), he meant the time for the happening of all the events his letter envisions, including the return of Christ, the destruction of evil, and the everlasting glory of the new world. He meant both "soon" and "End."

Does this mean he was wrong? Yes. Christians who reverence the Bible as Scripture, the vehicle of God's word, ought not to hesitate to acknowledge that its authors made errors. It is an aspect of the humanity of the Bible, a part of the meaning of the incarnation, that God uses human thought (with its errors) and human beings (with their errors) to communicate his message. Apocalyptic thought was one of the human ways of thinking about God and the world prevalent in the first century. One of the ingredients of apocalyptic thought was that the End was near. When John adopted apocalyptic as the vehicle of his message, he adopted its errors as well, just as would have been the case with any other form of thought available to him (or us). Just as John's view of the earth's extent in space was a first-century worldview, so John's view of the earth's extent in time was one of those available in the first century, namely a world soon to pass away or to be transformed in the apocalyptic climax of history. Just as John accepted a flat earth with corners as the spatial framework within which he expressed his message (cf. 7:1), so he accepted a world shortly to come to an end as its temporal framework. As he was wrong in the one case, so was he wrong in the other case. But in neither case does the error of his worldview nullify the validity of the message expressed. One must distinguish between gift and wrapper, baby and bathwater.

The error should not continue. Just as Christians need not promote flat earth societies on the basis of Revelation 7:1, so they need not feel bound to believe in the nearness of the End on the basis of 1:3. A reverent agnosticism concerning "times and seasons" is the more abiding biblical view (Mark 13:32; Acts 1:6–11). There is nonetheless something for the modern reader to receive from the early church's expectation of the near end of history: Without sharing their chronology, we can share their sense of urgency, the sense that our generation is the only generation *we* have in which to fulfill our calling. It was not necessarily naiveté, egotism, or presumption for the early apocalyptists to believe that God had led all history to its time of fulfillment in their generation. Erroneous as their chronology was, their apocalyptic expectation was, in its own way, an ex-

73

pression of that faith taught by Jesus that not only every generation but every individual life within it is of unique value in the
eyes of the Creator, without whose infinite care not a sparrow
falls (Matt. 10:29).

Revelation 1:4–8
Letter Opening

The letter proper begins in 1:4 with the traditional letter
formula as modified by Paul and adapted by John. The standard
Greek letter in John's time began with the stereotypical "A to
B, greeting" formula (cf. Acts 15:23; 23:26; James 1:1). Paul
adapted this formula in a distinctive manner, often elaborating
all three elements, but especially by replacing the conventional
"greetings" (which had become as colorless as our "hi") with a
theologically loaded double expression, "grace" (which sounds
like the conventional "greetings" in Greek: *chairein/charis*)
and "peace" (derived from the Jewish tradition, *shalom*). This
formula combined Greek and Jewish elements in a theologically significant way appropriate to the Jewish-Christian apostle
to the Gentiles and was continued in the next generation in the
churches of the Pauline mission (Eph. 1:1; Col. 1:1; II Thess. 1:1;
I Peter 1:1; cf. I Tim. 1:1; II Tim. 1:1; Titus 1:1). John's use of
this formula in his own letter shows that he belongs within the
broad stream of this later Pauline tradition. It also shows that
the formula had become customary for Christian leaders when
writing letters intended for reading in the public gatherings of
the Christian congregations for worship. The letter form
stamped on Revelation by these opening words is an important
reminder that the text we are interpreting is to be understood
in all its historical particularity as a letter (see the Introduction).

Sender (1:4a). The sender of the letter names himself simply "John," without official titles. He writes with authority (cf.
e.g., 22:18–19). Yet his authority is not of office and title but that
of a prophet who has been given a message for the churches,
and that of a pastor who knows and is known by his addressees.

Addressees (1:4b). The addressees are the churches in seven
cities of Asia, on the west coast of what is now Turkey. Since
there were more than seven churches in this area, seven is to

be taken as a symbolic number representing the whole church of John's area.

Greeting (1:4c–5). The pronouncement of grace and peace on the hearer-readers is from God, the seven spirits, and Jesus Christ. This tripartite formula is not the developed Trinitarianism of later theology: the "seven spirits" are the seven angelic beings said by John to be under the authority of both God and Christ (3:1; 4:5; 5:6; cf. Ps. 104:4; Heb. 1:7,14). In accord with the general theocentrism of Revelation, God is named as the one whose being and whose acts embrace all time. Although there is some similarity to the three-times formula frequently used for gods in the Greek-speaking world, there is an important difference. There, the formula was an expression of the deity's eternity and immutability. It was said, for example, that "Zeus was, Zeus is, Zeus will be" (Pausanias). But John speaks not only of God's being but of his acts: "he comes." As in the titular summary above, God is the ultimate One, self-defined by his revelation in Jesus Christ, so here again it is the christological statement that is elaborated. There are four features of this statement worthy of note.

1. John ascribes to Jesus a combination of traditional and innovative christological titles: "Christ" was already traditional, but "the faithful witness," "the first-born of the dead," and "the ruler of kings on earth" are new. The church continued to develop its understanding of the significance of Jesus after his death and resurrection. The post-Easter church's increased christological insight included the attribution of titles to Jesus he had never used of himself. This is certainly true of the last three titles used in 1:5, and may be true of the first, "Christ," as well. Here we can see the developing Christology of early Christianity taking shape. Christian prophets such as John played an important role in this process, for they not only spoke about Jesus, they spoke in the first person in his name, so that after Easter the risen Jesus continued, through his prophets, to make new christological claims, including the use of new titles. In preaching and teaching from Revelation, the pastor or teacher can help the congregation to perceive that Christian faith in Jesus is more than a matter of what he may have said about himself during his earthly ministry. The issue is rather the validity of the claims made for him in the early church, represented by the New Testament. John did not abandon the traditional titles for Jesus that had been meaningful in the previous

75

generation. But he did more than simply repeat them. He found ways to make the ultimate significance of God's act in Jesus clear to people who lived in the new situation of his own time and place. This is always the challenge of the preacher and teacher.

2. The titles given Jesus by John are not speculative but appropriate to the particular situation of his hearer-readers. For faith, the identity of Jesus is never an abstract question; it is always "Who is he *for us*?" The three new titles directly address the situation of John's readers. The phrase "the faithful witness" points to Jesus, not only as the revealer from heaven but as the one who also, like the Christians in John's churches, once stood before the Roman authorities. He had borne his witness, even at the cost of his life (cf. John 18:33—19:16; I Tim. 6:13). The word "witness" here, *martus* in John's Greek, is already on the way to becoming the technical term "martyr." Jesus as the "first-born of the dead" is likewise not speculative or abstract; it is directed to the situation of John's readers, who were being asked to witness to the lordship of Christ by giving their own lives (2:10; 12:11). What future did such a one have? Christ as the "first-born of the dead" is revealed as the one who gives the Christian martyr a future even beyond death. The phrase also indicates that the resurrection of Jesus was more than an isolated event of the past; it was the beginning of the eschatological event of the general resurrection of the dead. Jesus' resurrection was thus the key sign indicating that John and his fellow Christians were living in the last days, the time of the fulfillment of God's plan for history. The phrase "ruler of kings on earth" attributes to Jesus the title claimed by the Roman Caesars, whose claim to sovereignty John wants his readers to see as a false caricature of the real lordship of Christ.

3. The titles are not absolutely new; they were not arbitrarily created by John but adapted by him from his Scripture. (See Ps. 89:27, 36–37; the word "witness" occurs in the Hebrew text of v. 37, as the note in the RSV indicates.) John uses phrases from this psalm, originally written of the Israelite king, to interpret the meaning of Jesus, in the conviction, which he shared with all the early church, that the Scripture as a whole points to Christ as its fulfillment (II Cor. 1:20).

4. The christological statements, without detracting from the uniqueness of Jesus, represent a "shared" Christology. The same phrase (the identical Greek being slightly obscured in the

76

RSV) used as a christological title for Jesus, "the faithful witness" (1:5), is used of the Christian Antipas of Pergamum (2:13), who had died for his faith, presumably at the sentence of the Roman courts. Christ as the "first-born of the dead" has already experienced the resurrection that faithful Christians shall experience. Christ as the "ruler of kings" has a kingship, but so do Christians, as declared in the doxology immediately following.

Doxology (1:5b–6). In the Hellenistic letter the "greeting" was frequently followed by the "thanksgiving," in which the gods were invoked for the good health and prosperity of the addressee(s). Like the greeting, the thanksgiving was usually a formality, like "Dear" and "Sincerely" in our letter opening and closing formulae. As was the case with the greeting, Paul had also adapted the thanksgiving formality to his own purposes and filled it with theological content, as can be seen for example in Romans 1:8–10 and I Corinthians 1:3–5. Paul can sometimes make this thanksgiving into a doxology of praise to God, as illustrated by II Corinthians 1:3–4 and Galatians 1:5. John adapts this latter tradition. After the letter greeting of 1:4–5a, in the place where one might expect the thanksgiving, he places a doxology which is no formality but a significant theological statement. The doxological form of theology is not incidental. As elsewhere in Revelation, theology is done in the mode of worship rather than as analytical speculative discourse.

The doxology, normally directed to God, is here directed to Christ. The doxology praises him for his mighty acts for our salvation. The result is a doxological affirmation of the church: Like Israel in the Scriptures, the church is the beloved (Mal. 1:2!) community freed from its sins by the shedding of sacrificial blood (cf. e.g., Lev. 17:11). John has resisted the temptation of the oppressed to believe that they are innocent and only their oppressors are guilty. He knows that Christian existence is not innocent existence but forgiven existence; he knows that forgiveness came, as in the Old Testament sacrificial conceptuality, only at the cost of life (cf. e.g., Heb. 8—10, esp. 9:22). Like the Old Testament, John does not think that "blood" has any saving efficacy as a substance; it represents "life." Jesus is praised because he set us free from sin by giving himself, his life, for us.

Like Israel in the Scriptures, the church is a kingdom of priests (Exod. 19:6). The sense of 1:6 is not that Christ made a kingdom *for* us but that he constituted us, his people, to be a kingdom of priests. John throughout takes up the Scripture's predicates of Israel and applies them to the church, one of the many indications that, like Paul and other New Testament authors, he understands the church to be the continuing people of God, the biblical history of Israel continuing in the church (cf. Gal. 6:16; Phil. 3:3; James 1:1; I Peter 1:1, 17).

Once again, Christian existence is determined for John by sharing the ministry of Christ. "Christ" is the Greek word for "anointed" ("Messiah" in Hebrew), referring primarily to the anointed king (cf. e.g., I Sam. 10:1; Ps. 2:2), but also to the office of prophet (cf. I Kings 19:16; Isa. 61:1) and priest (cf. Exod. 29:1–9; Ps. 133:2). For John, "Christ" has not become a name but still connotes the office of God's anointed messiah as prophet, priest, and king. Christians share in this ministry. As we shall see below, John understands the church to be a prophetic community (see 11:1–13 commentary), and he here declares it to be a royal and priestly community. As a prophetic community the church mediates the word of God made known in Jesus to the world. As a priestly community the church mediates to the world God's reconciliation of the world in Jesus, the Sacrificed Priest, and instead of sacrificing to the emperor on the Roman altar, the church sacrifices itself on the true altar of God (cf. 6:9–11). As a royal community the church represents and signifies the rule of God as already present in the world.

All these affirmations demonstrate the fragmentary but real existence of the messianic ministry as already present in the church. John knows, and preserves, the Pauline tension between the "already" and "not yet" of Christian existence. This corresponds to the "already" and "not yet" of the coming of Christ. As in Judaism, the Christ is the one who is to come, and Revelation looks forward to this coming to establish the just reign of God on this earth (e.g., 19:6–16; 22:20). But Revelation and Christian faith not only look forward to the "not yet" but backward to the "already" of the coming of Christ. Despite all appearances, the Christ has in fact come. The meaning of "Christ" must therefore be redefined in terms of who Jesus actually was—the one who gave his life for others. Despite all appearances, the royal messianic community already exists and represents the reign of God in this world. The meaning of this community also must be redefined as love for the world that suffers even to death. Ecclesiology corresponds to Christology; the meaning of discipleship corresponds to one's idea of Christ.

Both the "already" and the "not yet" could be misunderstood when taken alone. Taking the "not yet" in isolation could lead to a neglect of the principal conviction of Christian faith, that the Christ has already come and that the meaning of "Christ" for Christians must be redefined in terms of who Jesus of Nazareth actually was. The danger inherent in this one-sided affirmation of the "not yet" can and does lead to thinking of the Christ yet to come as the warrior king who will establish God's kingdom with violence, rather than the suffering Man for Others, Jesus of Nazareth. John corrects this by repeatedly using the human name "Jesus" for the Christ and by portraying the Christ throughout as the slaughtered Lamb (see on 5:1–10). The potential misunderstanding of the "already" of Christian existence had become a dangerous reality in some of John's opponents in the churches. Revelation corrects this by an emphasis on the future in many passages, including the prophetic words immediately following. Yet John does not allow the abuse of realized eschatology to cause him to overreact and reject it entirely. The Christian life is not only a time of waiting; the songs and praises of Revelation show that the celebration has already begun.

Prophetic pronouncements (1:7–8). In verses 7–8 the doxology modulates into prophetic pronouncements of the future coming of Christ and its results. As in Paul's letters, where the initial thanksgiving served to "telegraph" the key elements of the content of the letter, so here this "motto"-like prophetic pronouncement helps the hearer-readers to determine in advance where the accents of the following communication are to be found. Both the form and the content are important for preaching and teaching from this text. Verse 7 is a fusion of Daniel 7:13 and Zechariah 12:10, a combination that had become traditional in the church and is found in Matthew 24:30 also. This is one of many instances in Revelation (cf. the Introduction) in which John's prophecy is expressed in words from Scripture, which he does not quote as a past authority but utilizes as the medium of expressing the present message of the risen Lord. His prophecy is not a matter of merely reporting words heard in a trance but of reflecting on his prophetic experiences and communicating them in words of Scripture and tradition.

The pronouncement declares that, in contrast to the first coming of Christ, this appearance will not be in obscurity but "with the clouds"; it will be an appearance from the sky visible to all. All shall see him and recognize his lordship, including his enemies who pierced him. The Zechariah text was limited to "the inhabitants of Jerusalem," but John universalizes it to include "all tribes of the earth." It is not clear whether their mourning (RSV "wailing") is the lamentation of repentance as in the original Zechariah context, or whether it is the wailing of those for whom Christ's appearance means only "judgment and calamity." John's general theology of universal reconciliation, and the specific analogy of 22:2 below, where John changes Ezekiel's "healing" to "healing of the nations," argues for the former. In this case John begins his book with a prophetic declaration that even Christ's enemies, the Romans who "pierced" him on the cross, will meet the returning Christ with lamentation and repentance, a powerful affirmation of the victory that Christ shall win over all people, including his enemies—a victory won through the love manifest in the cross. But perhaps John leaves the matter dialectically ambiguous, so that these words can be taken as either promise or threat (cf. "Reflection: Universal Salvation and Paradoxical Language").

Revelation 1:9–20
The Presence of the Risen Christ

As the body of the letter begins in 1:9, John shifts to the narrative form which Revelation shares with apocalyptic in general (cf. J. J. Collins SBL definition, *Apocalypse*, p. 9). Narrative is often the characteristic mode of a letter, in which the writer recounts to the reader a narrative of events (cf. II Cor. 7:5–16; 12:1–10; Gal. 1:11—2:21). The opening section of John's narrative is shaped by the questions implicit in any narrative: who? where? why? when? how? what?

Who? John is the only earthly member of the cast of the dramatic scene he is about to narrate. He chooses this point, instead of the letter greeting in 1:4, to identify himself. He needs no official titles; he is already known personally to his hearer-readers. He is the brother and fellow participant in the tribulation, the kingdom, and in the patient endurance which all Christians share "in Jesus." John writes with the authority of a prophet, but John's prophetic role does not have for him the dimension of over-againstness, does not separate him from the

80

members of his churches. He writes as a pastor who shares the life of his congregations.

This life is lived in three spheres that John and his fellow Christians share "in Jesus." By "tribulation," John does not mean the ordinary problems to which human life is heir but that time of terrible trouble which in the apocalyptic scheme must precede the End. John interprets the social discrimination and government persecution which threatened the churches as the beginning of the eschatological woes, the labor pains that must precede the birth of the new world (12:1–6; cf. Mark 13:3–8 for a similar view, which explicitly uses the imagery of labor pains). By "kingdom," John points not only to the future, when the rulership of God and his Christ will be manifest to all; his interpretation of the Christian life is not that of present tribulation but future kingdom: "Suffer now, rejoice later." Jesus is already king though crucified. Christians share "in Jesus" now in the kingdom, which is present though hidden and manifest in this world in the form of the cross. The Christian life is a tension-filled unity of tribulation and kingdom, which will yield at the eschaton to the pure kingdom of God. Within this framework of understanding, the Christian life is marked by "patient endurance," that is, by tenaciously holding on to the faith in the glad confidence that Christ's lordship is real, though at present invisible to empirical observation.

This life John shares with his fellow Christians as they all share it "in Jesus." As prophet, John does not mediate this life to them secondhand: They all share in it firsthand. John here takes up the Pauline way of understanding the Christian life as already participating in Christ, which he here designates "in Jesus" and later (14:13) "in the Lord." When John thought of his self-identity, he did not think egocentrically of his own psyche, but of the reality of Christ who formed the horizon and purpose of existence for both John and his fellow Christians. One with such a sense of "self"-identity can face tribulation with confidence and a quiet joy, and can encourage others to do so.

Where? John writes from Patmos, a small island about seventy-five miles west of Ephesus. Archaeological evidence indicates that in John's time Patmos was a fortified island belonging to Miletus, with a quality Greek school and shrines to Artemis and Apollos. There is no evidence of its being a "penal colony," but the island was used by the Romans as a place of banishment for troublemakers, real and potential.

81

Why? John has been officially banished by the government for being a leader in the Christian movement, in John's terms "on account of the word of God and the testimony of Jesus," his preaching activity. The grammar prohibits our understanding this phrase to mean that John had gone to Patmos for missionary preaching or in order to seek solitude to prepare for prophetic visions. The phrase "on account of" is always used in Revelation for the result of an action, not its purpose. John has been banished to Patmos because he had been preaching the Christian message. Since Antipas had been executed at Pergamum (2:13), and since John expected a bloody persecution to engulf all Christians everywhere, we may wonder at the relative lightness of John's own sentence. Pliny's letter (cf. Introduction) illustrates that Rome did not yet have hard and fast policies about how to deal with the new movement, and the severity of sentences apparently varied from governor to governor.

When? What John is about to narrate took place on "the Lord's day." Since this is the first occurrence of this term in Christian literature, we cannot be positive about John's meaning. Though "the Lord's day" has been interpreted as Easter and the eschatological Day of the Lord, it most likely refers to Sunday, the first day of the week, the new holy day of Christians, since earlier texts indicate that the church assembled to worship on the first day of the week as their holy day (I Cor. 16:2; Acts 20:7; cf. Pliny's letter above). This was the day when Jesus' resurrection was celebrated (Mark 16:2) and served to distinguish Christians from Jews, whose holy Sabbath was the seventh day, Saturday.

John's vision comes at the time when he knows the churches on the mainland are gathered for worship. Were he not banished, he would be there among them and during the worship service would deliver his prophetic messages as they were inspired by the Spirit. Prophecy was not an individualistic gift to isolated individuals; it occurred in the community's worship, where it could be critically evaluated and appropriated.

How? John describes the experience of receiving the vision as being "in the Spirit." This refers neither to John's own mood and personal feelings, which he does not discuss, nor to the general gift of the Holy Spirit to all Christians (Acts 2:38; I Cor. 12:13; Rom. 8:9–11), but to the special spiritual gift of prophecy (Rom. 12:6; I Cor. 12:10, 28; 13:2; 14:1–39). John does not describe the experience itself, but it involved both auditions (1:10) and visions (1:12).

As in the Old Testament, the prophetic vision comes from the divine initiative. John does nothing to cultivate it or manipulate it; there is no fasting, prayer, seeking. He does not seek it; it seeks him. The prophets were not mystics who sought "religious experiences"; they were messengers sought out by the God who willed to speak to his people.

What? John does not gaze at the scene and then note down what he sees, spectator-like; as a literary and theological artist, he consciously selects the language he uses to portray the vision. This language functions at more than one connotative level. First, there is the powerful, pre-conceptual impressionistic level. Quite apart from the details, the scene is overpowering in its grandeur as it presents the church's Lord as the transcendent ruler of the cosmos. In the conviction that Christ is the fulfillment of the Scripture as a whole (II Cor. 1:20), John chooses the language of Scripture to paint this picture of the risen Christ. The details are carefully chosen: The "long robe" is the priestly garment, taken from Exodus 28:4, 27 (cf. Wis. Sol. 18:24), while the "golden girdle" is the royal emblem of the king (I Macc. 10:89). As elsewhere, John is aware that the messianic office of Jesus includes the prophetic-revelatory, the priestly, and the kingly functions. The dazzling white hair is taken from the "one that was ancient of days" in Daniel 7:9. John's monotheism and theocentrism save him from the danger of identifying God and Jesus, or making them competitors, so he does not hesitate to use God-language of Jesus. The use of such language is an expression of his conviction that "God" is to be defined as "the one who has revealed himself definitively in Jesus." On the other hand, the "feet . . . like burnished bronze" and the "voice . . . like the sound of many waters" are taken from the description of the heavenly messenger in Daniel 10:6 (cf. Ezek. 43:2). Since John is not thinking metaphysically, this combining of angel-language and God-language in his portrayal of Jesus is not problematical: both serve to express the transcendent glory of the exalted Christ.

The picture of the seven stars in Christ's right hand also serves in the first instance to communicate the sheer cosmic magnitude of the church's Lord. The same hand that holds the stars touches John—literally unimaginable, another indication that we have here no mere report but a scene fraught with symbolic meaning. The commission John receives comes from the one who holds seven stars in his hand. This motif is not taken

83

from Scripture but has parallels in both the Mithras religion and the imagery of the Caesar cult. John probably chose it to express both an anti-astrology message and as a challenge to the claim of the Roman Caesars. The stars do not control our destiny and are not to be feared; Christ holds them in his hand. The claim that the Roman Caesars embody the rulership of the cosmos is a false imitation of the true cosmic ruler, Christ.

The only weapon borne by the exalted Christ is his word, the sharp two-edged sword that proceeds from his mouth. This is a scriptural motif taken from the promised deliverer in Isaiah 11:4 and the servant of the Lord in Isaiah 49:2. This corresponds to the fact that Christ's primary action in this cosmic scene, like that of the Creator in the beginning (Gen. 1:1—2:4), is to speak. The figure speaks words appropriate only to the living God of Israel: "I am the first and the last, and the living one." Again, there is no speculative interest here, but a particular message to the threatened Christians in John's churches: The One who calls them to be faithful even at the cost of their lives (2:10) is the one who embraces all, who will be there at the End to vindicate and receive them, the one who has already gone before them through the reality of death. No aloof deity this, but one who says matter-of-factly that he has taken death into his own experience, has overcome it, has the keys of death and hades. In Hellenistic mythology the keys of Hades were often thought to be in the possession of Hekate, who controlled the revelatory traffic between the other world and this one (Aune, "The Apocalypse of John and Greco-Roman Magic," pp. 484–89). John casts Jesus in this role. Death is portrayed here, as elsewhere in the Bible, as a personified power, the enemy that enslaves and robs (cf. 6:8; 20:14; I Cor. 15:26). Christians are not promised that if they are faithful they will be acquitted in the Roman courts and spared from the injustice of death; in and through death they are met by the One who has conquered death and abides as the living one.

Christ has appeared in order to commission John to write to the churches (1:11, 19–20). The Greek of verse 19 is best translated as referring to two items, not three: "Write your visions, both those that picture the present situation (chaps. 2—3) and those that picture the eschatological future that is already dawning (chaps. 4—22)."

The heavenly figure now explains that the lampstands among which he walks are the seven churches. Like the prom-

84

ised Servant (Isa. 42:6) and the Messiah himself (21:23–24), the church is pictured as having a mission, to be the bearer of God's light to the nations (cf. Matt. 5:14–16). The church is not abandoned to carry out this mission alone; Christ walks among the lampstands.

John's initial response (1:17) was to be struck down as one dead, overwhelmed with dread at the holiness of the awesome mystery he experiences. Here is no frivolous, superficially happy response; the response is of one who recognizes that he cannot traffic casually with the Almighty. Yet authentic response cannot remain immobilized, even by contemplation of God's holiness. The hand that holds the stars touches him and gives him a job to do. Christ appeared, not to dazzle but to communicate a message. John obediently writes. We now turn to consider that message.

Revelation 2:1—3:22
Messages to Seven Churches

The unit of which the "letters to the seven churches" are a part begins at 1:1 and extends through 3:22; it should not be interpreted apart from the Christophany of 1:9–20 to which they are integrally related. Each "letter" reflects the particular geographical, cultural, and religious situation of the city to which it was written, as well as the current conditions in the congregation of that city. Yet none of the messages in chapters 2—3 are independent letters addressed to a single church. Revelation is one unitary composition addressed, like all the messages, to all the churches, as is made clear by 1:4 and 2:7 and the identical note at the end of each message. The "letters" might better be called "prophetic messages." They share the same apocalyptic thought-world as the rest of Revelation but are written in more straightforward language, and they obviously speak to the this-worldly situation and concerns of the hearer-readers. They thus serve to set the parameters for understanding the visions to follow and to involve the hearer-readers in the apocalyptic message of Revelation as a whole, before the scene is transferred to the other world in 4:1. The direct address of the messages of chapters 2—3 may help the

85

preacher and teacher to show that Revelation addresses the real world of church life and its glories and problems, before launching into the visionary, transcendent world of the later chapters.

Preaching and teaching based on the "letters to the seven churches" has traditionally treated them individually. But since all the messages are addressed to all the churches and have an identical structure, the preacher or teacher interpreting texts from Revelation 2—3 will want to consider the unit as a whole.

Form and Content of the Seven Messages

All the messages are structured in an identical pattern of eight elements:

1. Address to the angel. John is directed to write to the seven churches (1:11), but in chapters 2—3 each message is addressed, instead of to the church, to its "angel"; this address is continued through the messages in the second person singular, with only an occasional shift to the plural form (2:10, 23). In 3:4, for example, the "you" is singular: the *angel* has a few people in Sardis who have not "soiled their garments." This unexpected phenomenon of addressing *churches* through their *angels* has sometimes been accounted for by understanding "angel" to refer to a human being, the episcopal or prophetic leader of each congregation. Since the basic meaning of "angel" is "messenger," it is true enough that the word can be used of a human being, such as John the Baptist (Matt. 11:10) or the messengers sent by Jesus (Luke 9:52). Such a pedestrian understanding ignores the meaning of "angel" throughout Revelation and reduces its level of discourse to that of straightforward communication on the human level. This is certainly false. Here, as elsewhere, the communication takes place on the transcendent plane. John operates out of the apocalyptic tradition within which earthly realities have their counterparts in the heavenly world. Just as each nation has its representative "angel" in the heavenly world (cf. e.g., Dan. 10:2-14, 20-21), so each congregation has its representative "guardian" angel in the heavenly world. The church is more than a human "worthy cause"; it participates in the reality of the eternal world. There was considerable angel-speculation in the churches of Asia in the generation after Paul (cf. Col. 2:18). John shares this world of ideas, but is concerned to reduce the status of angelic beings to that of the church members themselves: angels too are servants of God, who can be obedient or disobedient. They can be admonished, as in the messages to the seven churches, but they are not to be worshiped (cf. 19:9–10; 22:8–9). This mode of address has the effect that the members of John's churches only indirectly "overhear" the message spoken to the church's "angel," though it is clear that the message addressed to the "angel" is "what the Spirit says to the churches" (2:7).

2. The city. Each message names the city of the church to which it is addressed. The seven churches represent a selection, for other churches existed in the area at the time, for example, at Colossae. The number seven is to be taken as symbolic of completeness and strengthens the idea that Revelation is addressed to all the churches in Asia. It is not clear why these seven were chosen to represent the whole church, though they are all connected by being located on the main Roman road at intervals of about thirty or forty miles. Also, each of the cities named had a Roman law court, a location where Christians had been or could be charged with membership in the Christian sect, which was suspected of being subversive; and at least the first three churches addressed were sites of temples dedicated to Caesar (Ephesus, Smyrna, Pergamum).

The addressed churches were in sizable cities. Ephesus was the capital of the province and vied with Pergamum and Smyrna for the title of "the first city of Asia." By the end of the first century, Christianity was an urban phenomenon. The Christians in John's churches were not simple peasant people of the back country; they resided in the principal cities of their time, struggling with the issues of how the Christian witness could be made real and viable within the political and cultural life of a sophisticated urban population. The contrast between two cities, "Babylon" and the new Jerusalem, forms the burden of John's visions in the body of the book to follow (chaps. 4—22). Whether Christians who lived in the mundane cities of Asia would orient their lives to the "great city" of "Babylon" or the "Holy City," the new Jerusalem, is a major theme of Revelation and a structural factor in its composition (cf. Introduction).

3. Prophetic messenger formula. The standard prophetic messenger formula in the Old Testament was "Thus says the Lord, . . ." with the message following in the first person. The prophet did not speak as a reporter of what he had been instructed to say, using indirect address in the third person, but spoke directly in the person of the Lord who had commissioned him or her. John adopts that style and its accompanying for-

87

mula, the repeated "The words of him who . . ." (RSV) being exactly identical to the Septuagint translation of "Thus says the (Lord), ..." Characteristic of Christian prophecy, the speaker's slot in the formula (the "Lord" [Yahweh] in the Old Testament) is filled with the exalted Lord of the church's faith, the Lord Jesus.

4. Christological ascription. At the beginning of each letter is a christological affirmation taken from the attributes of the Christophany in 1:9–20. When these are exhausted, John supplements them with attributes that are particularly appropriate to his theology or to the church he is addressing. Thus in 3:7 Christ is designated "the holy one, the true one," in accord with his practice of using God-language of Christ. In 3:14 Christ is called the principle by which God created the world, like preexistent wisdom in the Old Testament (Prov. 8, esp. 22, 27, 30), an expression of John's emphasis on the creation throughout. In 2:18 the only instance of "Son of God" in Revelation appears, again not a feature taken from the initial Christophany but from Psalm 2, for later in the same message to Thyatira (2:26–27) John will use the language of the Second Psalm, which pictured the Israelite king as "son of God." In 3:14 Christ calls himself the "Amen," an unusual use of the Old Testament word for confirming the statement of another. Since Paul had used "Amen" of Jesus as the one who fulfills and confirms all the promises of God in the Old Testament (II Cor. 1:20), and since John is in the Pauline stream of tradition, he may be intentionally using this title to express his view that in Jesus the Old Testament as a whole finds its fulfillment.

We see that these christological statements at the beginning of each letter are neither casually chosen nor mere decorations, but they serve a theological purpose. The letters contain ethical instructions and warnings, the commands of the risen Christ for living a faithful Christian life in a trying situation. Such commands cannot stand alone; they are not general or obvious moral truths. Their truth is bound up with the truth of the vision of 1:9–20, that the crucified one is the exalted Lord vindicated by God and made Lord of all. Here, as elsewhere, the ethical imperative is founded on the christological indicative, the Christian life is founded on the fact and reality of Christ.

5. The divine knowledge. The exalted Lord says "I know . . ." to each congregation, whether in threat or reassurance. John is influenced by his Bible's portrayal of God as the one who knows all, who is both aware of the suffering of his people (e.g., Exod. 3:7) and who penetrates beyond the surface to the heart's hidden secrets (e.g., I Sam. 16:7). John stands in the tradition of biblical prophets who declared that God knows the situation of those to whom the prophecy was directed (e.g., Jer. 48:30; Hos. 5:3; Amos 5:12) and in the Christian prophetic tradition of those who charismatically expose the depths concealed in the lives of the worshipers (I Cor. 14:24–25; cf. Luke 7:39; John 4:19), because he is the spokesperson for the risen Lord who shares the divine attribute of omniscience (2:23; cf. 5:6). The penetrating eye of the one who says "I know" reveals the true situation of each church, sometimes reversing the church's own estimate of itself. Smyrna supposes it is "poor," but is really rich (2:9), while exactly the opposite situation obtains in Laodicea (3:17).

6. The "body." The "body" of each "letter" is composed of praise and/or blame, promise and/or threat. Only two churches receive unqualified praise (Smyrna and Philadelphia). See below for the message of the body of the letters.

7. The call to attention and obedience. A characteristic element in Old Testament prophetic forms was the call to attention, "Hear!" (Isa. 1:10; 7:13; 28:14, 23; 48:1, 14; Jer. 2:4; 5:21; 6:18; 7:2; 10:1; 13:15; Hos. 4:1; 5:1; Amos 3:1, 13; 4:1; 5:1; 7:16; 8:4). The word carries its full meaning of not only listening but acting on what is heard (as in "I tried to tell you, but you wouldn't *listen* to me"). John incorporates this call to hear/obey in the closing words of each message: "He who has an ear, let him hear what the Spirit says to the churches." The formula is one of the few places where John's prophetic idiom echoes the words of the historical Jesus—or where the words of Jesus in the Synoptic Gospels have been adapted to the familiar forms of Christian prophets who spoke in his name (cf. Matt. 11:15; 13:9, 43; Mark 4:9, 23; Luke 8:8; 14:35). We note again that John does not distinguish the risen Christ and the work of the Spirit; what the risen Jesus says is what the Spirit says to the churches.

8. Eschatological promise to the victors. Each letter concludes with a promise of blessing, expressed in apocalyptic terms, to the Christians who "conquer." As the christological affirmation with which each message begins represents a flashback to the Christophany of 1:9–20, the promise to the "conquerors" with which each message concludes represents a flash-forward to the eschatological glory of chapters 20—22. The Christian life called for in chapters 2—3 is not adherence

89

to moralistic norms but a life lived in view of the reality of the Christ event in the past and the victory of God in the eschatological future. The seven messages are thus integrally linked to the apocalyptic eschatology of the body of the book.

The "conqueror" will "eat of the tree of life . . . in the paradise of God" (2:7); shall "not be hurt by the second death" (2:11; cf. 20:6); will receive "the hidden manna" and "a white stone, with a new name written on the stone which no one knows except him who receives it" (2:17); will be given "power over the nations" to "rule them with a rod of iron" and "the morning star" (2:26–28). The "conqueror" will be dressed in white garments, and his or her name will not be blotted out of the book of life, but will be confessed by the exalted Lord himself before God and the angels (3:5). The "conqueror" will be inscribed with the name of God and of the new Jerusalem, where he or she will be built into the eschatological temple as a pillar (3:12), and will sit with the exalted Lord on the eschatological throne (3:21; cf. 2:27).

Some of these promises may reflect the particular situation of John's churches. The "white stone" of 2:17, for example, may originally reflect a magical use of amulets and/or the entrance ticket to social/business occasions from which Christians who hesitated to participate in pagan society were excluded. Other promises, the "hidden manna" (2:17), for example, reflect the Jewish despair over the destruction of the temple by the Babylonians in 586. At that time, the sacred Ark which contained some of the manna (Exod. 16:31–34; cf. Heb. 9:4) was hidden and never recovered, but would be revealed at the eschaton. All the lamentation and hopes and overtones of feeling associated with the Wailing Wall and the longing of the People of God for the restoration of the true worship of God in the true temple are compressed into the image of the "hidden manna." This is combined in Christian tradition with the eucharistic imagery of eating the true bread with the Messiah at the ultimate messianic banquet already anticipated in the eucharistic celebrations (3:20–21; 11:19; cf. John 6:1–65, esp. 49–51). This is no idle hope, for those who "conquer" will participate in this eschatological fulfillment and finally taste the hidden manna.

90

"Conquering," winning the victory, is a key word in Revelation's Christology and understanding of the Christian life. As the summary accomplishment of Jesus' work on earth can be expressed simply that he "overcame"/"conquered" (3:21; 5:5), so the faithful Christian life can be summarized as "conquering"/"overcoming." As revealed in Jesus, the meaning of "winning" is dramatically reversed.

Christian Life and Responsibility as Pictured in the Seven Messages

The "bodies" of the seven messages provide us a window into the life of the church in Asia at the end of the first century. As elsewhere in the New Testament, we see no idealized picture but the mixture of faith and unfaith, responsibility and irresponsibility, which always characterizes the church in this world. Christians are addressed not as individuals striving for perfection but corporately, as members of communities of Christian mission and witness.

Tribulation. The life of Christians is lived in the midst of the pressures from a hostile world, which John calls "tribulation." This tribulation is not some spectacular future event but has already begun in John's own time. For John and all the churches, tribulation is the constant context within which the Christian is called to be a faithful witness, but it is particularly evident in some situations (1:9; 2:9, 13). In John's view tribulation is about to intensify into a terrible persecution, which will engulf all Christians and is the prelude to the End (2:10; 3:10; cf. 7:14).

The members of John's churches are adherents of a minority religion in an environment of conflicting religious pluralism. Hostile Jewish synagogues (2:9; see the Introduction) and hostile pagan religions, especially the emperor cult, place the Christians in the situation of being outsiders in their own culture. Deciding that loyalty to Christ meant having the responsibility of exercising Christian witness by refusing to participate in pagan functions would have severe social and economic consequences, and could well lead to being accused before the local Roman courts of being a member of an anti-Roman sect.

John sees the conflict between the church and the synagogue, and between the church and the established, respected cultural religions, as the this-worldly reality of a deeper conflict being waged in the transcendent sphere. Thus the synagogues in Smyrna and Philadelphia are "synagogues of Satan" (2:9; 3:9), and the impressive temple to the emperor in Pergamum is "Satan's throne" (2:13). When Christians are jailed by the Ro-

91

mans, it is "the devil" who is really at work (2:10). On the other hand, the church is the setting where the Spirit speaks and the power of God is at work (2:7, 23; 3:8). The church is not spectator to the cosmic battle between God and the forces of evil but experiences it in its own life. These conflicts will be pictured on a massive visionary scale in chapters 4—20, but are already presupposed in the messages to the churches in chapters 2—3. The messages to the churches of chapters 2—3 cannot be isolated from the later visionary section of Revelation as though they were straightforward moralistic instruction.

Division. The churches are plagued by external conflicts and by internal tensions. They are visited by Christian religious leaders who understand themselves as being "apostles" (2:2). This does not mean that these itinerant apostles were claiming membership in the group of the Twelve (cf. 21:14 and I Cor. 15:5–7, which distinguishes "apostles" and "the twelve") but that they understood themselves to be authorized messengers, missionaries, and teachers for the church at large (cf. Acts 14:14; Rom. 16:7; II Cor. 8:23; Phil. 2:25). Their teaching conflicts with John's, and he commends the Ephesian church for rejecting them (cf. Paul and a similar situation at Corinth, II Cor. 11:1–15). It is noteworthy that the congregation tests such claims to leadership, since apostles, prophets, and leaders belong to the church and not vice versa (cf. I Cor. 3:21–22); and they are to be critically examined by the corporate body of Christians (cf. I Cor. 12—14; I Thess. 5:19–22), so it is not "tossed to and fro and carried about by every wind of doctrine" (Eph. 4:14). It is the church that finally decided what is and what is not apostolic, that is, authentic Christian teaching.

John also refers to "Nicolaitans" (2:6, 15), those who follow the teaching of "Balaam" (2:14), and the followers of a prophet "Jezebel" (2:20). Since these are described in identical terms, they are probably all designations of the same group or movement. "Balaam" and "Jezebel" are obviously John's own symbolic designations drawn from the story of the opponents and seducers of God's people in the Old Testament story and Jewish tradition (Num. 22—25; 31:16; I Kings 16:31; 18:1–19; 19:1–2; cf. II Peter 2:15; Jude 11). Jezebel was the royal promoter of foreign cults. Baalam, in Numbers 22—25, was the obedient spokesperson of God, but on the basis of Numbers 31:16 Jewish tradition had made him into a false prophet, one of the ringleaders in tempting Israel to participate in idolatrous religion (Philo,

Vita Moses I.48–55; Josephus, *Antiquities* IV.126). He understood both "Balaam" and "Jezebel" to be foreigners who seduced Israel into idolatry. John chooses these figurative names not from xenophobia but to represent them as not belonging to the People of God, as being agents of the foreign religion. It may be that the "Nicolaitans" were named for a real historical figure, their leader Nicolas; but if so, we know nothing else about him, though later Christian legend identified him with the Nicolaus of Acts 6:5. More likely, "Nicolaitans" (literally: "conquerors of the laity, the people") may, like "Balaam" and "Jezebel," be John's own symbolic name for his opponents, since "conquer" is a key word in John's theology and since "Nicolas" is the rough equivalent of "Balaam" in Hebrew ("ruler of the people").

The "Nicolaitans," "Balaam," and "Jezebel" promoted the "progressive" doctrine of accommodation to the culture around them. The question of the manner and degree of the Christians' participation in the ordinary business of the world in which they lived, especially as it dealt with the issues of whether they could attend pagan festival meals and eat meat "contaminated" by its association with the sacrificial cult of some pagan deity, had troubled Christians in other times and places and had received a spectrum of differing answers (cf. Acts 15:28–29; I Cor. 8—10). John saw the issue entirely in either/or terms: to participate in such activities was to take part in the false worship of pagan religion. In contrast, the Nicolaitans and related groups taught that Christians should attend the cultural festivals, buy and eat the sacrificial meat sold in the marketplace, and participate in the cultural lifestyle. For Israel's prophets and for John, such accommodation to pagan ways was a betrayal of the faith, equivalent to idolatry and fornication, to which John may not have been alluding only figuratively (cf. I Cor. 6:9–20). John's opposition to the opposing groups was not small-minded dogmatism about the finer points of doctrine; it was related to his understanding of the Christian life as a whole. For the Nicolaitans and related groups, John's view was reactionary and traditional, since for them it was the Christian's right and responsibility to join in the practices that combined Christianity and the cultural religion. They did not understand themselves as un- or anti-Christian, but as gifted leaders, equipped with the charisma of the Spirit, helping the church to adapt to new times. What they saw as the response to the crisis, John saw as

93

a further manifestation of it. What they considered to be the answer, John considered to be another serious dimension of the problem.

These groups apparently also advocated a "realized eschatology" which affirmed that Christians already participated in the new age and were thus released from the constraints of life in the old aeon. The "riches" of which the Laodicean church boasted were probably not only or even primarily material riches but the spiritual riches enjoyed by Christians who supposed they were already living in the fulfilled time of prophetic phenomena and spiritual bliss (cf. I Cor. 1:5–7, and 4:8 for Paul's sarcastic response to another church which had this view of the richness of its own spiritual life). In John's view the biggest internal danger to the churches was a combination of two misunderstandings: an understanding of the Christian life which relegated religion to the internal realm of one's "real self," instead of one's external conduct, and an orientation to the present as the time of fulfillment rather than to the future, sure hope of God's coming kingdom.

How could the troubled churches of Asia decide between the conflicting claims about the nature of the Christian life? The group John opposes was led by charismatics such as himself. The churches of Asia needed to have an authoritative response to their questions about Christian responsibility in their ambiguous situation, but charismatic, prophetic phenomena themselves were not adequate to settle the question of authentic teaching. In the churches of Asia charismatic stands over against charismatic, prophet opposes prophet—just as had been the case in the Scripture (e.g., I Kings 18; Jer. 27—28). The churches had to make decisions about which of the charismatic groups had authentic insight into the will of God for the community. Criteria were needed. The churches eventually decided that new teaching revealed through Christian prophets had to agree with the revelation made in the earthly life of Jesus, especially including his death on the cross. Jesus and his cross became *the* criterion of the authenticity of Christian prophecy, for the exalted Lord could not deny the once-for-all revelation made by his incarnation (1:5, 18; 5:5–6; cf. Rom. 12:5–6; I Cor. 12:1–3; I John 2:18–23; 4:1–2; II John 7–11). It is the responsibility of the church to apply this criterion. In the case before us, John's Revelation was accepted by the church as authentic revelation, and the revelations of the Nicolaitans, Balaam, and Jezebel were rejected, however impressive they may have seemed at the time. This is not an individualistic judgment in which each Christian may shop around in the cafeteria of charismatic phenomena according to his or her own tastes; it is a community decision by the church, as John already knew (2:2).

Works. It is in this context of the action of the Christian community in the face of the claims of the cultural religion that John's emphasis on "works" is to be understood. Repeatedly, the risen Christ declares that he knows the works of the Asian Christians (2:2, 19; 3:1, 8, 15), who will finally be judged by their works (20:12; cf. the commentary discussion there). John is not thinking in the Pauline terms of "faith versus works," of how the guilty sinner becomes acceptable before God or how God can incorporate Gentiles into the saved community without failing in his promises to Israel (cf. the argument of Romans and Galatians). "Believe" as a verb does not occur in Revelation at all; "faith" as a noun means "faithfulness" (2:13, 19; 13:10) or *the* faith, the content of faith (14:12); "faithful" as an adjective means not "believing" but "loyal, enduring, having integrity," and is used of Christ (1:5; 3:14; 19:11) and his word (21:5; 22:6) as well as of human beings (2:10, 13; 17:14). In Revelation the whole word-group for faith and believing is thus never used in contrast to works, as in Paul, and never has the Pauline meaning of "obedience in personal trust that mediates our relationship to God." While it is true that John is not an explicit exponent of the Pauline doctrine of justification by grace alone through faith (the word "grace" does not occur in Revelation, except in the letter opening and closing formulae of 1:4 and 22:21), this does not mean that John is an advocate of "works righteousness." Like Paul, his concern is with responsible Christian conduct; John's word for this is "works."

This insistence on the importance of Christian action shows that even in his situation of persecution, threat, and expectation of the near End John does not understand the Christian life to be simply passive waiting. The reference to "service" in 2:19 is more than incidental. John calls his churches to do more than endure; there is a ministry to be performed in the meantime.

Repentance. Some churches are commended for their conduct in the face of crisis, their "works" (Ephesus, 2:2; Thyatira, 2:19; Philadelphia, 3:8), while others are reproved (Sardis, 3:1-2; Laodicea, 3:15). All except Smyrna and Philadelphia are called to repentance. Repentance is not a once-and-for-all act

95

that brings one into the Christian community but is the constant challenge to the community. It is not a matter of feeling sorry in a religious mood about past misdeeds but reorientation to a new model of life based on the gospel, the good news that God has already acted in Jesus for our salvation. The call to repentance is thus not chiding but opportunity. Even the Laodicean Christians can repent and sit with Christ on his throne, rejoicing with all God's people at the messianic banquet (3:20–21).

Holding firm. In John's situation the Christian life is expressed chiefly in *hypomone* (RSV: "patient endurance," 1:9; 2:2, 3, 19; 3:10). The quality of Christian action it expresses is not passive resignation; it is an active holding firm "for the sake of my name" (2:3, 13; 3:8), having courage in the face of interrogation by the Roman officials (cf. the letter of Pliny in the Introduction). Elizabeth Schüssler Fiorenza translates it "consistent resistance" to oppressive power (*Book of Revelation*, p. 4). The word is derived from a verb which means "stand one's ground, not to give in" (cf. Matt. 24:13; Mark 13:13). Some of the Asian churches are praised for manifesting this quality (2:2, 3, 19; 3:10): In the face of the cultural pressures, they hold fast to their confession of Christ as the only Lord—some of them even to the point of dying (2:13). There was much to admire in the Asian Christians. Preachers and teachers in later generations, when the church is not such a powerless community threatened by the hostile government and culture, need to ask how *hypomone* can be translated into appropriate forms of Christian life and witness. In settings other than oppression and persecution, "patient endurance" as the essence of Christian responsibility in the world can be misunderstood as all too passive.

Love and spiritual gifts. Since Revelation has the reputation of being a violent and unloving book, it should perhaps be emphasized that the risen Christ, through John, commends some of the Asian Christians for their love (2:4), and that like Paul, John considers love among the supreme expressions of the Christian life. "Love," of course, is not a sentimental emotion but the active care for others manifested in Jesus' own life. It is equated with "works" in 2:4–5. The church at Thyatira is praised for its love expressed in deeds (2:19). The Ephesian church receives blame because it has abandoned the love it had at first (2:4). This does not mean that their "enthusiasm" had waned. John is not speaking of enthusiastic worship services, which seem to have continued among the Ephesians and John's other churches. The reputation of Sardis as a "live" church (3:1) and the Laodiceans' view of themselves as "rich" (3:17) probably refer to the charismatic enthusiasm of their realized eschatology (cf. Paul's ironic comments to the Corinthians, I Cor. 4:8; II Cor. 4:12). Like Paul earlier, John acknowledges that his churches were well supplied with charismatic phenomena, but charges them with abandoning the love that had characterized their Christian lives earlier. Other, more spectacular manifestations of what they supposed was the spiritual life had become more important than the commonplace, selfless care for others represented by love in its Christian meaning. As in Paul's teaching, the kind of love Christ has for sinners (1:5, cf. Rom. 5:5–11) and even for the city which crucified him (20:9—Jerusalem is nonetheless "the beloved city") is the basis for Christian love for others. John does have visions of terrible violence which befall the unrepentant, and these must receive their due (see chaps. 6—9, and "Reflection: Interpreting Revelation's Violent Imagery"). Yet these violent pictures must not blind us to the fact that John also has a vision of the love of God that embraces and redeems even the enemies, and this love is the basis for commending Christians to love as they have been loved.

Theological basis. The word of the risen Jesus that closes this section (3:21) provides a striking summary of Revelation's theological perspective on Christian responsibility:

1. *God* rules from the throne. God, not an apocalyptic scheme, is sovereign. This is an appropriate transition to the vision of the throneroom to begin in chapter 4.

2. *Christ* "shares" the throne with God in the present. The God who rules is the God who represents himself in Jesus. Jesus attained to the throne by "conquering," by giving his life for others and for the truth of the gospel. Chapter 5 will present this in powerful imagery.

3. *Christians* will share this same throne, and attain it by the same "conquering." This is an implicit call to follow Jesus' pattern of martyrdom, a call to ultimate human decision. Yet this future rule and victory is called the gift of God. Human responsibility and gift of God are not alternatives; each is raised to the ultimate level by this declaration.

97

PART TWO

God Judges the "Great City"

REVELATION 4:1—18:24

A new major section begins at chapter 4 and extends through chapter 18 (cf. the outline and discussion of the structure of Revelation in the Introduction). Following an introductory vision of the glory of God the Creator and Redeemer, the major content of this section portrays the series of eschatological woes that, according to apocalyptic thinking, must form the prelude to the victorious establishment of God's kingdom at the End. These are represented by the seven seals (6:1—8:1), the seven trumpets (8:6—11:19), the seven bowls (15:5—16:21), and the fall of "Babylon" (17:1—18:24). This extended series of pictures of judgment begins with a premonition of the fall of Rome/"Babylon" (6:1-2; cf. commentary) and returns to it as the definitive picture of God's judgment on the evil world power that has usurped his authority (17:1—18:24; cf. commentary). Yet John does not wait until he has completed the visions of judgment to announce salvation and encouragement but intersperses the visions of catastrophe with heartening pictures of the victory already won and anticipations of the victory to come (7:1-17; 14:1-5; 15:2-4). This is good literary and communications strategy—an unrelieved series of twenty-one woes would generate a sensory overload that would dull the impact it attempts to make. This structure is good Christian theology as well, for John is an exponent of the Christian faith that the Christ is not the one who comes only at the end of history but the one who has already come, and salvation is not experienced only beyond the eschatological woes but is already experienced in the midst of the throes of historical struggle.

This section is both continuous and discontinuous with the preceding. Discontinuity is signaled by the change of scene from earth to heaven. Like the Old Testament prophets, John is caught up into the heavenly court, where he overhears the divine council (cf. I Kings 22; Isa. 40; Jer. 23:18; cf. Job 1—2). He remains there through the seal visions and trumpet visions of chapters 6—9. From chapter 10 on, John's standpoint sometimes appears to be back on earth, yet all is still seen from the transcendent perspective of the eschatological future.

The shift of perspective at 4:1 involves a new way of seeing the church. Revelation began with John on the earth with his hearer-readers, involved in the struggle of ordinary Christians to be loyal to Christ in their ambiguous situation. The messages to the seven churches of chapters 2—3 were often very critical of the Christians in the churches of Asia. From 4:1 on they are almost idealized, as in the scene in 14:1–5. Christians are no longer distinguished into good, bad, and indifferent but are uniformly assumed to be faithful and obedient. Everything is now seen from the heavenly, eschatological perspective.

Continuity with chapters 1—3 is provided by the connection with the motif of the heavenly throneroom in the concluding lines of the final message to the churches (3:21), and by the fact that John is addressed by the same voice that had addressed him in the vision of chapter 1—the voice of the exalted Christ (4:1).

"After This"—The Future/Present of 4:1—18:24

Revelation 4:1 signals a decisive turn to the future. As chapters 2—3 had portrayed "what is," chapters 4—22 picture what "will be" (cf. 1:19). John refers to the short-term future of his own hearer-readers, not the centuries-long perspective from which later readers tend to see his prophecy (see "Reflection: Interpreting the 'Near End' in Revelation"). In particular, John is not predicting some future "rapture" of the church. (The word "rapture" does not, of course, occur in Revelation.) On the contrary, he consistently portrays the church as present on earth during the days of eschatological tribulation shortly to come (2:10, 22–25; 3:10; 6:9–11; 7:1–8, 14; 8:3–4; 12:17; 14:12–13; 16:15; 17:6; 18:4). John here communicates what happened to him in his visionary experience; he does not predict what will literally happen to others. Being caught up into the heavenly world to receive revelations is a common feature of apocalyptic literature (e.g., II Cor. 12:1-4; Apoc. Abram. 8-12; II Enoch 3—22). No one interprets these heavenly trips as predictions of a future "rapture." John's revelation is to be interpreted within this common framework of ancient apocalyptic thought.

Chapters 4—18 disclose the eschatological future. The sealed book in God's hand (5:1) contains the ultimate future, the outcome of all things, the final scenes which contain the key to the whole story of history and make it all worthwhile. The future is real and already exists in God's hand. Yet it is sealed, and John weeps because neither he nor anyone else can break the seal and know the mystery of God's future (5:2-4).

The future orientation of the visions which begin at 4:1 does not mean that the remainder of the book is a straightforward prediction of the chronological future. John's thinking is not so linear. The keynote throneroom scene of 4:1—5:14 focuses on the central figure, who is repeatedly described as the One who spans all time, to whom past, present, and future are all one (4:8; cf. 1:4, 8; 21:6; 22:13). Thus the visions of "what must take place after this" (4:1) portray not only the diachronic future but synchronically represent what always is/will be as one tensive picture.

Revelation 4:1—5:14
The Heavenly Throneroom

As is the case with the other two major parts of the book, this part begins with a scene portraying the heavenly glory of God and the Lamb, 4:1—5:14 (cf. outline in the Introduction). Preaching and teaching should take into account the unity of these two chapters.

John is caught up into the heavenly throneroom, where he beholds One seated on the throne. Although no description is given of the figure on the throne, the setting is described in detail. Present before the throne are seven torches of fire identified as the seven spirits of God, four living creatures, and twenty-four elders on twenty-four thrones. Amid the splendor of heavenly worship, which includes the prayers of the Chris-

101

tians on earth (5:8), the Lamb appears, takes the sealed scroll from the hand of the one seated on the throne, and as he opens the seals the eschatological events begin.

This scene is the theological fountainhead and anchor point for the whole document. The bulk of John's writing will be composed of visions of the catastrophes represented in the traditional apocalyptic imagery of the seals, trumpets, and bowls of chapters 6—18, hence its gloomy reputation. Yet before portraying these eschatological woes, John wants the hearer-reader to see what he has seen: At the heart of things God rules in sublime majesty, the God who has defined himself as the Lamb who suffers for others. The eschatological plagues to be portrayed in chapters 6—18 unfold from the hand of the Lamb in chapter 5, the hand of the crucified and risen one.

The Throneroom of the Universe (4:1–6a)

John's description turns immediately to the throne (4:2). In contrast to other apocalyptic literature, he spends not a syllable on curiosity-titillating descriptions of the heavenly journey itself (cf. Paul's similar reticence in II Cor. 12:1–4). All attention is focused on the throne. Three of every four occurrences of the word "throne" in the New Testament are found in Revelation (47 of 62). The manner in which throneroom imagery and vocabulary dominates John's vision indicates that he is influenced by that stream of tradition that began with Ezekiel's daring vision of the throne-chariot of God (1:4–28), with which Revelation 4:3–8 has many contacts: the description of the throne, the living creatures, the rainbow, the thunder and lightning, the figure on the throne. Ezekiel's vision of the throne-chariot had a deep influence on later apocalyptic, so that, for example, the vision of the throneroom in I Enoch 14 also draws on Ezekiel and thus resembles John's very closely. In early Judaism some rabbis attempted to prohibit the reading of Ezekiel's vision because it was considered a means of inducing visionary experiences in the reader, as dangerous as hallucinogenic drugs would seem to us. Despite these warnings, a stream of Jewish mysticism developed from this tradition called Merkabah ("chariot") mysticism. John's vision is thus not a reporter's account of something he "actually" saw; here, as elsewhere, it is the literary expression in traditional terms of his prophetic experience, carefully composed to communicate his theological meaning.

In John's vision there is a throneroom for the universe, and

102

the throne is not vacant. The universe is not a chaos nor is it ruled by blind fate. Someone is in charge. The words "one seated on the throne" occur twelve times in Revelation; it is John's way of saying "God." Like the drama as a whole, this scene is theocentric. Knowing the future is not a matter of obtaining information but of knowing God who holds the future. The ultimate future is not an item of information to be analyzed but a person to be encountered. Despite his heavy dependence on Ezekiel, there is no description of the one who sits on the throne, in contrast to Ezekiel 1:3–28. John intentionally withholds any description of the central figure on the throne, leaving a blank center in the picture to be filled in by the figure of the Lamb—yet another means of affirming that God is the one who defines himself by Christ.

These repeated references to the throne serve as a reminder that some of John's hearer-readers live in the presence of "Satan's throne," as he has already mentioned (2:13), the imperial claims of Rome expressed especially in the Caesar cult. "Throne," like "kingdom," is an explicitly political term. John's vision of the one throne of God contains an implied political polemic, a claim to reveal who *really* rules. Overtones of Caesar's counterclaim to the throne are found in John's depiction of God's sovereignty: The repeated "Worthy art thou" (4:11; 5:9, 12) directed to God/Christ reflects the acclamation used to greet the emperor during his triumphal entrance. The title "Lord and God" (4:8) is paralleled by Domitian's insistence that he be addressed by this title. The twenty-four elders may be influenced by the twenty-four lictors who surrounded Domitian (see Aune, "Influence," p. 13). The act of the twenty-four elders placing their crowns before God's throne in 4:10 calls to mind Tacitus' report that "the Parthian King Tiridates placed his diadem before the image of Nero in order to give homage to the Roman emperor" (cf. Fiorenza, *Invitation,* p. 76). Yet, as elsewhere in Revelation, the correlation of imagery from the imperial cult with that used to express faith in the sole sovereignty of God simply shows that all earthly claims to sovereignty are only pale imitations and parodies of the One who sits upon the one throne. Christians dare not give this homage to another.

The picture of God's throne is filled in by evocative references to other elements in the scene, descriptions which set up chains of associations in the minds of the hearer-readers. John does not relay a detailed description which we can only pas-

103

sively accept or reject; he invites imaginative participation in envisioning the scene by giving us language that evokes multiple layers of meaning simultaneously (cf. Introduction).

Flashes of lightning and peals of thunder. This is the language of theophany, imagery borrowed from the storm god and used by Israel to portray God's appearance at Sinai (Exod. 19: 16) and his repeated appearance in prophetic visions (Job 36: 30–32; Ps. 77:17–18; Ezek. 1:4, 13, 14, 24). Though unseen and indescribable, God is certainly and terribly *present.*

The book. The sealed book in the right hand of the figure on the throne contains the eschatological events which begin to happen as the seals are broken, beginning in 6:1. This image of a sealed scroll in heaven functions by evoking a plurality of images in the hearer-readers' imagination:

(a) the scroll of the Law, which contains God's will and the judgments against those who violate it, an image corresponding to the elements in this vision which suggest a heavenly counterpart to the synagogue;

(b) the book of the prophets containing God's threats of future judgment and promises of future victory, sometimes portrayed as sealed up for a future day (Isa. 8:16; 29:11; Dan. 12:4);

(c) the prophetic scroll given to Ezekiel, written like this one on both sides (Ezek. 2:10);

(d) the heavenly tablets of destiny which contain the gods' decisions about the future, a motif of Babylonian religion often adopted in Jewish apocalyptic (e.g., I Enoch 81:1–3);

(e) the book of life, in which the redeemed are inscribed (Pss. 69:28; 139:16; Dan. 12:1; I Enoch 104:1; Luke 10:20; Phil. 4:3; Heb. 12:23; John makes use of this image in 3:5; 13:8; 17:8; 20:15; and 21:27);

(f) the heavenly books in which the deeds of human beings are recorded for future judgment (Dan. 7:10; II Esdr. 6:20; I Enoch 47:1; II Bar. 24:1; cf. Rev. 20:12);

(g) last wills and testaments were normally sealed with seven seals; this document evokes the image of a will that is to be executed by being opened.

The seals. The scroll is sealed with seven seals. A seal is a personal imprint, made by the signet ring pressed into clay or wax. Like the signature in modern society, it is an extension of the person. What I seal or sign, I guarantee by "placing myself on the line," I attest to and bind myself. The sealed scroll connotes mystery and inaccessibility and also the Sealer, one who personally stands behind the document whose word it is.

The seven spirits of God. This image connotes, kaleidoscopically, the angels of God who minister in his presence and are sent out to all the world, the "eyes" of God by which he keeps watch over the universe, and the fullness of God's spirit by which he is present to his creation. This image thus alternates between furnishings of the heavenly throneroom ("torches"), divine beings in the heavenly court ("spirits," "angels"), and an aspect of God's own being ("eyes," Spirit). The variety of references to this image are not to be decoded into one meaning (1:4; 3:1; 4:5; 5:6; cf. Zech. 4:2, 10); they illustrate the polyvalent, fluid imagery characteristic of John's revelatory language.

The sea. Just as the earthly temple had a "sea," so does the heavenly (cf. I Kings 7:23–26; II Chron. 4:6). Again, John's language evokes multiple layers of meaning. Common to the creation mythology of the Near East was the motif of the defeat of the chaos monster, represented by the sea. Even the Genesis story echoes the myth of the Creator's giving us a solid earth on which to live by driving the raging waters back (Gen. 1:1–10). Yet they are only held in check, not finally destroyed. Chaos always threatens to return and engulf the good creation. God's judgment on the world by the flood is an instance of precisely this (cf. Gen. 7:11). The Red Sea, from/through which Israel was saved and Egypt judged, was interpreted in the prophets as an expression of the anti-creation chaos monster (Isa. 51:9–10; cf. Rev. 15:1–4). John sees the hostile threat to creation as no threat. It is in God's presence—smooth as glass and under control. In the new creation it will vanish altogether (21:1).

The rainbow. John is still using imagery borrowed from Ezekiel to communicate his vision. Yet the appearance of the rainbow in 4:3 is more than a mere reflection of Ezekiel 1:28. Having just brought the reminder of the sea/chaos monster before the hearer-readers' imagination, with all its connotations of the flood of God's judgment, John then lays hold of the full scriptural meaning of the rainbow symbol: the God who judges has made a covenant with all creation. After the judgment comes the new beginning for all humanity (Gen. 9:8–17; note the universality of the repeated "all flesh" and "every creature," "all future generations"). Before the violent eschatological woes begin, we are given the sign of hope by the Creator who has covenanted to bring his creation safely through to the promised fulfillment.

The living creatures. Around the throne are four living creatures representing all aspects of created life (see below).

105

The other thrones. God alone is the true sovereign of the universe. This is the central message that reverberates throughout Revelation (1:8; 4:8; 11:17; 15:3; 16:7, 14; 19:6, 15; 21:22). Yet God "shares" his rule, his throne, with others: He does not exercise his rule in an arbitrary unilateral manner that makes automatons of his creatures.

Christ shares the throne of God (3:21). In this scene, God's sovereignty, expressed in his holding the sealed scroll of the eschatological future, will be exercised by the Lamb (5:6–7). Quite apart from the linguistic issue of how John's strange Greek phrase should be translated, the location of the Lamb "in the very middle of the throne" (5:6, NEB) is theologically correct, for John understands the throne to be occupied by "both" God and the Lamb (cf. 5:13; 7:9, 17; 22:1, 3). This language is not intended to conjure up some mental picture of double occupancy of the throne of the universe or of a parceling out of its rule between God and Christ. It is John's way of declaring that the throne of the Lamb and the throne of God are one and the same—God is the one who has defined himself in Jesus Christ; that when Christians say "God," the one they refer to is the one definitively revealed in Jesus, the Crucified.

The heavenly throneroom contains *the* throne of God/ Lamb and also twenty-four thrones occupied by twenty-four "elders." In both Jewish and gentile social structure, the ruling council was often designated as "elders," which has more to do with authority than with age. The triumphant authority of these twenty-four is signified by their crowns and white garments. "Crown" has already been associated in the hearer-reader's mind with "being faithful unto death," martyrdom (2:10); "white garments" will receive the same connotation (6:11; 7:9). These twenty-four represent in John's mind a kind of heavenly counterpart to the continuing People of God on earth (twelve tribes of Israel, twelve apostles, cf. 7:1–8; 12:1; 21:12–14), who are called to "reign" through faithfulness even to the point of death. They represent the church on earth in that they have the prayers of the saints in their censers, which they offer up before God as incense in the heavenly worship (5:8). God "shares" the throne not only with Christ, the Lamb, but also with his people (3:21), who are destined to participate in ruling the eschatological kingdom (1:6; 5:10; 20:6; 22:5). Although the twenty-four elders sit on thrones and wear crowns, they are in no sense

106

competitors to the sovereign rule of the one God, as their sub-
jection in 4:10 illustrates.

God the Creator of All (4:6*b*–11)

Around the throne are four living creatures. Their descriptions
are a collage of details from Ezekiel 1 and Isaiah 6, both of
which draw upon the traditional picture of the cherubim. The
Israelites adopted this imagery from the winged bull or similar
mythological animals that figured in Mesopotamian and Canaanite mythology as guardians of the throne of both heavenly and
earthly kings.

John is not interested in (or even aware of) the sources of
this imagery. He is concerned with what they represent. Here
we have represented before the heavenly throne all categories
of animal life, the whole animal kingdom of God's creation: wild
animals, domestic animals, human beings (not, be it noted, as
the "crown" of creation, but as a good part of it), and birds. In
each case an apex of creation is portrayed. Again, John is parallel to a Jewish tradition which declares, "Man is exalted among
creatures, the eagle among birds, the ox among domestic animals, the lion among wild beasts; all of them have received
dominion" (*Midrash Shemoth* R. 23, as quoted in Sweet, p. 120).
These living creatures, who, like the twenty-four elders, participate in God's own sovereignty over the creation and exercise
some responsibility for the creation, are yet themselves *creatures* and join in praise to the *Creator* (4:11). As in a Greek
drama, the songs sung by the heavenly chorus provide a clue to
the central meaning of the action. Here the song is a hymn to
God the Creator, with emphasis on God as the creator of *all that
is,* and as having willfully *intended* to bring the universe into
being. Why this emphasis?

John's opponents in the churches, against whom the polem-
ics of chapters 2 and 3 are directed, seem to have some gnostic
characteristics. They may have had a dualistic view which affirmed the other, spiritual world and disdained this world, as did
the later Gnostics. John, inspired by the Spirit and caught up
into the other world, hears there a constant song of praise to
God as the creator of *this* world. John, like apocalyptic generally, is not otherworldly; he is the opponent of those who reject
this world for some other. His fervent eschatological faith is not
an alternative to faith in God as the loving creator of this world
but the outcome of this faith. In a situation of persecution or

107

threat, John has no interest in a dualistic escape hatch; he insists on the rigorous faith and theology demanded by faith in one God who is the creator of all.

The Christological Redefinition of Winning (5:1–7)

Within the throneroom scene, John's eye fastens on the sealed scroll in the right hand of the One seated on the throne (5:1). He hears the angel's question resound through the universe and weeps when he learns that our future must remain a closed book. John's crying is interrupted by the announcement that the Lion of the tribe of Judah, the Root of David, has conquered and can open the book.

Great lion of God. This is the announcement of the victory of the Messiah, and it is worthy of celebration. The "Root of David" is derived from such texts as Isaiah 11:1, which announces a branch from the root of David, and was understood in the first century to promise a David-like warrior Messiah who will fight God's battles and wreak vengeance on "God's" (our) enemies. The venerable, violent image of the lion had also been used for the Messiah, from the earliest days of Israel's proto-eschatological hopes (Gen. 49:9–10) into the first century. The Testament of Judah 24:5 understood the lion of Genesis 49:10 to be the Messiah; II Esdras 12:31–32, almost exactly contemporary with Revelation, declares matter-of-factly that "the lion . . . is the Messiah."

It seems so right. At the hands of history's evil empires, God's people have been lambs for the slaughter long enough (cf. Ps. 44, esp. v. 11!). What we need is God's messiah, full of righteous indignation and God's power, to turn the tables, punish the oppressors, and establish justice. The "Great Lion of God" is the answer to our prayers (it's about time!) and cause for celebration.

Agnus Dei. John looks at the appointed place in the vision where the Lion was supposed to appear, and what he sees is a slaughtered lamb. Although readers of the Bible may have become so accustomed to it that the effect is lost to us, this is perhaps the most mind-wrenching "rebirth of images" in literature. The slot in the system reserved for the Lion has been filled by the Lamb of God.

108

This is the first occurrence of "Lamb" in Revelation. It is absent from all the christological language and imagery of the opening chapters; John has reserved it for its dramatic entrée precisely here. It is John's definitive title for Christ, occurring twenty-nine times in Revelation (only once elsewhere in the N.T., John 21:15; "lamb" in John 1:29, 36; Acts 8:32; I Peter 1:19 is another Greek word, *amnos,* not Revelation's *arnion*).

Two images of the Messiah, "Lion" and "Lamb," appear in this vision. The relationship between them is *crucial* to understanding all of Revelation's theology. Interpretation of Revelation has presented several options:

First the lamb, then the lion. A chapter in a book representative of a kind of pop-eschatology is entitled "The Lamb Becomes a Lion" (Lindsey). The author presents Jesus as having "two roles": his "first coming" as a lamb and his "second coming" as a lion. Those who do not respond to the love offered by Jesus in his first coming get the apocalyptic violence of the second. This is the polar opposite of the meaning of the text of Revelation, in which the lion image is reinterpreted and replaced by the Lamb. It represents a retrogression from a Christian understanding of the meaning of Messiahship to the pre-Christian apocalyptic idea. In Revelation the Lamb is the "slaughtered" Lamb, slain not only on the cross but on the transcendent altar. In Revelation the participle "slaughtered" is always in the perfect tense, representing the *continuing* effects of a once-for-all past act. (Modern English lacks a true perfect, but cf. the older "Joy to the world! the Lord *is* come.") A similar understanding of the Crucified One in Paul's and Mark's theologies is expressed in the use of the perfect participle "crucified" for the living Christ after the resurrection (I Cor. 1:23; Mark 16:6). Crucifixion was not an incident which once happened in the cosmic career of the Messiah and then was superseded by the resurrection and exaltation; it is the definitive act which stamps its character on the identity of the Christ, and is thus definitive for the identity of God. Love was not a provisional strategy of the earthly Jesus, to be eventually replaced by transcendent, eschatological violence when "they've had their chance" and love has not "worked."

Lamb to some, lion to others. Another way of relating "Lion" and "Lamb" is to think of the Christ as having both lion and lamb aspects, for example showing his lamb side to believers and reserving his lion nature for unbelievers. Again, there is no suggestion in Revelation of this parceling out of the Christ into part-lion, part-lamb.

109

The lamb is really a lion. Another effort to come to terms with this imagery is to understand "Lamb" as simply another image for the power and violence of the lion. C. H. Dodd is representative of a small group of scholars who advocate this interpretation (see Dodd, pp. 230–38). Basing his interpretation on Jewish texts in which the Messiah is symbolized as a young ram or warrior sheep (Test. Jos. 19:8; I Enoch 89:46; 90:19; cf. Test. Benj. 3:8), Dodd concludes that the powerful "Lamb" of Revelation is simply another version of the violent Messiah expected in Jewish apocalyptic.

Dodd is correct in emphasizing that the Lamb of Revelation is indeed a powerful Lamb, with seven horns and seven eyes. But his interpretation has two insuperable problems. First, the texts on which it is based are now widely considered to be late interpolations (cf. Charlesworth). Second, his interpretation fails to do justice to the essential characteristic of the Lamb, which is that it has been and remains *slaughtered* (cf. above), and to the fact that John's word for "lamb" is never the usual word for "lamb" in the New Testament *(amnos);* John uses a diminutive *(arnion),* having the *-ion* ending something like English *-kins* and *-y.* While "Lambkins" is in English too sweet and childish to express the seriousness of John's thought, his consistent use of the diminutive does picture the vulnerability and victimization of the defenseless Lamb upon the altar (as in the LXX of Jer. 1:19, and cf. Isa. 53:7–12), at the opposite pole from the violent warrior Messiah of apocalyptic expectation.

The "lion" is really the lamb, representing the ultimate power of God. This is the meaning of John's dramatic rebirth of images. It is as though John had adopted the familiar synagogue practice of "perpetual Kethib/Qere," whereby a word or phrase that appears in the traditional text is read as another word or phrase: "wherever the tradition says 'lion,' read 'Lamb.'" To use another analogy, this one from mathematics, it is like putting a minus sign before the parentheses of a complicated formula—the old materials are retained, but their valences are all reversed.

The Lamb is indeed powerful, for as the Messiah he represents God, takes the scroll from his hand, and puts it into effect. Breaking the seals of the scroll does not mean merely making known but making effective. The Lamb has seven horns (fullness of power!) and seven eyes (fullness of insight!) and is thus the fulfillment of the hopes of the scion of David of Isaiah 11. What God does for humanity through the Lamb is not a three-party transaction (God, Jesus, and humanity) but a two-party transaction: God and humanity. This is John's understanding, and this is why his evocative images of God and Christ tend to

110

fade into each other (cf. the discussion above about Christ "sharing" the throne of God). The "seven eyes" of the Lamb (5:6) are the seven spirits *of God.* John wants his hearer-readers to grasp how close the relationship is between Christ, God, and the Spirit, to relate the living Christ to the Spirit who speaks in the churches, and to relate this Spirit to the crucified and exalted Christ.

Since the Lamb operates by the ultimate power, the power of God, the Lamb *conquers.* As "Lamb" is the key christological noun in John's vocabulary, so "conquer" *(nikao),* also translated "overcome," "prevail," "win the victory," "triumph," "win the right," is the key christological verb. It occurs twenty-three times, twice as often as in all other New Testament books combined. The Lamb indeed "conquers" (3:21; 5:5; 17:14), as do faithful Christians (2:7, 11, 17, 26; 3:5, 12, 21; 12:11; 15:2; 21:7). Indeed, John explicitly points out that "conquering" is what binds together Jesus and his followers (3:21), and that Christians "conquer" not only by what they do but by what Jesus has done (12:11).

"Conquering" in both cases, that of the Christ and that of Christians, means no more or less than dying. It never in Revelation designates any destructive judgment on the enemies of Christ or Christians. Jesus stood before the Roman court, was faithful unto death, and this was his victory and his reign. John calls Christians to the same messianic conquest. "Conquer" *(nikao)* has in John's situation not only the military, violent connotation which he redefines but also a forensic, legal connotation which he likewise redefines: "In the context of the Apocalypse as a whole, 'conquering' means being acquitted in a court of law. The acquittal of the faithful is paradoxical. It is expected that they will be found guilty in the local Roman courts and executed. But the testimony they give and their acceptance of death will win them the acquittal that counts—in the heavenly court, in the eyes of eternity" (A. Y. Collins, *The Apocalypse,* p. 14). For Christians, what it means to "win" has been redefined by the cross of Jesus.

Universal Victory and Praise (5:8–14)

Both halves of the breathtaking scene John calls before our imagination in chapters 4 and 5 end on an absolutely universal note. The last words of the heavenly chorus of 4:11 worship God as the Creator of *all;* the choir that sings the final chorus of 5:13 in praise to the Lamb is comprised of the *whole* creation. The

111

grand vision of chapters 4 and 5 proceeds in concentric circles from God through Christ to the living creatures, to the twenty-four elders, to an innumerable host, to include absolutely everything that is: one creation celebrating the one God as Creator and Redeemer. Absolutely no one and nothing is excluded from this picture. Given this mind-expanding picture, it is impossible to see any part of the universe as ultimately rebellious and lost, just as it is impossible to see any part of the universe as existing apart from the creative will and activity of the one creator God. "All," "every" applies in both cases (4:11; 5:13). (See the "Reflection: Universal Salvation and Paradoxical Language.")

It is difficult to fit this final scene into a chronology (cf. the comments above on the future/present of 4:1—18:14 and Introduction). It is thus important to remember both that the scene pictured here is from beginning to end a scene of worship and that Revelation was intended for reading forth in the congregation assembled for worship (cf. 1:3 and the Introduction). In worship past and future collapse into the present. The hymns of chapters 4 and 5 allow the worshiper to participate in the ultimate past, signaled by creation language, and the ultimate future of God's universal victory, without expending too much analytical worry about how this scene of universal salvation fits into John's chronology. The hymn of all creation to the Creator and Redeemer has a proleptic dimension to it. Having joined in this grand chorus, the hearer-reader is now prepared to appropriate the violent message of judgment presented in the opening of the seven seals and will not misunderstand the penultimate pictures of judgment as representing God's last word, the word of salvation which already resounds in this scene.

REFLECTION

Interpreting Revelation's Violent Imagery

When the Lamb opens the sealed scroll, catastrophic violence is unleashed upon the earth and its inhabitants. The world is devastated by war, famine, plague, and death (6:1–8). People are killed because of their faithfulness to God and cry out for vengeance (6:9–11). Sun, moon, and stars are struck; mountains and islands are displaced, as everyone from king to slave tries to escape the approaching wrath (6:12–17). The earth is struck with hail and fire mixed with blood (8:7) and sea and rivers turn to blood (8:8–11; 16:3–4). Demonic locust-like creatures stream out of the abyss to torment humanity, and people cry out for death but continue to suffer (9:1–11). A twilight-zone supernatural horde of two hundred million cavalry pour across the Euphrates from the East (9:13–19). Those who worship the beast are tormented with sulphurous fire in the presence of the holy angels and the Lamb (14:10–11). Horses wade for two hundred miles in bridle-deep blood (14:20). The kings of the earth mount a final battle against God and his Messiah, and vultures are gorged with the flesh of both the lowly footsoldiers who fight the world's battles and of their high and mighty commanders (16:14–16; 19:17–18).

Not only is mind and imagination overwhelmed by the quantity and unrelenting intensity of the violence perpetrated against both humans and the cosmos itself, the theological problem is compounded by the fact that the source of violence is God and the Lamb, sometimes invoked with cries for vengeance. This whole range of imagery has posed a severe problem for interpreting Revelation as a Christian book, particularly when compared with the pictures of Jesus in the Gospels. The picture of sinners being tormented forever in the presence of the Lamb (14:10) seems to present a different world from the picture of the Jesus who prays for his tormentors and teaches his disciples to do the same (Luke 23:34; Matt. 5:43–44). Here and elsewhere, the Bible's message is not honored by ignoring the problems it presents. No real answers can be forthcoming until the question is allowed to emerge in all its sharpness. It thus seems advisable to reflect on this issue in one comprehensive discussion dealing with the interpretation of such imagery wherever it occurs in Revelation. The following observations, perspectives, and principles may be found helpful in interpreting the violent/"vindictive" language of Revelation. John's violent/"vindictive" language can be properly interpreted by attending to (1) the givenness of John's situation, (2) John's appropriation of tradition, (3) his use of language, and (4) his theology.

The Givenness of John's Situation of Suffering

John's thought did not begin with visions about future suffering; it began with the fact of suffering in his own present. Apocalyptic thought gives experienced suffering a meaning by placing it in a cosmic context, functioning as hermeneutics of the present, not speculation about the future. The sociological and psychological realities of such a situation must be taken into account. As illustrated by Israel's imprecatory psalms (Pss. 35; 55; 69; 109; 137), a community that feels itself pushed to the edge of society and the edges of its own endurance will, in its worship, give vent to the natural feelings of resentment, even revenge, as it anticipates the eschatological turning of the tables. Even then, cries for "revenge," rather than being personal, are but a plea for the justice of God to be made manifest publicly.

John's Appropriation of Tradition

It is not as though John had devised this violent language and imagery himself. In both form and content most of it was adopted and adapted by him from his tradition. Some important elements of this tradition are these:

The ancient Near Eastern combat myth. In the background of much of the religious imagery that pervaded John's world was the mythical story of creation in which the chaos monster (the Sea, Tiamat, Lotan [=Leviathan]) was subdued and held at bay at creation, but was still there at the "edges" of the secure created world, still threatening and disrupting the ordered creation. The evil of the present world is understood as the remnants of uncreation, so that the present world has a built-in tension. There will be a final abolition of the uncreation, and a new creation will emerge. But just before the final victory of the Creator, the forces of chaos will make a final reassertion of their threat, causing great havoc to the creation before chaos is finally destroyed forever. The final victory includes pictures of violence.

The apocalyptic scheme of the "messianic woes." Jewish apocalyptic developed a "standard" pattern which interpreted the present troubles of the faithful community as the leading edge of the period of suffering which must come just before the final victory, just as labor pains precede birth. In II (Syriac) Baruch 26:1—30:5, for instance, twelve disasters are announced as preliminary to the coming of the Messiah, resurrection, and judgment. John's theology was worked out within the framework of traditional apocalyptic thought, which included the "messianic woes" as an integral part of the plot. John takes over this language, including its macabre details. For instance, the image of horses wading up to their bridles in blood (14:19–20)

114

was not original with John but was already a proverbial picture of the woes of the last days (I Enoch 100:3; cf. II Esdr. 15:35–36). The world heaves and groans in labor pains as it brings forth the Messiah and the new age. The terrible period of suffering is not the last word but the harbinger of good news. It is in this sense that the announcement of the coming violence of God's judgment can be called "good news" in 14:6–7.

The language of Scripture. In attempting to come to terms with the pervasive violence of the language of Revelation, it must not be forgotten that here too John is not creating *ad hoc* but is drawing from Scripture. Almost everything in the violent pictures of the seals, trumpets, and bowls of chapters 6—19 is derived from biblical pictures and is described in biblical language. The language and imagery of the exodus naturally becomes John's means of expression of the eschatological deliverance from the contemporary (Roman) "Pharaoh." By labeling the eschatological disasters "plagues" (15:6), which God will visit on the arrogance of the contemporary "Pharaoh"/"Egypt" before the evil empire will "let my people go," he interprets the present Roman pressures and their anticipated intensification as an extension of the biblical story into his churches' own experience.

The terminology of God's "wrath" (6:16–17; 11:18; 14:10; 16:19; 19:15) is not John's creation, but a dimension of a deep stream of biblical theology (only a sampling, including the great prophets of Israel, the Gospels, and Paul: Exod. 22:21–24; Deut. 9:7–8; Pss. 2:5; 78:21–22; 90:7–9; Isa. 1:24; 9:19; 13:9, 13; 51:17, 22; Jer. 4:4; 10:10, 25; 25:15; Ezek. 7:8, 12; 13:13; 20:8, 13; Hos. 5:10; 13:11; Micah 5:15; Matt. 3:7; John 3:36; Rom. 1:18[!]; 2:5; 5:9; 9:22; 12:19; I Thess. 1:10; 2:16; 5:9). The stream of biblical theology represented by these texts does not picture a petty deity overcome by emotional outbursts; rather it pictures the relentless, inexorable punishment of sin by a God of justice.

The biblical prophets' woes against Babylon as the enemy of God's people are transmuted into the eschatological woes against the "Babylon" of John's time (e.g., Isa. 13; Jer. 51:1–19). The source of John's language is his Bible; it does not come merely from his bitterness against his oppressors. Again, imagery from the imprecatory psalms is used in portraying God's wrath against the contemporary embodiment of evil (Ps. 69:24 ‖ Rev. 16:1).

John also makes extensive use of the theophany language of

115

his Scripture. Some of the imagery (earthquakes, hail, etc.) is intended to communicate the awesome glory accompanying the appearance of God rather than the punishment of humanity. It is not punishment language, but theophany language: The earth reels because it cannot *stand* in the presence of God. (Cf. such scenes as 8:7 and 11:19, and cf. Exod. 9:23–25; 19:18–19; Judg. 5:4–5; I Kings 19:11–13; Pss. 18:7–15; 29:3–9; Ezek. 38:22; Joel 3:16.)

The other side of this is to show human dependence; water, sun, the elements are not under human control. As human beings, we live in Somebody Else's world, and this truth is eschatologically demonstrated, *pictured,* for us. In the portrayals of the terrors of earthquake, plague, and other catastrophes that afflict the cosmos just before the final victory, the community confesses its faith that it does not control the universe and its destiny; it does acknowledge that that destiny is in the hands of an indescribably awesome power over which we have no control. *This,* and not the fate of those portrayed as suffering the final woes and its justice or injustice, is the "point" of such imagery—as in Exodus and the Psalter!

John's Use of Language

Visionary/metaphorical. None of the violence in the scenes of chapters 6—16 is literal violence against the real world; it is violence in a visionary scene of the future, expressed in metaphorical language (9:7!). The bloody hail and fire launched from heaven against the earth (8:7) are pictures of something, and something terrible, and though not "just" pictures, they are still pictures. The sword and fire by which the evil of the earth is judged (and even "tormented") are not literal swords and fire but metaphors for the cutting, searing *word* (1:16, 11:5).

Confessional. John's imagery portraying violent judgment upon God's enemies is the insider language of the confessing community expressing praise and gratitude for salvation. The language of worship and prayer is not objectifying description of the fate of outsiders but the confession of the faith of insiders.

The language of the plague stories of Exodus, one of the quarries from which John hews his own imagery, is confessional language glorifying God's deliverance of Israel. Its function is not to make statements about God's lack of care for the Egyptian mothers who mourn the loss of their firstborn sons, and the children themselves. The story is told from inside the faith of the confessing community, and makes its "point" from this one perspective. To misconstrue such language as making objective statements about the fate of the Egyptians from which inferences about the character of God could be drawn is to misconstrue the genre of the language (cf. the discussion of non-objectifying and non-inferential language in the Introduction).

Psalm 91:1–8 is one of many examples of the Bible's confessional language of the worshiping community:

> He who dwells in the shelter of the Most High,
>   who abides in the shadow of the Almighty,
> will say to the LORD, "My refuge and my fortress;
>   my God, in whom I trust."
> For he will deliver you from the snare of the fowler
>   and from the deadly pestilence;
> he will cover you with his pinions,
>   and under his wings you will find refuge;
>   his faithfulness is a shield and buckler.
> You will not fear the terror of the night,
>   nor the arrow that flies by day,
> nor the pestilence that stalks in darkness,
>   nor the destruction that wastes at noonday.
> A thousand may fall at your side,
>   ten thousand at your right hand;
>   but it will not come near you.
> You will only look with your eyes
>   and see the recompense of the wicked.

Such language is non-inferential; it does not presuppose a logical system within which inferences about the fate of the ten thousand that fall at your right hand can be made. Such language functions to make only one point—God's protective care for the confessing worshiper. It must never be forgotten that Revelation was written to be read in a service of prayer and praise of worshiping congregations and is expressed in language that functions within that context.

John's Theology and Purpose

Sin, repentance, judgment. The violent imagery repeatedly expresses John's conviction of universal human sinfulness. As in the plagues of the exodus story, events intended by God to call people to repentance (cf. 11:13) only serve to reveal how hardened are their hearts (9:20). Like Paul's, John's theology assumes too that Christians, insiders, are also sinners (1:5). John

117

pictures sinful humans, reeling under the judgment of the holy God, not innocent or self-righteous Christians suffering at the hands of sinful Romans. The catastrophes—terrible, tragic events—are repeatedly placed in the category of God's judgments: 6:10; 11:18; 14:7; 16:5, 7; 17:1; 18:8, 10, 20; 19:2, 11; 20:12, 13. These eschatological terrors are therefore an expression of John's sense of justice. Considering the situation, this is done in a remarkably non-smug manner. The us/them mentality, while present, is not absolute: *we* are also judged as sinners; *they* are not excluded from salvation.

Christological transformation of traditional imagery. The traditional imagery of apocalyptic terror is adopted and used by John, but like everything else in his revelation it is transformed within his christological perspective. The imagery of the lion is still used, but the Messiah is the slain Lamb. As in mathematics when one changes the valence of the sign outside the parentheses, the formulae within the parentheses are retained, but all their values are reversed. The same imagery is used, but its valence is changed.

Every event of apocalyptic violence in chapters 6—19 must be seen as *derived from* the scene of chapters 4—5. This means that *all* of 6—19 transpires from the hand of the Lamb . . . "all is situated in the cross of Jesus Christ . . . these texts must not be read in themselves but only in relation to that love which sacrifices itself for those who hate it" (Ellul, p. 123). The *Lamb* is the controlling image throughout. The Messiah is still clothed in the bloody garments (19:13) of the eschatological victory, but the blood is his own (1:5). The scenes are scenes of "wrath," but it is the "wrath of the Lamb" (6:16). Death and Hades still rampage through the final scenes (6:7-8), but the Messiah holds the keys to Death and Hades (1:18) and will finally cast them—not their victims—into the lake of fire (20:14).

Universal salvation. The violent imagery is presented within a Revelation which also has scenes of universal salvation. (See "Reflection: Universal Salvation and Paradoxical Language.") While the world may reel under the hammer blows of God's wrath, it is also redeemed and released from the power of Satan (20:1-6). The kings of the earth may be destroyed and their flesh eaten by vultures (19:17-21); they are also redeemed and make their contribution to the new Jerusalem (21:24-26). "Only when we acknowledge that Revelation hopes for the conversion of the nations . . . will we be able to see that it does

118

not advocate a 'theology of resentment' but a theology of justice" (Fiorenza, *Invitation,* p. 119).

The above perspectives may permit the awe-full imagery of the eschatological woes in Revelation to appear in a new light. None of this is intended to water down the terror of their imagery but to allow it to function in its full force.

Revelation 6:1—8:1
The Heavenly Worship: Opening the Sealed Scroll

The Sevenfold Pattern

The portrayal of eschatological woes that now begins is loosely structured into three series of sevens: seals (6:1—8:1), trumpets (8:6—11:19), and bowls (15:5—16:21), with various interludes and digressions. The series of trumpets unfolds from the seventh seal, so that the seals and trumpets form one interrelated unit. These two series have a neat, identical pattern. The first four elements of each series present a concise description of four interrelated catastrophes. In the fifth and sixth sections a more elaborate description is given, as the woes intensify. Between the sixth and seventh episodes comes an interlude filled with anticipatory and retrospective visions of God's eschatological victory in Christ. The third series, the visions of the bowls of God's wrath (separated from the first two by the insertion of much material which does not fit into the pattern of sevens [12:1—15:8]), preserves only a rough approximation of the "sevens" pattern. Although the unifying structures of the Apocalypse are "a web interlaced in different ways" (Thompson, p. 16) that cannot be represented in a two-dimensional chart, something of the overall pattern of the three septets can be seen in the following diagram.

The First Four Seals:
The Four Horsemen of the Apocalypse (6:1–8)

In typical apocalyptic imagery (cf. e.g., Mark 13:8, par.), John portrays the beginning of the End as the eruption of war, plague, and death into the Roman world. To be sure, these

119

Structure of the Seven-Fold Pattern of Woes

	7 SEALS		7 TRUMPETS		7 BOWLS
	Chapters 6—11				Chapters 16—18
The Initial Unit of Four Catastrophes	6:1-2 — white horse, bow, crown conquer	8:7 — hail, fire, blood		16:2 — sores	
	6:3-4 — red horse, sword take peace from earth	8:8-9 — fiery mountain in sea, 1/3 sea became blood		16:3 — sea to blood	
	6:5-6 — black horse, balance	8:10-11 — star falls on 1/3 of rivers wormwood > water		16:4-7 — rivers to blood	
	6:7-8 — pale horse, sword, famine, plague, wild animals	8:12 — 1/3 sun, 1/3 moon, 1/3 stars		16:8-9 — sun	

Chapters 12—15

The Woes Intensify as the End Approaches			
6:9-11	martyrs under altar, "how long," "little longer"	8:13	"woe, woe, woe" demon locusts from dark pit
6:12-17	earthquake, sun and moon, stars fall, all fear	9:13-21	200,000,000 demon cavalry from Euphrates

INTERLUDE			
7:1-8	sealing 144,000/great multitude	eating scroll (10:1-11) 2 witnesses (11:1-3)	

The End			
8:1	silence	11:15	end announced and celebrated but not described

16:10	darkness		
16:12-16	kings of east cross Euphrates to prepare Armageddon		

(pattern broken)

16:17-21	theophany "God remembered great Babylon"		
17—18	then elaborate the 7th bowl Babylon as a continuation and elaboration of the Fall of Babylon		

tragedies have always terrorized human history. Yet, however useful John's pictures may be for later theologians' efforts to interpret history's pageant of suffering, John has a more specific purpose than to offer a general theology of history. The four horsemen portray the judgment of God on human arrogance and rebellion as manifest in the persecuting Roman power.

The image of the archer on the white horse, who is "crowned" and goes forth to "conquer," is intended to evoke in the hearer-readers' minds a specific, dreaded threat. Just as "men wearing green berets flying in Cobra helicopters" evokes a specific image in the twentieth century, so the combination of white horse and mounted archer called up only one picture in the imagination of the first-century reader—the dreaded Parthians. They were the only mounted archers in the first century; white horses were their trademark. Parthia was on the eastern border of the empire, and was never subdued by the Romans. In the Roman mind they represented the edges of civilization, a different kind of enemy, somewhat like the Yellow Peril in the consciousness of many western Europeans and Americans. The defeat of the Roman armies in the Tigris valley by the Parthian general Vologeses in 62 was still remembered in John's time. John will use this potent image again (9:13–16; 16:12). Here, the picture of victorious Parthians functions as the announcement of the beginning of the end of Roman sovereignty, to be replaced by God's rightful sovereignty (11:15–19). The picture of Parthian conquest of Rome forms an *inclusio* with the closing scene of this long section of eschatological woes, the detailed depiction of the fall of "Babylon" in 17:1—18:24, thus effectively bringing all the violent scenes of 6:1—18:24 under the one rubric, "God judges the 'Great City.'"

With the appearance of the rider on the red horse, the Pax Romana disappears, replaced by anarchic internal violence (6:3–4). The third horseman initiates famine, and the Roman prosperity is replaced with food rationing at eight to sixteen times the normal price for staples, while the prices for oil and wine are not changed. The wealthy continue to live as usual; the crisis hurts the poor (6:5–6). The fourth horseman represents death in all its violent forms: sword, famine, plague (often called simply "death," as here), and wild animals. That the catastrophes presented here are eschatological, and not "merely" historical tragedies is seen from the dimensions of the coming slaughter (one-fourth of humanity!) and from the fact that the rider on the fourth (literally "green," apparently meaning "sickly pale") horse is not a this-worldly being at all, but the transcendent power of death, followed by personified Hades, the world of the dead.

As elsewhere, John begins with the troubles of his own times, and gives them a prophetic interpretation by painting them in colors drawn from the Scripture, as its images are kaleidoscopically recombined in his fertile imagination. The four horsemen represent the rebirth of imagery found originally in Zechariah 1:7-15 and 6:1-8. (John will use related imagery from Zech. later in 11:1-14.) The combination of "sword, famine, and plague/death" is found in Jeremiah 14:12; 15:2; 21:7; 24:10; 29:17-18; 42:17; 43:11, with "sword, famine, wild animals and plague" found in Ezekiel 14:21 (cf. 5:12, 17).

This initial series of plagues has christological overtones. In fact, the first rider was often understood to be Christ by interpreters from Irenaeus in the second century through the Middle Ages, and by some modern interpreters (Ellul, pp. 147-48). Interestingly enough, it was a theologian-artist, Albrecht Dürer, who, in his series of woodcuts (1498), correctly saw that the first horseman belongs to the same series as the other three, and turned the tide of interpretation of the first horseman from Christ to an agent of eschatological judgment. Yet the medieval interpreters had good reasons for thinking of the first horseman in terms of Christ. Like Christ in the picture of 19:11-16, this figure rides a white horse, and he is "crowned" (even though the Greek word translated "crown" is different). The figure in 6:2 looks all the more like Christ in that he rides in victorious triumph (*nikao* is used of him, as it has just been definitively used of Christ in 5:5-6). Further, the imperative verb "come" used to call forth each of the four horsemen is identical to the promise and longing for Christ to "come" eschatologically in 22:17, 20.

Even though this first, definitive horseman does indeed belong to the series of agents of eschatological catastrophe and thus cannot mean the Christ, these christological overtones of the imagery are nonetheless important. The connotations evoke a premonition and almost subliminal anticipatory response to the figure in 19:11-16, who shall finally destroy the persecuting evil power represented by Rome. Thus the figures of 6:1-2 and 19:11-16 would form an *inclusio,* a theological bracket suggesting in yet another way that all the eschatological

123

plagues are in the hand of Christ and are to be interpreted christologically: in the light of Christ-as-Lamb rather than in the traditional lion imagery of violence (cf. "Reflection: Interpreting Revelation's Violent Imagery"). The destruction unleashed by the four horsemen is not directly done by Christ, but neither are the horsemen independent agents of destruction. They are *permitted,* with God/Christ being the actors hidden in the repeated "divine passive" verb *edothe* (v. 2 "it was given," v. 4*a* "was permitted," v. 4*b* "was given," v. 8 "were given"). Further, the resemblance of this first figure to Christ is another expression of John's view that the destructive power unleashed in the world is only a pale imitation, a parody in fact, of the true power of God/Christ. The actual actors in the eschatological drama, the direct perpetrators of the eschatological woes, are the forces of evil in the world, demonic anti-God forces permitted and used by God as agents of divine judgment. These forces which *seem* to be powerful are actually mere parodies of the ultimate power of God represented in the Lamb. The rider on the white horse does look deceptively like Christ, but his "conquering" is the this-worldly power of death that kills others, not the true power of the Lamb who dies for others.

The Fifth Seal: The Cry of the Martyrs (6:9–11)

With the opening of the fifth seal, the focus narrows and intensifies, characteristic of the pattern. The scene of the activity portrayed only seems to shift from earth to heaven, for in fact all the seals portray the events of earth from the heavenly perspective. People are being killed on earth, but one sees this only from the point of view of the heavenly altar. The imagery may be traditional, and those slain may include Jewish martyrs and the first Christian martyrs of the Roman state of 64 under Nero. But John has a specific group in mind: the Christians who are to die in the great persecution he sees as already beginning. Their death places them in the same category as Jesus (the word translated "slain" is the same word used for the slaughtered Lamb in 5:6) and the church on earth that continues to bear witness to the Christian gospel, since they were killed "for the word of God and the witness they had borne" (6:9). This is the same phrase used repeatedly in Revelation for the Christian message (cf. 1:2, 9; 19:10; 20:4).

124

How should the Christians of John's church interpret the death that had already occurred among them (cf. 2:13), and the many deaths that John foresees to come? In John's understanding their death is not meaningless tragedy but sacrifice on an altar. In the sacrificial worship of Israel with which John is acquainted from his Bible (and in which he had likely participated prior to the destruction of the temple) when the worshiper brings the sacrificial victim to be killed on the altar, its blood was poured out at the base of the altar (Lev. 4:7, 18, 25, 30, 34). Since life was thought to be in the blood of the animals, and of humans (Lev. 17:11, 14), and since "life," "soul," "self" were interchangeable terms, the lives or selves of sacrificed victims could be thought of as being at the base of or "under" the altar. Without intending to speculate on the nature of an "intermediate state" after death, but before the final resurrection, John uses this constellation of imagery to picture the "selves" of the Christian martyrs as already present in heaven, having been taken there through their death at the hands of the Romans. (Note again that John knows nothing of a "rapture" of the church. Christians ascend to heaven through suffering and death, as Jesus did; they are not taken to heaven to escape the sufferings of earth.) Once again he gives us a profound image with which to reinterpret the meaning of things. The chopping-block of the Roman executioner has become a cosmic altar. Christians who refused to sacrifice to the image of the emperor are nonetheless Christian priests who sacrifice themselves on the true altar of God. The image used metaphorically by Paul (Rom. 12:1) is filled with stark literalness in John's situation.

The carnage on earth continues, and the martyrs already in heaven, rather than smugly celebrating their own deliverance, cry out "How long?" to the Judge of the universe who continues to tolerate it. They have no doubt *that* the present injustice is not the last word, but do not understand why God does not bring it to an end now. They join their cries with those of Israel (e.g., Pss. 74; 79), and with the figures in Jesus' stories (Luke 18:1–8). There must be elements of personal feeling here— Christians too had feelings of resentment, bitterness, and revenge. But neither here nor in the teaching of Israel and Jesus can such cries be reduced to personal anger and desire for revenge. *Ekdikeo* ("avenge" in RSV) means both "avenge" and "procure justice for" someone. Here is a cry for God to reveal himself, a plea for a public vindication of God's justice, as in Psalm 79:5–10:

125

> How long, O LORD? . . .
> Help us, O God of our salvation,
>   for the glory of thy name . . . !
> Why should the nations say,
>   "Where is their God?"
> Let the avenging of the outpoured
>   blood of thy servants
> be known among the nations
>   before our eyes!

The Christians in John's churches who are trying to decide how they must respond to the pressures of the Roman emperor cult recognize their own anxious cry in the "How long?" reverberating through the heavenly scene. They are encouraged to persevere in their own witness, even to the point of death (2:10), when they see the victorious martyrs in heaven receive their white robes and when they hear the announcement that they must hold out only "a little longer" (6:11) until God intervenes. But they are not promised escape from the challenge to martyrdom. Those who have been killed are triumphant in heaven; those on earth can look forward to only an earthly future, however brief, in which yet more are to be killed (6:11). John's encouragement to martyrdom is utterly realistic.

The Sixth Seal:
The Cosmos Shakes at God's Approach (6:12–17)

In the typical apocalyptic pattern for the end of history, the eschatological woes begin with the this-worldly catastrophes of war, famine, and plague; they proceed through earthquakes and "natural" catastrophes and then intensify into cosmic proportions, in which the structure of the universe itself breaks down: stars fall, sun and moon no longer function. One can see an example of this pattern in the "little apocalypse" of Mark 13:5–36. So also in John's portrayal the progression of eschatological woes has proceeded through "normal" historical catastrophes (seals 1–4: war, famine, plague), through extraordinary historical pressures (seal 5: martyrdom), to the opening of the sixth seal in which the cosmos itself convulses. The small and great of the earth flee in terror from the great day of wrath to occur when God comes to judge the earth. While this scene is no more to be taken literally than the rest of John's metaphorical language, neither is it to be decoded in a "spiritual" sense to refer to the fall of oppressive political and social structures,

126

as though John had only dressed up his expectation of a social revolution in apocalyptic language. As a genuine apocalyptic thinker, John uses pictorial language for the end of this world to mean precisely that. The language is pictorial, but it signals to John's hearer-readers the approaching demolition of this world, as God himself comes in judgment and justice to establish his kingdom.

The language is the traditional language of theophany, used to picture the day of wrath of God's final appearance. Yet John does more than adopt the tradition; he transforms it in the light of his Christian faith. As in traditional apocalyptic, the wrath is to come and the world shakes at the prospect. All self-justifying confidence is removed. Who can stand? (6:17). Yet with one exquisitely paradoxical phrase John calls before the imagination of his hearer-readers both the terror of the coming judgment and the glad tidings that the judge is the One who has already paid the supreme penalty in behalf of the world. Though it is no less wrath for being so, the wrath is "the wrath of the Lamb" (6:16).

Interlude: The Church Militant and Triumphant (7:1–17)

One anticipates that the next event will be the breaking of the seventh seal and that the End will come. The pattern has run its expected cycle through the messianic woes and dissolution of the cosmos; all that can follow with the seventh seal is the appearance of God and the eschatological events themselves: resurrection, judgment, salvation in the heavenly world for the redeemed, damnation for the unfaithful. But John is more creative with his interpretation of apocalyptic traditions. Instead of the anticipated breaking of the seventh seal his vision lets us see the sealing of God's servants—another motif taken from tradition. Instead of seeing the expected End, what we see is the church. This is literary craftsmanship, but more than that—it is a reflection of the experience of first-century Christianity. They looked for the End and what came was the church, not as a substitute for the act of God but itself a dimension of God's saving activity. What seems at first to be a postponement or narrative digression turns out to be a skillfully constructed interlude, which pictures the church during the time of persecution and builds suspense before the final seal is broken. The seventh seal will in fact open into another series of seven plagues. But before continuing the woeful pattern of sevens at

127

another level, John gives us a dual vision of the nature and significance of the Christian community.

How big is the church? While some Christians of our time still think of "church" in terms of their local congregation, most are aware of themselves as members of an international community, numbering hundreds of millions, with a venerable history that reaches back through the generations and the centuries. How would the church appear to the eyes of the members of John's churches? Their congregations are small; on the margins of society; politically suspect; without impressive buildings, institutions, or respect from their neighbors. In their minds this was in sharp contrast to the synagogues (to which some of them had once belonged) with their sense of historical roots and worldwide fellowship. The Christians of Asia needed a vision of the church to which they belonged; John's dual vision addresses this need.

The Church Militant (7:1–8)

Four angels stand on the four corners of the earth (an item in John's first-century worldview which *no one* today takes literally!). They restrain the four destructive winds that threaten to continue God's violent judgment of rebellious earth. This image is forgotten; John never returns to tell of a plague of hurricanes or tornadoes. All his attention is focused on the sealing of God's servants.

John here takes up his repertoire of scriptural images and gives one of them, Ezekiel 9:1–11, a powerful reformulation. He has, in fact, already drawn from Ezekiel for both the material and the chronology of his presentation, and will continue to do so. The throne and living creatures of chapter 4 reflect the throne vision of Ezekiel 1; the eating of the scroll in chapter 10 corresponds to the similar scene in Ezekiel 3; the Gog/Magog imagery of chapter 20 is parallel to Ezekiel 38—39; and the new Jerusalem of chapters 21—22 reflects Ezekiel 40—48. Even the "four corners of the earth" of Revelation 7:1 is an adaptation of the same phrase in Ezekiel 7:2 ("land" and "earth" are the same word in Ezekiel's Hebrew and John's Greek). John's vision of the sealing of the servants of God in 7:1–8 corresponds to Ezekiel's: with the mark of God on their foreheads, faithful Christians are preserved through (not from!) the great persecution that is about to be unleashed upon them like a mighty devastating wind (7:1–3) or horde of demonic locusts (9:3–4).

128

"Sealing" not only evokes this powerful image from the Scripture, it has particular overtones within the Pauline stream of tradition to which John and his churches belong. Incorporation into the body of Christ by baptism (I Cor. 12:13) was sometimes pictured in Pauline churches as the seal which stamped the new Christian as belonging to God (II Cor. 1:22; Eph. 1:13; 4:30). In the midst of the Roman threat baptism comes to have a new meaning: those who bear the mark of God are kept through (not from!) the coming great ordeal, whatever the beastly powers of evil may be able to do to them.

John has woven yet another meaning into the image of the seal. He has not yet specifically mentioned the "beast," one of his primary symbols for the persecuting power of Rome (11:7; 13:1–18; 14:9–11; 17:3–17; 19:19–20; 20:4, 10). This "beast" will also give his followers a special mark on their foreheads (13:16–17; 14:9). Yet this is only another instance of the beast's parodying of the Lamb. Evil has no independent existence; its supposed power is only a counterfeit of the real power of the Lamb. For John, just as the true "conquering" is the power of loving self-sacrifice as manifested in the Lamb which can only be imitated by the worldly violent "conquering" exercised by the powers of evil (cf. comments on 6:1–2), so the "mark of the beast" is only a pale imitation of God's marking his servants.

Who are the 144,000 who are sealed? Since they are described as from every tribe of Israel (7:4), it has sometimes been thought that 7:1–8 represents Jewish Christians in contrast to the "great multitude from every nation" of 7:9–17. Yet this cannot be the case, since John identifies this group with the same number in 14:1–5, which cannot be limited to Jewish Christians. "Israel" is obviously not meant in a literal sense; there were no literal twelve tribes in the first century. Judaism had long since been more of a religious community with people of various ethnic backgrounds than a racial group identified by genealogy. The key argument for identifying the 144,000 as intended to represent the church as such, however, is the theological understanding of the church as the continuation of Israel. This view was widespread in early Christianity (e.g., Matt. 10:5–6; Luke 1:68–79; 2:29–32; John 1:47; 5:43–47; 11:52; Acts 2:14–21; 26:14–23; James 1:1), but was particularly strong in the Pauline tradition to which John belongs (1:6; 5:10; cf. Rom. 9—11; Gal. 3:29; 6:16; Eph. 2:11–22; I Peter 2:9). John considers the church to be the continuation of Israel, and speaks with

129

disdain of "those who say they are Jews but are not" (2:9; 3:9), that is, Jews who did not accept Jesus as the Messiah.

The number 144,000 is intended as symbolic theology, not literal mathematics. From our perspective it may sound limiting, exclusive, and rather small; but in the ears of John's hearer-readers the number is stunningly large. Along with "myriad" (literally, 10,000), "thousand" is the largest numerical unit found in the Bible. In biblical usage both are used primarily to mean "a very large number" rather than to be taken with literal precision (Exod. 20:6; Deut. 1:11; 7:9; I Sam. 18:7; 21:11; Pss. 3:6; 68:17; Dan. 7:10). A multitude of 144,000 is meant to convey the impression of a vast throng beyond all reckoning (precisely the same as 7:9!). John resists the temptation to think smugly of only the "faithful few" who are genuine Christians. This is in contrast to the more typical apocalyptic view. The author of Second Esdras understands the reality to be that "the Most High made this world for the sake of the many, but the world to come for the sake of the few" (8:1) and has the angel of God say "I will rejoice over the few who will be saved" (7:60).

The church in this picture is not only big, it is complete. The number 144,000 is a complete, fulfilled number. (The 144 is obviously the multiple of 12 × 12, the twelve tribes of old Israel and the twelve apostles of the new Israel [cf. 21:12–14].) Judaism knew that the original unity of twelve tribes had been disrupted by the Assyrian deportation (II Kings 17; Jer. 16:10–15; Ezek. 47:13—48:29; Bar. 4—5; II Bar. 63; 67; Test. Mos. 2:3–9) and had never been restored, but at the eschaton God would reassemble the full complement of all Israel (Ps. Sol. 17:28–31, 50; 1QM 2; T. Sanh. 13:10; II Esdr. 13:40–47; II Bar. 78—87; cf. Matt. 19:28; Luke 22:30). John declares that the eschatological hope for Israel is realized in the church. His listing of the "twelve tribes" corresponds to none of the numerous lists in the Old Testament and is peculiar in that Dan is missing but both Manasseh and Joseph are included to round out the number to twelve. There are probably reasons for his peculiar list, which may come from his tradition. The tribe of Dan had a bad reputation in the Old Testament (Lev. 24:11; Judg. 5:17; 17—18; I Kings 12:29) and in later Jewish tradition was thought to be the tribe from which the Antichrist would come (Test. Dan. 5:6). Yet it is likely that none of this is important to John. As is the case with the New Testament's various lists of the "Twelve Apostles," the significant aspect is the number twelve representing the whole People of God, not the names of the tribes and apostles, which vary from list to list. God has sealed his multitude (144,000) of faithful people in baptism and will bring all of them, the whole "Israel of God," safely through the ordeal, even if they have to die—that is the message.

"Thousand" also has a military connotation, a division of the army. The "thousands of Israel" is used of Israel's army and has the same ring to it as "the battalions of Israel" (cf. Num. 31:14, 48; Deut. 1:15; I Sam. 8:12; 22:7; II Sam. 18:1, 4). John uses much battle imagery, transformed by the paradigmatic symbol of the Lion who has become the Lamb. He here pictures the church in its aspect of earthly struggle, the "church militant."

The Church Triumphant (7:9–17)

John's vision never portrays the actual martyrdom of Christians. The preceding scene pictures the sealing of faithful Christians in advance of the great ordeal. Then the point of view shifts from earth to heaven, where we see a countless host of peoples from every nation and language exulting in the worship of God. They are identified as "the people who have been through the great persecution" (7:14, JB). As 7:1–8 presents the church militant on earth, sealed and drawn up in battle formation before the coming struggle, 7:9–17 presents the church after the battle, triumphant in heaven. As in 6:9–11, those who have "conquered" are dressed in the white robes of the victors; as there, martyrdom is seen only from its heavenward side. Again, they have "won" only from the heavenly perspective of the Lamb's redefinition of winning; on earth they have been killed.

John's mind-jarring rebirth of imagery continues in paradoxical juxtapositions and deformation of language. The robes of the martyrs are white because they are washed in the blood of the Lamb (7:14). Their own death is not an accomplishment of which they can boast. It is Christ's death, not their own courage and determination, which has given them their victor's garment. Their death becomes one with the Lamb's death; Christology and discipleship fade into each other (cf. 12:11). And the Lamb who gave his life's blood for others is also the Shepherd who rules from the midst of the throne (7:17). In surrealistic pictures that resist any reduction to consistent

131

prosaic statements, John lets us see the suffering love of the One who dies for others enthroned and ruling at the heart of the universe.

The Seventh Seal: Silence (8:1)

When the seventh seal is opened, we are at the anticipated End. But we are met with silence, a long pause of half an hour. After the emotional intensity of the "Hallelujah Chorus," Handel inserts a long rest just before the final "Hallelujah." This is good psychology as well as good music. In John's case it is good theology as well. We have come to the last seal, but the End is not described—that must come later. Like the primeval pre-creation silence that prevailed before the first day of creation (cf. II Esdr. 7:30; Wis. Sol. 18:14–15; II Bar. 3:7), the final Day of the Lord is also preceded by deafening silence. John may have Zephaniah 1:7 in mind: "Be silent before the Lord GOD! For the day of the LORD is at hand."

Revelation 8:2—11:19
The Heavenly Worship:
Sounding the Seven Trumpets

The Prayers of the Church in the Heavenly Worship (8:2–5)

From 4:1 on, John has been caught up into heaven in order to give his fellow Christians, who remain on earth during the tribulation of the last days, the heavenly perspective on the sufferings they are called upon to endure and the greater ones to come. He is about to present the next, more intensive series of plagues represented by the seven trumpets. Before proceeding with his visions of disaster, John sets the whole in the context of heavenly worship.

As in previous scenes, the hearer-reader gets a glimpse into the worship which eternally takes place in the heavenly temple (4:1—5:14; 7:9–12; cf. 6:9–11). The worship of the earthly church is never directly pictured. Though the word "worship" (*proskuneo,* literally "prostrate oneself before") is used in Revelation more than in any other book in the New Testament, it is always used for the true heavenly worship of God or the false worship of the beast on earth. The sole exception is 14:6-7, where it is used in an eschatological command from heaven for the "earth-dwellers" to worship the true God rather than the beast. The verb "pray" is not found in Revelation, and the noun "prayers" only in 5:8 and 8:3-4, each time within a picture of the heavenly worship. "Give thanks" *(eucharisteo)* is found only at 11:17, used of the twenty-four elders, there pictured as part of the heavenly worship at the End, not of the church's worship on earth now. The extensive references to the life of the church on earth in chapters 2—3 never refer to its worship.

Yet the earthly church does pray. The "book" of Revelation was composed to be read forth in a worship service of prayer and praise. The struggling church on earth knows that it prays; during the hard times of persecution it may wonder what happens to its prayers. John's revelation lets the worshiping church see its prayer from the heavenward side. As the incense ascends before the heavenly throne, the distressed Christians on earth recognize their own prayers. This has the effect of revealing the earthly church as participating in the worship of heaven and creating one continuous community embracing the heavenly temple and the struggling churches of Asia. This is John's apocalyptic pictorial version of the "communion of saints." Through its worship and prayer, the church is intimately linked with the real world, the world of God.

Although John does not here detail the content of the prayers, suggestions elsewhere in Revelation indicate they were not merely a subjective outpouring of feelings but were also acclamations of praise and thanksgiving to God and Christ (4:8-11; 5:9-10, 12-14; 7:10-12; 11:17-18; 15:3-4; 19:1-8). There are prayers too for the "coming" of God's kingdom and justice (6:9-11), the eschatological "coming" of God/Christ (22: 20; cf. I Cor. 16:22).

The prayers are "heard"; they have an effect. The effect is not merely a subjective release in the worshiper; the prayers of the saints on earth cause things to happen on earth (8:4-5; cf. 9:13-14). The saints' prayers do not result in a deliverance from historical troubles but the deliverance of the world and history, by the eschatological appearance of God's kingdom.

The prayers of John's church are thus in step with a traditional Jewish prayer, the Kaddish:

> Magnified and sanctified be his great name in the world that he has created according to his will. May he establish his kingdom in your lifetime and in your days and in the lifetime of all the house of Israel, even speedily and at a near time.

Vivid "details" are filled in from the imaginative palette of the apocalyptic tradition, but essentially the persecuted Christian's prayer in John's churches is the prayer "Thy kingdom come" (Matt. 6:10; Luke 11:2)—and it does, at the conclusion of the series of trumpet woes (11:15–19).

John testifies that the prayers of his fellow Christians for the coming of God's kingdom will be answered. But the immediate result of their prayers is not the glorious coming of the kingdom—though that is the ultimate result—but the precipitation of the series of eschatological woes. The path to the kingdom goes through, not around, the woes of history.

The First Four Trumpets:
The Final Troubles Intensify (8:6–12)

Like the liturgy of the earthly temple, the worship in the heavenly court includes not only the burning of incense but the sounding of trumpets (II Chron. 5:12–13). A number of other images had become associated with trumpets in Jewish tradition. They represented the call to festive assembly and battle, announced warning and victory, were instrumental in the holy war in which God alone gave the victory, were sounded on New Year's Day and the accession of a king, and were an element in the sound and fury of the theophany (Exod. 19:16; Num. 10:2–10; Josh. 6:4; Ezek. 33:3; Joel 2:1, 15; Amos 3:6). The prophets thus easily adapted the image of sounding the trumpet for their pictures of the eschatological Day of the Lord and the related motifs of assembly, battle, judgment, and the new order, with the result that "the last trumpet(s)" became a standard feature of the eschatological signs (Isa. 27:13; Matt. 24:31; I Cor. 15:52; I Thess. 4:16).

The last trumpets are sounded by the seven angels, John's version of the traditional seven archangels or spirits of the heavenly court traditional in Jewish apocalyptic. The imagery shifts rapidly between seven eyes, spirits, stars, or angels, all representing God's own omniscient power by which he communicates with and rules the world (cf. 1:4; 8:2). This is further indicated by the repeated passive verb "it was given" *(edothe)*, the concealed subject of which is God, and by the fact that all

134

the plagues come from heaven (8:7, 10, 12 and 9:1, with 9:13–14 adding a final reminder that the heavenly altar from which the prayers of the saints ascend is the effective source of the plagues). The terrors about to intensify upon the earth are not caused by independent powers of which Christians need to be afraid nor which they might attempt to placate. All proceeds ultimately from the sovereign hand of the one God.

Like the seven seal visions, the seven trumpet visions are not a prediction of distant future events but fit into the apocalyptic pattern of the woes that must precede the victory of God at the End, which John saw as rapidly approaching in his own day (see the "Reflection: Interpreting the 'Near End' in Revelation"). This second cycle is not a chronological continuation of the first but a retelling of the first cycle at a more intensive level. In the first cycle one-fourth of the earth's inhabitants were struck (6:8); in this cycle the scale goes up to one-third (8:7, 9, 11, 12). To inquire whether this is a third of the original whole, or a third of what remained after one-fourth had been struck would be a wrong question; John works with the imagination, not calculators. John has a rich store of scriptural and traditional apocalyptic images and has not attempted to make the different series of plagues consistent with each other. Thus all grass is burned up in 8:7, but is still there in 9:4; the stars are struck in 8:12, although they have already fallen in 6:13. The pictures function to communicate a surrealistic impression of the terror of the final judgments and not as a series of events which one may somehow fit into a single consistent pattern, even in the imagination.

John sees the terrors to come as analogous to the plagues with which God struck Egypt in the exodus story: as the means of God's liberation. Points of contact with the Egyptian plagues are seen in the hail and fire of 8:7 (Exod. 9:23–25), the sea becoming blood in 8:8–9 (Exod. 7:20), the darkness of 8:12 (Exod. 10:21), and the locust-like beings of 9:1–12 (Exod. 10:12). Casting the imagery in the mold of the exodus story places it in the framework of judgment but also in the framework of God's liberating activity. Even the plagues can be seen as good news and can be endured because the ultimate exodus is about to occur!

The plague imagery is transposed into a transcendent, mythological key and projected onto a cosmic screen; not only the Egyptian oppressors are struck down within history but all

135

oppressive worldly powers are judged, as history itself is brought to an end. The world itself has been corrupted by human sin (cf. Gen. 3:17–18; Isa. 24:4–6; Rom. 8:19–23), so human beings are not alone in the suffering of the eschatological plagues. The cosmos itself is struck, as the land (8:7), sea (8:8–9), rivers (8:10–11), and the heavenly bodies (8:12) experience the onslaughts of divine judgment.

A shift in narrative style occurs at 9:1, between the fourth and fifth trumpet vision. Characteristic of John's pattern (see above), the first four visions of the series form a concise unit, while the fifth and sixth are told in more detail and represent a further intensification of the eschatological troubles. In addition to being enumerated as part of the trumpet series, the last three "trumpets" are also specifically designated by the apocalyptic term "woe" and have their own dramatic introduction: A great eagle/vulture (the word *aetos* was used for both), bringer of death and carrion-eater, circles ominously over the corpse-trench of earth and screeches out the impending doom (8:13).

The Fifth Trumpet: First Woe—Demon Locusts (9:1–12)

This vision does not literally correspond to any event in John's past, present, or future. With a montage of images from mythology and tradition, he bombards the hearer-readers' imaginations with yet another evocative image of eschatological woe. The vision opens (9:1–2) with a fallen star-angel who opens the abyss which disgorges the swarm of demon locusts. (The stars, personified as deities in ancient paganism, were sometimes identified with angels in the Old Testament and in Jewish tradition; cf. Job 38:7; Test. Sol. 8; 18; Sefer ha-Razim 5.) The vision concludes (9:11) with the declaration that the demon locusts are led by their "king/emperor," the angel of the abyss. The whole vision is thus framed with motifs from the myth of the fall of the evil angel(s) which in various forms had already been used in traditional apocalyptic. Canaanite mythology knew the story of how one of the gods, Athtar the "Day Star" (Venus), had been proposed to take the place of Baal, but did not succeed and had to come down to earth where he reigns as "god of it all." In Isaiah 14:4–20 this mythical pattern is mockingly applied to the pretensions of the king of Babylon, who is pictured as aspiring to attain the divine throne but instead was cast down to the pit of Sheol, the abode of the dead. In verse 12 the Babylonian king is taunted: "How you are fallen from heaven, O Day Star [*Hêle'l*, "Luminous," translated "Lucifer" in the KJV], son of Dawn [*Shahar*, the name of a Canaanite deity]!" Although the myth originally and in Isaiah 14:12 had nothing to do with the idea of Satan and the origin of evil, this connection was later made in (Jewish and) Christian tradition (II Enoch 29:4-5; Life of Adam and Eve 12—16; Wis. Sol. 2:24; Gos. Bart. 4:51-55; Irenaeus, *Against Heresies* IV.40.3). In other Hebrew and Jewish adaptations of the myth, a whole order of angels came down from heaven and corrupted earth by teaching humanity various skills (such as writing!), but the good angels defeated them and imprisoned them in the abyss (cf. Gen. 6:1-4; I Enoch 6—10; 54; II Bar. 56). In various versions of the myth evil angels were not destroyed but placed in the pit for future judgment (II Peter 2:4). An additional apocalyptic motif was that the evil which is now restrained will experience a resurgence just before the end, will explode in one final futile paroxysm before being destroyed forever. John uses this general pattern in his apocalyptic understanding of history as a whole, particularly in his description of the final events in 19: 11—20:15.

The vision of 9:1-12 represents another example of John's adaptation of this myth. The evil powers now restrained in the abyss will be released just before the End. Before their own final destruction, they serve God's purpose by inflicting the eschatological plagues on the rebellious world. As in the preceding trumpet visions, the passive *edothe* formula ("was given," "were permitted") continues to express the hidden activity of the sovereign God.

The terror of the locust plague, still known in Africa and the eastern Mediterranean, becomes in John's imagination the this-worldly launching pad for his portrayal of the demonic terror of the eschaton. John reflects the shifting of the imagery of the locust plague from the historical to the transcendent mythological plane that had already occurred in Joel 1—2. This-worldly locusts devour vegetation but do not harm humans. The locusts of John's vision disregard vegetation and attack human beings. This-worldly locusts proverbially have no king (Prov. 30:27). In 9:11 the "angel of the bottomless pit" is called *basileus* ("king"), used also for the Roman emperor (thus JB translates ". . . their Emperor, the angel of the abyss . . ."). He is also called "Apol-

137

lyon," a pun for "Apollo," the divine name the Emperor Domitian liked to use for himself. Further, the locust was the symbol for the god Apollo. Typical for John, the imagery here is not consistent as in a system of steno symbols—Rome is both subject to and demonic instrument of the divine judgment (cf. on chaps. 17—18, "The Fall of Babylon and the Lament"). Through (but not from!) it all, those who bear God's mark are preserved (9:4).

The Sixth Trumpet:
Second Woe—Demon Cavalry (9:13–21)

In an *inclusio* that frames all the plagues within the context of God's response to the prayers of the saints, 9:13 points back to the scene in 8:2–5. As in the first seal, 6:1–2 (see commentary thereto), John uses the almost paranoid Roman fear of the Parthian threat on the eastern boundary of the empire as the raw material for his vision of the final devastation before the End. The "bound angels" at the edge of John's world is another allusion to the mythical pattern of fallen angels discussed above (9:1–12). By picturing the incursion of the unimaginably vast army of demonic cavalry (200 million!) into the civilized world as the result of releasing these angels, John again elevates a historical anxiety to the level of eschatological myth. The bizarre description of the horses is reminiscent of the Parthians, but they belong to the other, demonic world.

"Repentance" is a key word in this terrible scene (9:20–21). Despite the horrors of the last days, rebellious humanity does not repent. In the face of such suffering and the dramatic evidence that they are not in charge of the world, human beings, like the Pharoah/Egyptians of the exodus story, do not repent but are only further confirmed in their rebellion. Though attacked by beastly hordes, they continue to worship the demonic cultural images and to live by the ungodly values that result. The word "repent" calls a particular meaning to the mind of John's hearer-readers. If the situation and terminology described in Pliny's letter to Trajan is also representative of John's time (see Introduction), "repent" meant from the Roman side the turning away from commitment to Christ as Lord in order to conform to the emperor cult. Just as faithful Christians refused to "repent" in the Roman sense, the Roman world refuses to repent in the Christian sense by turning away from the false values of their culture to worship the Creator.

138

Interlude:
The Church of Prophets and Martyrs (10:1—11:13)

As chapter 7 was the interlude between the sixth and seventh seals, so 10:1—11:13 forms the interlude between the sixth and seventh trumpets. As chapter 7 offered a twofold perspective on the church (militant/triumphant), so 10:1—11:13 offers a further twofold perspective on the church (prophets/martyrs). In both cases the interlude is more than "filler"; it serves the double function of giving a powerful vision of the role of the church during the time of persecution and increasing suspense before the sounding of the last trumpet.

The Bittersweet Vocation of Christian Prophecy (10:1–11)

John sees a mighty angel descending from heaven whose description combines elements elsewhere used of both God and Christ. Like Yahweh in the Old Testament, he is clothed in the cloud of the storm deity (Job 37; Ps. 18:7–15; Zech. 10:1) and speaks like a roaring lion (Amos 3:8). Like God enthroned as the sole sovereign of the universe in 4:1–3, he is surrounded by the rainbow sign of the covenant with creation (4:3 ‖ 10:1) and has a book in his right hand (5:1 ‖ 10:2). Like the description of the exalted Christ in 1:12–20, his face shines like the sun (1:16 ‖ 10:1). The description of the legs of the figure of Christ ("burnished bronze, refined in a furnace") also seems to be reflected in the legs of the mighty angel ("like pillars of fire"), a word picture which also evokes the description of God (or the angel of God; cf. Exod. 13:21 ‖ 14:19) who led Israel through the wilderness in the exodus story (cf. Rev. 12:6, 14!). The figure of the angel is thus transparent to the figures of God and Christ who speak through him. As in 1:1–2 and throughout Revelation, the images of God, Christ, Spirit/angel collapse into each other. The ultimate Revealer is God, who defines and represents himself in Christ and communicates with the prophet by means of the angel. Although the figures are kept somewhat distinct, the imagery overlaps in such a way that God/Christ/angel are all presented to the mind's eye by the one picture.

No emphasis should be placed on the description of the book as a "little" book, a diminutive (used only three times in the New Testament, all in this chapter) of the usual word for "book" or "scroll" in Revelation, and used interchangeably with it in 10:10. This is, in fact, the same word used for the scroll in

139

the hand of God in 5:1. The contrast is not between "large" and "small" but between "sealed" and "open." The sealed scroll of God's purpose for the endtime (5:1; cf. Dan. 12:4, 9) is no longer sealed. The Lamb has won the right to open it and has done so (5:1-10; 6:1—8:1). The connection of this scene with Daniel 12:1-10 is extremely important, for it is the key source for John's reformulation of Old Testament imagery. There a mighty angel speaks of a great tribulation to come, followed by resurrection and judgment, and commands that the revelation be sealed until the time of the end. Then two other angels appear, one on each bank of the stream. (John's fluid imagery has one figure of cosmic proportions with one foot on the continent and one on the ocean.) In the Old Testament scene, Daniel asks the poignant question of suffering apocalyptic communities, "How long?" The angelic figure raises both hands to heaven and swears by the eternal God that the endtime period would be three and one-half years ("time, two times, and half a time," Dan. 12:7; cf. Dan. 7:25; 8:14, and the later recalculations in 12:11-12). This is the Danielic picture John receives from his Bible: mighty angels standing on water and dry land, arms uplifted, swearing by God, a long delay, a sealed book to be opened at the endtime period of three and one-half years. In the light of John's conviction that he lives in the eschatological time begun by the advent of the Christ, his inspired prophetic imagination reconfigures these elements into one dramatic picture of an angel with an *un*sealed book in one hand and the other lifted up to heaven and swearing by the Creator that there will be no more delay. The time of waiting and hoping is over; the time of fulfillment already dawns. But before it arrives, there is the pre-dawn darkness of the final tribulation, the "time of trouble such as never has been" of Daniel 12:1 which must be negotiated. John believes he and his churches are already entering into this final terrible period. The 1260 days that he derives from Scripture is not for him speculative prediction but encouragement: Hold firm to your faith, the tribulation will not last long!

Before we learn how the opened book of God's revelation is to function, the scene is interrupted by seven thunders. John prepares to write the visions of the seven thunders, just as he had written the visions of the seven seals and the seven trumpets, but he is forbidden to do so. No interpretation of this prohibition is provided, but two complementary interpretations seem to be suggested by the context and by John's theology.

1. As was the case with Paul, the claim to have some divinely inspired insights into God's purposes does not mean that the Christian prophet claims to know everything (I Cor. 13:12; cf. II Cor. 12:4). John acknowledges that his revelation is only fragmentary. His God is the God of Israel who reveals what his people need to know in order to live faithfully before him, but does not deal in speculative revelations, so that he preserves the divine mystery (Deut. 29:29). In scene after scene John has testified that the sealed book of heavenly mystery (5:1) is now opened, but in this scene he hears a command to seal up divine truth with a seal that is *never* broken. John's claim to provide a revelation of Jesus Christ (1:1) does not include the claim to know everything, does not remove the distinction between divine knowledge and human ignorance and fallibility, even for a prophet who has toured heaven.

2. God interrupts the apocalyptic system of sevens and decides that there will be "no more delay" before the End, even though the traditional apocalyptic scheme of sevens might call for further disasters. This is like other New Testament apocalyptic (Mark 13:20) and in contrast to extra-biblical apocalyptic writings in which the apocalyptic system is more absolute than God, who has no choice but to follow it himself (II Esdr.). John does not present us with an enslavingly consistent logic or inexorable, impersonal fate but with a God who is free to revise the system en route. This is the God of the Hebrew Scriptures who responds to his creation and even repents (Jer. 9:5; 18:8; Jonah 3:9). A person, not a cosmic computer, is seated on the throne of the universe.

John is not merely the spectator and reporter of this scene; he becomes a main character, for the opened book in the hand of the mighty angel is meant for him. He is commanded to take it and—not read, but—*eat* it! Again, what seems a bizarre incident is seen on closer reflection to be John's re-imaging of biblical pictures. John has been following Ezekiel rather closely (cf. above on 7:1–8, "The Church Militant"). As a part of his call to be a prophet, Ezekiel was given a book of "lamentation, mourning, and woe" and told to "fill his stomach" with it (Ezek. 2:8—3:3). Ezekiel ate the book, which as word of the Lord was as sweet as honey in his mouth (3:3; cf. Pss. 19:10; 119:103). John sees himself as a prophet in this tradition. He is called to "de-

141

vour" the book that contains the plan of God for his creation, the bittersweet message of judgment and salvation. Every person who struggles to preach and teach the word of God knows this taste, this satisfaction, and this sickness in the stomach.

The Prophethood of All Believers (11:1–13)

As a prophet, John belonged to a special group within the church (see Introduction, "By a Christian Prophet"). Yet John is concerned to communicate that the prophetic ministry is not confined to persons like himself who receive dramatic revelations. In the Israelite community as documented in the Hebrew Scriptures, the Holy Spirit, often identified as the Spirit that inspires prophecy, was not thought of as given to the community as a whole but only to special persons *within* it. Yet the Old Testament expresses the hope that the prophetic gift would be democratized, that the People of God as such would receive the prophetic gift (Num. 11:24–29; Joel 2:28–29). The early church believed that they were living in the time of the fulfillment of those hopes and promises, which they expressed in different ways: all members of the Christian community participate in the body of Christ and thus in the breath/Spirit that animates the body; and thus they receive the gifts of the Spirit, including prophecy (I Cor. 2:12–14; 12:4–13; 14:1–5; cf. Rom. 8:9–11; 12:6–8). All Christians receive the Spirit at baptism (Acts 2:38) and thus inherit the promise that the gift of prophecy will be distributed to the whole believing community (Acts 2:17–18, quoting Joel 2:28–29). After Jesus' departure the Paraclete/Spirit will continue to speak new truths in the name of Christ (John 14—16). John too believes that the Spirit that inspires prophecy functions within the whole Christian community, not individualistically in special persons such as himself. He can thus apply prophetic descriptions such as "servants" to Christians as such (cf. 1:1a, 1:1b; 2:20; 7:3; 10:7; 11:18; 19:5; 22:6). In the vision of 11:1–13, John pictures the whole church in their role as the eschatological prophetic People of God; he affirms the "prophethood of all believers."

Although the symbolic connotations of this evocative picture are subtle and complex, the general picture is quite clear: pagans trod down the holy city for 1260 days, but the temple and those worshiping in it are spared. During these same 1260 days of the endtime tribulation, the two witnesses, representing the church, exercise their prophetic ministry. They are killed by the powers of evil, but vindicated by God who raises them and calls them into the courts of the heavenly temple.

The initial unit of this vision may be a traditional fragment of a previous prophecy. Many scholars have thought it likely that 11:1–2 originated as a Zealot prophecy during the last days of the war against Rome in 66–70, when the Roman troops had taken the city but had not yet penetrated to the last refuge of the Zealot defenders, the inner court of the temple. A detailed description of those terrible days was given by Josephus, who was present among the Romans. He recounts how Zealot prophets delivered oracles until the very last, interpreting the Roman advance as the testing of Zealot faith by God and declaring that the heavenly troops would swoop in at the last minute and deliver the faithful Zealots and vindicate their militarist version of apocalyptic faith. It is difficult to think of John as having originated this element of his prophecy, since the temple was already destroyed when he wrote and since it fits somewhat awkwardly into his vision. The theory of the incorporation of a Zealot prophetic fragment would account for this awkwardness. We have seen that John elsewhere repeatedly takes up older prophecies from Scripture, transforms them, and incorporates them into his prophecy.

Whatever its past, the picture of measuring the temple is now an integral part of the whole visionary scene of 11:1–13 (joined to the following picture by the period of 42 months/ 1260 days common to both). For John, the temple is not a literal building, as it was in the presumed Zealot prophecy; it is the Christian community who worship God (cf. 3:12, and the description of the Holy City in 21—22 without a temple building, where God makes his dwelling in the community of redeemed saints). This idea, of course, was already present in the Pauline tradition in which John and his churches stand (I Cor. 3:16–17; the "you" is plural). The "measuring" of the temple is to mark it out for protection, both in the original Zealot version (if there was such) and in John's understanding. The "marking" of the temple is thus another image for the "sealing" of the church in 7:1–8. Yet here, as there, it is necessary immediately to point out that being "sealed" or "measured" for God's protection does not mean that Christians will be shielded from suffering and death but that they are stamped with the sign of God's security, even if they have to die. As in the analogous vision of the role of the church in chapter 7, John thus proceeds immedi-

143

ately to a picture of the prophetic church as a martyr church.

The two figures are "prophets" (11:10) whose ministry is "to prophesy" (11:3). Of course this does not mean that they spent three and a half years making predictions; "prophesy" means "speak and act for God." The prophets who act in God's authority are also immediately (11:3) designated *martures* ("martyrs"/ "witnesses," the same word in John's Greek) and their ministry is summed up in the word *martyria* "testimony" (11:7). As prophets, their ministry is martyrdom. In John's context martyrdom is not something in addition to being a prophet; it is inherent in the prophetic role itself. In the pages of the Old Testament some prophets suffer as an integral part of their prophetic vocation—Ezekiel and Jeremiah come immediately to mind—but suffering is not characteristic of prophetic ministry as such. On the contrary, in some circles the prophets were considered quite beyond the realm of ordinary human suffering, making havoc of their enemies through their divinely given miraculous power. This was the picture of both Moses and Elijah in the Hebrew Scriptures (Exod. 3—34; I Kings 17—II Kings 1). But with Jeremiah's actual experience of vulnerability and suffering at the hands of Babylon as the beginning point, there developed in later Jewish tradition the firm idea that the true prophet must suffer as the badge of his authenticity. Isaiah, for example, who strides through the pages of the Old Testament narrative rather triumphalistically, is pictured as the suffering martyr in the literature of the first century (Mart. Isa. 5:1). Matthew 23:29–35, Acts 7:52, and Hebrews 11:32–38 also reflect this development. In John's tradition, to say "true prophet" was already to say "one who suffers as the hallmark of his or her vocation." "Prophet" and "martyr" were not two words but one.

It is important to understand these words in their biblical senses when interpreting Revelation. "Martyr" in our time is used in the vocabulary of international terrorism for suicidal fanatical devotees of political causes and in popular psychology for persons of low self-esteem who invite or imagine persecution. "Witness" and "testimony" has in the jargon of pietistic Christians become synonymous with "relate my own personal religious experiences, telling 'what the Lord has done for me.' " Revelation's meaning is quite different. John makes extensive use of the martyr/witness word group, which derived from the courtroom.

144

"Witness," "martyr," and "testimony" preserve their legal connotations and already have the overtones of "holding fast to one's Christian convictions when tried before the pagan courts," even to the point of death, thereby giving testimony to the truth of the Christian message. In this sense Jesus was the prototypical martyr (1:5; 3:14; 22:20). Language about Jesus (and his martyrdom) is used interchangeably with language about Christians (and their martyrdom): 2:17 ‖ 19:12 and 3:12; 2:26–28; 3:21; 12:13 ‖ 12:17.

The doctrine of God the Almighty affirmed throughout Revelation is also implicit in John's theology of martyrdom (1:8; 4:8; 11:17; 15:3; 16:7, 14; 19:6, 15; 21:22). A god who is only relatively stronger and better than we are, a god who is part of the world process and is himself subject to it, cannot ask for absolute commitment, nor can we give it. To give absolute loyalty to, to be willing to die for, that which is only relative is to make an idol of it, even if this idol be called "God." God's almightiness was no item of doctrine for John but the basis for his call to a commitment which might mean sacrificing life itself.

The two martyr-prophets of 11:1–13 thus represent the church in John's imagery, the whole church of the eschatological times. Their ministry takes place during the time of the church, the last three and one-half years before the End. Their ministry takes place in Jerusalem, the "holy city" (11:2), often used to represent the People of God, including the dramatic final vision of 21:1—22:5. The theological symbolism is chosen by John to point to the church. The "two olive trees" and "two lampstands" are reflections of Joshua the priest and Zerubbabel the king, of Zechariah 4, John's major source for the imagery in this vision. They represent the channels through which God's power becomes effective and are thus appropriate symbols for the church. That the church is a community of "priests" and "kings," assuming the priestly-royal role of Israel (Exod. 19:6), is one of Revelation's themes throughout (1:6; 5:10; cf. 20:6). The witnesses are called "lampstands" (11:4), explained as "churches" in 1:20. From Second Isaiah (42:6; 49:6; 51:4) through the teaching of Jesus (Matt. 5:14) and Paul (I Thess. 5:5; Phil. 2:15), the People of God are pictured as the bearers of God's light to the nations. When they are killed, people in every city gaze on the dead bodies of the witnesses (11:9)—this is a picture of the church scattered throughout the empire.

The two witnesses represent the church, but in a particular aspect appropriate to the time of eschatological persecution in which they are called to witness: They are pictured as the eschatological prophets Moses and Elijah. Some streams of Jewish tradition understood that one or both of the two Old Testament prophetic figures who had not died but had been taken bodily to heaven must return to prepare the way before the coming of God or the Messiah could occur at the End (Mal. 4:5–6; II Esdr. 6:28). Though Moses' death is reported in Deuteronomy 34:5, the indication in the next verse that God buried him secretly gave rise to the tradition common in the first century that he had not died but, like Elijah, had been taken directly to heaven. Early Christianity had to come to terms with the Jewish view that the eschatological times could not dawn until Moses and/or Elijah had returned, and did so in a variety of ways (Mark 9:2–13; Luke 1:15–17; 4:25–26; 7:11–17). *John meets this condition by casting the faithful church in the role of Elijah and Moses.* Like both Moses (in Jewish tradition) and Elijah (II Kings 2:11), they are vindicated by God by being taken up to heaven. Like Moses (who was considered the *prophet par excellence* by first-century Judaism [cf. Deut. 18:15–18; 34:10–11; Hos. 12:13]), the two martyr-prophets turn water to blood and strike the earth with every plague (11:6; cf. Exod. 7:17–19). Here once again the persecution and troubles of the endtime are interpreted as God's latter-day "plagues" against the rebellious "Egyptians" (cf. v. 8—the persecution of Christians takes place in "Egypt"). Like Elijah they have power to shut the sky and stop the rain (I Kings 17:1; cf. James 5:17) and like Elijah send forth "fire" to destroy their enemies (II Kings. 1:10–12). Jesus' disciples had once mistakenly wanted to do the same to the Samaritans who rejected them (Luke 9:51–56), but they were rebuked by Jesus, who simply absorbed and accepted the rejection of the Samaritans. Likewise in Revelation the "false prophet" who gets people to worship the beast mimics Elijah by making fire come down from heaven (13:13). In contrast, two prophet-martyrs of 11:1–13, while they are cast in the role of Elijah and operate with the prophetic power of God, do not, Elijah-like, bring down fire from heaven. Fire proceeds from their *mouths:* it is their powerful word of witness, a fulfillment of the promise to Jeremiah: . . . "behold, I am making my words in your mouth a fire, and this people wood, and the fire shall devour them" (5:14; this tradition was already applied to Elijah

146

in Sir. 48:1). Just as their Lord's "terrible swift sword" of justice is the sword that proceeds from his mouth, his judging and purifying word (1:16; 2:12; 19:15), so the "fire" with which his servants "torment" (11:10) their oppressors is their unbearable word. Our society sometimes pretends not to believe in the power of words, but in our better moments we know that words can wound and kill and that words can bind up wounds and restore life.

The suffering of the oppressed Christian community is not here understood as mere passivity, a doing-nothing until the End comes. The prophetic ministry of the church, that is, its testimony by its own suffering, is, like their prayers (5:8; 8:3-4; cf. 6:9-11, interpreted as an active agent in bringing about the eschaton and final victory of God. These prophetic witnesses are thus powerful, operating with the power of God; namely, their word of testimony, their willingness to give their lives. These two things represent John's christological redefinition of power, corresponding to his transmutation of the Lion Messiah into the Lamb, the crucified prophet of Nazareth. Their "power" over their enemies is thus not arrogance nor is it vindictive. Their ministry is conducted in "sackcloth" (11:3); the repentance proclaimed by the church is not only for others. There is no smugness in this orientation to martyrdom.

What John has been describing is perceivable to the eyes of faith only. To all ordinary observation, the "witnesses" have no power at all. In 11:7 the "beast" opposes them, "conquers" them, kills them ("beast" mentioned here for the first time in Rev. is to receive full treatment in chaps. 12—13). The faithful Christian martyr/witnesses are easily dispatched by the pagan courts. Yet they do not die without completing their testimony; their death is not a meaningless tragedy (cf. 12:11). John holds up an utterly realistic picture before the churches, who must decide how to respond to the Roman pressures: God will not intervene to deliver them; faithfulness does not deliver them from death but causes it. The beast and all casual observers will consider the death of the witnesses adequate proof that Rome, who has the power, has won. Yet "conquer" here is used in the parody-language of the beast, whose "conquering" can only be a weak imitation of the Lamb's power.

The beast does not have the last word. Three and a half days   147
transpire. (Three and a half had already become a traditional apocalyptic number, cf. Luke 4:25 and James 5:17, where the

less than three years of I Kings 17:1—18:1 has become three and one-half to correspond to this tradition.) At the end of this brief period the same event happens as is pictured in Ezekiel 37, God restoring his vanquished people, pictured as a "valley of dry bones" (John using Ezekiel again!): "A breath/spirit of life from God entered them, and they stood up on their feet" (11:11; cf. Ezek. 37:5, 10). They hear exactly the same words addressed to John in 4:1, "Come up here," and ascend to heaven in the sight of all their enemies. For the church, the experience of being called into God's heavenly world is no escapist "rapture"; in John's revelation Christians go to the presence of God through tribulation and martyrdom, not instead of it. In the present the kingdom of God is hidden and ambiguous, but the eschatological Day comes when it will be public and clear. John is already making the transition to his next scene, the last trumpet and the coming of the kingdom. The completion of the faithful church's ministry of martyrdom and its vindication by God is the signal for the final theophany and judgment (11:13), as once again John prepares to describe the final scene of history.

The Seventh Trumpet:
The Kingdom Comes as Salvation and Woe (11:14–19)

The last trumpet sounds, and the glad announcement is proclaimed in heaven that God, the rightful sovereign of the universe who has always been king *de jure,* has now become king in fact, has taken his power and begun to reign. In this proleptic vision, God is praised as "the one who is" and "the one who was," but the customary third member of the formula, "the one who is to come" (1:4, 8; 4:8), is missing, because in the "now" of the vision he *has* come. The word usually translated "kingdom" is an active noun, designating an action, not an object or territory: "kinging," "acting as king," "ruling," "rulership." The prayer "Thy kingdom come" is the prayer for God who is the sovereign of the universe to exercise his power, put down the rebellious claimants to sovereignty over the world, vanquish all that opposes his will, and establish his gracious reign of justice over all his creation. It is a magnificent image, and John dares to announce that it will be fulfilled in reality. In John's vision of the future, his churches are allowed to hear the thanksgivings and praises that already echo through the heavenly world; and in their own worship they can themselves already join in the celebration, even as they continue to pray "Thy kingdom come."

148

There is also a dark side to the announcement. The coming of the final kingdom is also the coming of the last "woe" (cf. 8:13; 9:12; 11:14). There may be some point in the fact that the final "woe" is never identified. While judgment is an inseparable aspect of John's pictures of the End, he does not have a dualistic view in which God's punishment and justice are co-eternal with his grace and mercy. (See the "Reflection: Universal Salvation and Paradoxical Language.") Nonetheless, the final picture of this series not only portrays the good news of the arrival of God's kingdom but also announces wrath, the rage of nations, and the destruction of those who destroy the earth (11:18).

At the end of the first series of seven, the last seal had no content at all—only silence (8:1). With the last trumpet vision John is less hesitant to describe the End. His picture remains quite general, however. He is not yet ready to give the full details of the final picture, which he is withholding for the detailed visions of 19:1—22:5. Only one tantalizing glimpse, a detail to provoke the imagination, comes into focus in his vision: In the heavenly temple John makes out the contours of the Ark of the Covenant! This had disappeared at the time of the destruction of the first temple by Babylon. The second temple, standing in Jesus' day but not in John's, destroyed by the latter-day "Babylon," had contained a Holy of Holies as the designated place for the Ark, but it was empty. Various legends had grown up about the destiny of the original Ark, which was supposed to reappear in the eschatological restoration of the temple. When John sees the Ark of the Covenant in the heavenly temple in this scene of the final coming of the kingdom, not only is it the ultimate sign that the prayer "Thy kingdom come" has been finally answered, all the Wailing Wall prayers of all the ages also finally find their fulfillment.

Revelation 12:1—14:20
Exposé of the Powers of Evil

The impact of the surrealistic drama communicated in chapters 12—14 comes not by analyzing it, but by hearing it read, or reading it, with imagination and insight. This can be facilitated, but not replaced, by understanding something of the unit's literary context and structure, the cultural context of

149

the mythological pictures contained in it, and by a discussion of the characters and action of the drama.

Behind the Scenes at the Drama (12:1—13:18)

Literary Context and Structure

With the sounding of the seventh trumpet in 11:15–19, we were brought (once again!) to the End. All that is supposed to happen at the eschatological victory of God happens: the kingdom comes, God himself comes, the dead are raised, the last judgment is held, the good are rewarded, the corruptors of creation are destroyed, there is a sense of restoration and fulfillment. Chronologically, things can proceed no further: we have been through the final plagues (twice!) and are now at the End. There is a sense in which the document could end here, as the first hearer-readers may well have supposed it would. And yet . . .

We are now met with an extended section that is not at all a chronological continuation of the preceding visions nor is it their conclusion. Nor is it the kind of "interlude" that John regularly inserts between the sixth and seventh units of a series. The series of visions in 12:1—14:20 is the central axis of the book and the core of its pictorial "argument." We experience something of a surrealistic flashback and flash-forward through the events that have just been pictured in the visions of the seven seals and seven trumpets, going back to the time of Jesus and beyond into the primeval, pre-creation world of God's eternity (13:8), and then forward again to the eschaton and beyond, a verbal/visual Sistine Chapel panorama (literally: "vision of everything") from before the creation till the end of time. In John's view the Christians of Asia need to keep the decisions they must make in perspective, and he provides it. After this mind-stretching revelation of his hearer-readers' earthly struggles from the perspective of eternity, John will return once more to his pattern of a final series of seven plagues before the End (15:1—16:21), only this time he will indeed mean "last."

Chapters 12—14 constitute one unit, a cosmic operatic drama in which all the characters and actions are exaggerated, larger than life. Chapters 12—13 pull away the curtain that hides the transcendent world from ordinary sight and offers a behind-the-scenes view of the powers of evil at work in the present, while chapter 14 proleptically presents a behind-the-scenes view of the victory of God in salvation and judgment.

Cultural Context of the Mythological Pictures

Not far from John's island prison is the island of Delos, sacred to the Greeks because, in a story known to all John's hearer-readers from childhood, there the divine Apollo had been born. His mother Leto had fled there to escape the dragon Python, who wanted to kill the newborn son of Zeus. Instead of being killed, Apollo returns to Delphi and kills the dragon. The basic outline of this plot is found in the mythical folklore of many peoples. It is a variation of the story of how the forces of darkness, disorder, and sterility/death rebelled against the divine king of light, order, and fertility/life, attempting to overthrow the divine order, kill the newborn king, and/or seize the kingship and establish the rule of darkness. This story, like all such myths, is an expression and interpretation of the human story as part of the cosmic conflict between good and evil, just as it expresses the common experience of humanity that there is always a new day after the darkness of night: The darkness-dragon attempts to destroy the sun god, but is himself killed as the new day dawns.

The Roman emperors found the myth politically useful. Apollo was understood as the primeval king who had reigned over a "golden age" of peace and prosperity. Augustus, the first emperor, interpreted his own rule in terms of this tradition, claiming that his administration was the Golden Age and casting himself in the role of the new Apollo. Nero erected statues to himself as the god Apollo. There were coins on which the radiance of the sun god emanates from the emperor's head. A grateful citizen of the Roman world could readily think of the story as a reflection of his or her own experience, with the following cast: the woman is the goddess Roma, the queen of heaven; the son is the emperor, who kills the dragon and founds the new Golden Age; the dragon represents the power of darkness, "our old wickedness" (Vergil, *Eclogue* IV.15) that oppose the goodness of life.

The Characters of the Drama

John takes up the story and literally recasts it, providing new identities for the characters. More precisely, he uses the old myth as a means of identifying the characters already on the stage of history with their cosmic counterparts. His hearer-readers needed no help in identifying *who* the contemporary rulers were; John wanted to expose them for *what* they were—

151

agents and embodiments of the transcendent powers of evil. Images from two worlds come together here: images of buying and selling, persecution, the pain of labor and giving birth are combined with images of a dragon who falls from the sky, a beast who ascends from the watery abyss, and an earth that has chosen sides in the cosmic conflict. With prophetic insight, John knows that it "takes two worlds to make sense out of one." What we have is neither the mythical story of events in some other world far away in time and space, unrelated to the struggles and decisions John and his parishioners are called upon to make, nor is it the code-language of allegory, in which every item in the scene corresponds to some item in John's contemporary history. The old mythical story is retold in such a way that the events and institutions of John's own history shimmer through it. The mythical story reflects and evokes images and events of his hearer-readers' experience, allowing them to see their struggles in a transcendent context.

The characters fall, not surprisingly, into two absolutely polarized groups with no middle ground. On the one side are the forces of good:

The woman. No Christian acquainted with the Gospels can read this story of the woman who labors to bring forth the child who shall rule the nations without thinking of Mary, the mother of the Messiah, whose divine child is saved from wicked Herod by divine intervention (Matt. 2:1–15). Yet to interpret John's evocative symbolic language in this limited fashion would reduce it to a steno-symbol code. John the artist uses language more creatively. The woman is not Mary, nor Israel, nor the church but less and more than all of these. John's imagery pulls together elements from the pagan myth of the queen of heaven; from the Genesis story of Eve, mother of all living, whose "seed" shall bruise the head of the primeval serpent (Gen. 3:1–16); from Israel who escapes from the dragon/Pharaoh into the wilderness on wings of an eagle (Exod. 19:4, cf. Ps. 74:12–15); and Zion, "mother" of the People of God from whom the Messiah comes forth (Isa. 66:7–9; II Esdr. 13:32–38). She reflects the historical experience of the People of God through the ages, Israel and the church, and yet she is the cosmic woman, clothed with the sun, with the moon under her feet, and crowned with twelve stars, who brings forth the Messiah. A passage in the Dead Sea Scrolls (1QH 3:4) also pictures the elect community Israel bringing forth the Messiah. Albrecht

152

Dürer's woodcut captures the subtleties of this combination of a this-worldly mother and a transcendent queen of heaven.

The Messiah. The woman's child is identified as the one spoken of in the Second Psalm, already understood in both the Judaism and Christianity of John's day as speaking of the Messiah. Psalm 2:7–9 pictures God as saying (in the original context, to the new Israelite king), "You are my Son. . . . I will make the nations your heritage. . . . You shall break them with a rod of iron." John (like the Septuagint) changes the Hebrew bible's "break" to "shepherd" ("rule" in RSV), transforming what might still seem like a harsh picture of the Messiah's rule into his characteristic "Lion into Lamb" christological terms (see on 5:1–14). "Shepherd all the nations with a rod of iron" is not a picture of brute force but of the future absolute and universal rule of the Messiah. If Revelation teaches anything, it is that the power by which God brings the kingdom is the power of suffering love revealed in the cross.

Christians. Other characters in the drama are the "brethren" of 12:10, who are likewise offspring/"seed" of the woman (another echo of Gen. 3:15), and therefore "brethren" not just of each other but also of Christ, the primary "seed" of the woman. Like Christ, they too are "sons of God" (2:18; 21:7), they too are persecuted by the empire, they too offer their witness by suffering martyrdom, they too win the victory over the dragon (12:11) and they too are vindicated and taken up to heaven. In this imagery Christ is not only the church's Lord but also its elder brother whose life, death, and vindication/exaltation is the paradigm for the Christian's life. They are characterized (13:10) as those who have *hypomone* (steadfast endurance), faithfulness: faith in the sovereignty of God as the hidden Actor in the whole drama (see below).

"Earth." The earth is not just the stage, the neutral scene where the human and angelic drama is played out, but an actor in the drama (12:16).

Michael and the angels. Actions from the heavenly side are taken by angelic figures—in this scene a total of seven (!), another indication that John thought of chapters 12—14 as a single unit (12:7; 14:6, 8, 9, 15, 17, 18). The prominence of angelic action reflects the idea current in various streams of apocalyptic thought that God did not administer the affairs of the world directly but delegated authority to the angels, each angel being charged with responsibility for a particular nation. Sometimes

153

God reserved Israel to his own special authority (Deut. 32:8–9), sometimes the captain of the angelic hosts, Michael, was placed in charge of Israel. Michael then became the heavenly champion and sponsor of the People of God, as in Daniel 10:21; 12:1, and is the only angel named in Revelation.

God the hidden actor. God is never mentioned as a direct actor in the cosmic drama, but is referred to only obliquely in these chapters (cf. 12:5–6). And yet it is clear that the behind-the-scenes drama revealed in John's vision has its own behind-the-scenes dimension not directly portrayed. The hidden Actor in everything is the Lord God Almighty (19:6) who is sovereign over all. John expresses this by using the variety of linguistic modes that had become current in Judaism to express the action of God without pronouncing the divine name: the use of the passive voice (12:5) and the use of the indefinite third person plural, literally "they" (12:6). Particularly striking is John's repeated use of "was given" or "is/was allowed" with reference to the "beasts," with God understood to be the sole Sovereign who "allows" (13:5, 7, 14, 15). The use of such language provides John a manner of expression which affirms that God is not directly responsible for evil but that Satan has no independent power in this world, only that "allowed" or "given" him by the one Lord of all.

It is in this light that 13:9–10, and other "predestination" texts should be read. These lines, adapted from Jeremiah 15:2 and 43:11, do not express resignation or fatalism but are confessional language's affirmation of the sovereignty of the Creator who is present and active in his creation, even in the absurd situation of the persecution in Asia.

Opposite the cast representing the forces of good are the villains of the cosmic drama:

The evil "trinity." John by no means has a developed doctrine of the Trinity, but his conception of the divine activity does have the elements from which such later conceptions developed: the one God, the Creator, represents himself and acts definitively in this world in and through the Christ, the Lamb, and makes his word and power known in the church and the world through the Spirit, thought of by the prophet John primarily as the Spirit that inspires prophecy. Corresponding to and parodying the divine reality John sees a counterfeit "trinity": the dragon, the beast, and the false prophet (16:13 shows he thinks of these three as a unit).

154

The dragon. In the Pauline tradition Paul's own view of the trans-individual supra-personal powers of evil was taken up and developed: ". . . we are not contending against flesh and blood, but against the principalities, against the powers, against the world rulers of this present darkness, against the spiritual hosts of wickedness in the heavenly places" (Eph. 6:12). John stands in this tradition, and gives it vivid pictorial dramatization.

The dragon is the parody of God the Creator, the counterpart to 4:1–11. Like God the Creator, his place was in the heavens (12:7; cf. Eph. 6:12 "heavenly places" and 2:2 "the prince of the power of the air") and he has a "throne" which he may grant to others (13:2). Like the chaos monster of ancient Near Eastern mythology that was defeated and held at bay at creation (Leviathan, Lotan, Tiamat), he has seven heads, as does the death monster in Testament of Abraham 17:14. John has already associated the dragon with Python, the opponent of Zeus and Apollo in the Greek myth. He also draws on Old Testament tradition (e.g., Jer. 51:34 and Ezek. 29:3–5; 32:2–8; Dan. 7:7 [the source of the ten horns]), in which previous prophets had identified the historical enemies of God's people with the mythical dragon. By identifying the "dragon" with Satan, the devil, the ancient serpent (12:9), John shows that he intends to symbolize all the anti-God forces from Eden on, whatever they may be called.

The beast from the sea. The other two members of John's "evil trinity" are his adaptations of the Jewish tradition according to which God created two mythical creatures, Leviathan the sea monster and Behemoth the land monster (I Enoch 60:7–25; II Esdr. 6:49–54; II Bar. 29:4; Baba B. 74ª). The beast from the sea, with its seven heads, ten horns, blasphemous names, and features of the leopard, bear, and lion of Daniel 7:1–8, is the composite and culmination of the traditional sea monster and all the beasts of Daniel's vision. As in Daniel, "beast" means "historical empire." In John's time, the fourth beast of Daniel was often interpreted by Jews as signifying the Roman Empire (e.g., II Esdras). John clearly wants his picture of the beast to evoke in the imaginations of his hearer-readers images of Rome and her emperors, especially Nero, the first emperor to persecute the church (see Introduction, "Christians and the Emperor Cult"). This is made unmistakably explicit in 17:9–10, where the seven heads are the seven hills of Rome, as well as seven "kings" (emperors), and the woman seated on the

155

beast "is the great city which has dominion over the kings of the earth" (17:18; cf. 13:8). The heads bear "blasphemous names" because the emperors assumed the titles of divinity—"Son of God," "Lord," "Savior," even "God," as their coins and inscriptions make clear. "One of its heads seemed to have a mortal wound, but its mortal wound was healed" (13:3). This is a transparent allusion to Nero, who took his own life by stabbing himself in the throat, but was believed to still be alive and returning in bloody vengeance (see Introduction, as above).

Since sacrificial lambs were killed by cutting their throats, the parody with the Lamb is clear. As the dragon represents the powers of chaos versus the Creator, so the beast from the sea is a parody of the Christ. As Christ is the representative of God and works by his power and authority, so the beast receives power and authority from the dragon. As the Lamb bears the marks of slaughter, but lives, so does the beast. John repeats this three times, 13:3, 12, 14! The beast "conquers" (13:7), but his "conquering" by the power of the sword and the death of others is a pale imitation of the real power of the Christ who conquers by love expressed in his own death. The beast "rules" for a very short time (3½ years; 13:5) in contrast to the thousand-year prelude to the eternal reign of Christ. The contrast with Christ is made explicit in 13:8, where there are again only two groups: the followers of Christ and those who worship the beast. Yet the beast is not merely "Rome" in an objective, reductionistic sense. It is the inhuman, anti-human arrogance of empire which has come to expression in Rome—but not only there.

The beast from the land. John explicitly identifies this second beast that "rose out of the earth" as the "false prophet" (16:13; 19:20; 20:10). It is the Satanic counterpart to and parody of the Holy Spirit at work in the churches, thought of especially as the Spirit that inspires prophecy. In imitation of the true prophetic church, this beast is a fake Elijah who does signs and makes fire come down from heaven (cf. I Kings 18:20–39 and the exposition of 11:4–13 above). As the Holy Spirit leads people to worship God "and" the Lamb (the God who has defined himself in Christ), so the false prophet promotes the worship of the beast "and" the dragon (Satan who has represented himself in the imperial cult, 13:12–15). As the Holy Spirit that speaks through the Christian prophets leads people to live a life in tension with the cultural norms of this world, the false prophet enables people to fit into the economic structures of this world

156

only if they receive his "mark" (13:16–17). As the Holy Spirit is related to the risen Christ and speaks with his voice (2:1 ∥ 2:7 and in each of the seven messages of chapters 2—3; cf. 5:6), the false prophet even looks superficially like Christ. But when he speaks, it is the very voice of the devil-dragon that is heard (13:11).

Just who is this "beast/false prophet"? Scholars have often identified it with the local Roman officials or the *koinon* (Greek), the *commune* (Latin), the council consisting of local officials from major towns of the Roman province of Asia. As the first beast from the sea represented the Roman Caesar or governor who literally came up out of the sea upon his arrival on the coast of Asia, so the beast from the land represents the indigenous officials who promoted the Roman government, especially as expressed in the Caesar cult—so the argument goes. Alternatively, this beast has been identified as the priests of the Caesar cult who are reported to have duped the populace by their light and fire miracles, tricks of ventriloquism, and contrived images that let the image of the beast (image of Caesar) "speak" (13:15; cf. Scherrer). John makes no miraculous claims for the true prophets, whose witness is given in suffering, not in triumphalistic miracles (11:5–6 are part of the visionary imagery and do not correspond to anything John reports as occurring in his church). *False* prophets traffic in miracles (Mark 13:22; II Thess. 2:9). Some scholars have understood the *prophetic* features of the beast from the land and its specific designation as the "false prophet" to point to John's opponents *within* the church—the teachers and charismatic prophets who encouraged Christians to accommodate themselves to Roman culture, ideology, and cult as an aspect of their "progressive" theology (e.g., Minear, *I Saw a New Earth*, pp. 119–27).

Since John is not communicating in code-language or steno symbols, it is useless to try to decide whether the beast from the land "represents" the Roman governors, the *commune*, the Roman priesthood, or false Christian prophets and teachers. The beast has characteristics of all of these. All who support and promote the cultural religion, in or out of the church, however Lamb-like they may appear, are agents of the beast. All propaganda that entices humanity to idolize human empire is an expression of this beastly power that wants to appear Lamb-like.

157

The Action of the Drama

We are now equipped to hear the story as John's first hearer-readers would have heard it and, overhearing the message it communicated to them, grasp its meaning for our own time and place.

The foiled attempt of the dragon (12:1–6). The woman who represents the People of God labors to bring forth the Messiah. In this scene that blends two worlds, God's agent of salvation, the One who shall shepherd all nations with absolute authority, is represented by the innocence and vulnerability of a baby. As the dragon waits to devour the newborn child, all the forces of evil, in this world and beyond, are concentrated against this saving act of God. The child is born and taken up to God—so quickly does the story move from the Messiah's birth to death and resurrection. There can be no doubt that, although the dragon does not "get" the child, who is safe at God's throne, the way to God's presence was not by escaping death. Precisely by dying, Jesus defeated the dragon and was exalted to God's right hand. The meaning of this kind of victory did not have to be spelled out to John's hearer-readers, who faced their own decisions about how to deal with the dragon's activity in their midst.

The woman flees to the wilderness (12:6), as the People of God had found refuge from the dragon/Pharaoh in the exodus story John often uses as a model. The woman is "in the wilderness" for 1260 days (3½ years, 42 months; cf. Dan. 7:25; 8:14; 9:27; 12:7,11,12), the brief period of eschatological troubles just before the End, the time of trouble that John sees already dawning in the imperial persecution.

The dragon defeated in the real world (12:7–12). The picture of the dragon being cast out of heaven is not the "explanation" for the origin of Satan—the Bible does not deal in such "explanations." (See the "Reflection: Interpreting Revelation's Satan Language.") As proclaimed in the heavenly voice that (like the choir in a Greek drama) interprets the action on stage, the expulsion of Satan from heaven is the result of the victory of Christ on earth (12:10–11). As in the similar vision reported in Luke 10:18, the "time" of the fall of Satan from heaven is "now" (12:10): in the story line of the vision, the time of the Christ event. The story thus has nothing to do with the squelching of a rebellion of hyper-ambitious angels in some pre-creation mythological story. It is Michael, commander of God's

158

armies, who takes the initiative, as the visionary counterpart to God's saving act on earth in the event of Christ and his cross. This too was a matter of God's initiative, not merely a *re*action to human rebellion—the Lamb was slain "from the foundation of the world" (13:8). Christians are not passive spectators—they are involved in the defeat of Satan. Their blood flows together with the blood of the Lamb, as they make their own testimony/ martyrdom as Jesus did his (12:10–11).

The action which takes place in heaven is a reflection of events in this world: the life and death of Jesus, the witness of Christians who are "faithful unto death" (2:10). Although John uses mythical language, there is a sense in which John has reversed the order of myth as understood in the pagan world. There, earthly history is only the by-product of events in the heavenly world among the gods. In Revelation the scene of God's saving activity is on this earth, in the life of Jesus and the lives of Christians. The incarnation, crucifixion/resurrection, and testimony of Christians happens on earth, and *that* results in the defeat of the evil powers in the transcendent world.

Although the devil and his angels are already defeated in the real world, the transcendent world of God's reality, they have been cast down to *this* world, angry and frustrated. Like a poor-loser football team hopelessly behind with only three and a half minutes to go, having already lost, they determine to do as much damage as they can in the remaining brief time. This is precisely how John perceives the situation of his suffering fellow Christians—and those trying to decide whether to suffer or to yield to the cultural pressure. To line up with the Roman cult is to cast one's lot with an enemy already defeated. All that is necessary is to hang in there (*hypomone!*) until the End. The only way to lose in such a situation is to switch sides or to quit.

The dragon persecutes the woman on earth (12:13–16). The "child" has met the dragon, conquered it by his death, and is now exalted to God's throne. The woman, the People of God, mother of the Messiah and the messianic community, the church, remain on earth. The dragon has been defeated and expelled from heaven and vents his last wrath and frustration on the woman. The Christians of John's churches recognize themselves and their demonic opponents in this picture: it is not just their Roman officials, who after all are fellow human beings victimized by the powers of evil, who are their persecu-

159

tors, but Satan himself who is the power behind the earthly Roman throne. The dragon, who represents the primeval anti-creation forces of the watery abyss, opens his mouth to sweep the woman away with a flood. (John's hearer-readers felt themselves deluged with a flood of persecution, or in John's view would soon recognize themselves in this frightful picture.) The earth, no neutral bystander in this drama, comes to the woman's rescue. "Nature" itself is the good creation of God and is on the side of the People of God—as the stars in their courses fought against Sisera (Judg. 5:20), as ". . . creation will join with him [God] to fight against the madmen" (Wis. Sol. 5:20).

With such pictures, John has no intention of encouraging the beleaguered Christians of Asia to expect miraculous help to save them from persecution and death—the model of Antipas (2:13), not to speak of Jesus (1:5, 18; 2:8; 5:6), and the message of the whole book (2:10! 11:1–13!) makes that impossible. John wants to show that though "nature" may seem to be unfeeling or even hostile, the "natural" world that is the context of our daily lives is God's good creation that shall finally be redeemed (21:1—22:6; cf. Rom. 8:19–28) and is even now rallying to the aid of God's people.

The beast from the sea appears to conquer the saints (12:17–13:10). Frustrated at his impotence in trying to destroy the Christian community as such, the devil vents his fury on individual Christians (12:17*a*). Having failed in his direct attack, the dragon summons an ally from the sea (12:17*b*) and gives his throne and authority to it (13:2). As we have seen, the visionary monster who appears will certainly have evoked pictures of the oppressive Roman authorities in the minds of John's hearer-readers. The beast is "allowed" (God the hidden sovereign!) to make war on the saints and to "conquer" them (13:7). Here is another example of the realism of John. He holds out no false hope of rescue from death for those who remain faithful. John has the stories of Daniel in mind (cf. 13:15; Dan. 3:5–6), where the faithful *are* rescued from death at the hands of the evil empire (Dan. 3 from the fiery furnace; Dan. 6 from the lions' den). Yet John understands that even the author of Daniel did not advocate faithfulness because it leads to deliverance from suffering (see Dan. 3:17–18)!

160

The beast from the earth and its promotion of emperor worship (13:11–18). The demonic "trinity" is also a kind of hierarchy: Satan empowers the Roman imperial beast from the sea, which in turn grants authority to the beast from the earth. As the first beast was characterized by political features, the beast from the land appears clothed in all the accoutrements of religion: it works miracles, promotes worship, looks somewhat like the Lamb (13:11), encourages folk to make an image of the beast and to worship it, is designated the "false prophet" (16:13; 19:20; see above). John never denies the reality of the impressive miracles worked by this beast, knowing in accord with biblical theology in general that the truth of faith is not proven or disproven by displays of miraculous power or the lack of it (Exod. 7:11, 22; 8:7; Deut. 13:1–5; Matt. 7:21–23; Mark 13:22; II Cor. 10—13; II Thess. 2:9).

The most notorious act of the "false prophet" is to mark everyone—rich, poor, small, great, slave, free—with a mark on the hand or forehead, without which no one can participate in the economic life of the community (13:16–17). Since this text about the "mark of the beast" has through the centuries been a happy hunting ground for religious quacks and sensationalizers, and for all who have understood John to be predicting the long-range future, it is important to give some clear guidelines for preaching and teaching.

1. The passage is important, and its misuse by calendarizers and religious hobbyists who regard the number 666 as something of a religious crossword puzzle should not deter more serious interpreters from seeking its authentic meaning. A perusal of all John's references to the mark of the beast (13:16–18; 14:9–11; 16:2; 19:20; 20:4) indicates that it is one expression of his "dualism of decision." As a sign of ownership and security, the Lamb marks his followers on the forehead with the seal of the living God, his name and the name of his Father (7:1–8; 14:1–5). The beast imitates the Lamb, marking his followers on the forehead or the right hand. For John, there are only these two groups, these two choices—everyone bears one mark or the other, and conspicuously! There are no anonymous Christians, no middle-of-the-road, no non-aligned.

2. The "mark of the beast" occurs as part of a visionary drama. It is to be taken seriously but not literally. Just as John does not want his hearer-readers literally to suppose that their spiritual enemy and threat is a monster with seven heads, so he does not want them literally to expect any time, then or later, when it would be impossible for Christians to buy or sell unless they had a certain mark on their hand or forehead. Yet the

161

picture is to be taken seriously, for it represented something all too real to the members of John's churches who felt the economic pressure inherent in Christian commitment. Guild membership often involved participating in pagan ceremonies. Business contracts often went to those who "patriotically" supported the Roman administration's gift of peace and prosperity. Even the coin of the realm bore the image and religious claims of the emperor.

3. The mark of the beast is a number, "a man's name" (13:18, NEB, TEV), which is to be explained by the ancient practice of gematria, common in John's setting. In contrast to modern English, all the languages used in John's time and place represented numbers by letters of the alphabet (cf. "Roman numerals"). In Greek, Hebrew, and Latin, every letter was thus also a number. This means that every word is also a numerical sum obtained by totaling all its letters. It is thus easy to go from a word to its number; there is only one possibility, which anyone who can spell and add can readily compute. The opposite process, however, is not easy at all. Given a number, there are many possible words whose letters might add up to that number. This means that gematria functions only for those who know the word it designates in advance. The number does not serve to identify the name, *but to say something about its significance.* When Revelation was read forth in the worship of the Asian churches, the call for wisdom to calculate the number of the beast (13:18) was not a challenge to identify *who* the beast, the persecuting authority was—they knew that well enough already—but to recognize *what* it was, that it was in fact the beast empowered by Satan, not the cultural savior it claimed to be.

4. The number 666 has a generic significance that made it particularly appropriate for John's purpose. John shares the broad apocalyptic tradition in which *seven* is the complete number, and has used it as such throughout. The seventh seal, trumpet, and bowl is always the last, that represents the coming of God and his kingdom. But six is often the penultimate number, the number of lack and incompleteness. It is also the number of judgment. As the kingdom of God comes in the seventh and last of each series, the judgment of God comes in the sixth seal, trumpet, and bowl (6:12–17; 9:13–21; 16:12–16)—and John himself and his parishioners live in the time of the sixth emperor, the time of idolatry and eschatological plagues (17:10).

162

"Six-six-six" is thus the intensive symbolic expression of incompleteness, idolatry, judgment, non-fulfillment, evil itself raised to the third power. The number communicated as symbol, not by analysis.

There is an element of evocative mystery in the symbol that functions whether or not a particular referent is also in mind. Thus the symbol of the beast and his mysterious number can continue to have evocative power in situations where the original reference has long since been forgotten. Since the symbolic meaning of John's imagery is clear whether or not we can identify the particular meaning evoked in the imaginations of John's audience, we do well to be wary of the "obsession with decoding 666," against which Paul Minear warns us (*I Saw a New Earth*, p. 123). The exhortation of verse 18, "It is the moment to have discernment" (Ellul's translation), challenges the modern interpreter not to historical decoding but to discerning where in our own time propaganda is used to idolize political power.

5. Yet it is likely that John intended his readers to think of a particular individual, one already known to them, by this number which is designated as "a man's name" (13:18 NEB, TEV). Nero is by far the most likely candidate supported by the majority of historical scholars, since the letters "Neron Caesar" in the Hebrew spelling add up to precisely 666: Nun (50) + Resh (200) + Waw (6) and Nun (50) + Qof (100) + Samech (60) + Resh (200) = 666. There are two possible objections to this view, namely that (a) the calculation involves Hebrew and John is writing in Greek, and (b) the name must be spelled with an additional letter (Nun = 50) on the end of Nero ("Neron" above) to reach the correct total (666). But John, who probably came from Palestine, elsewhere makes wordplays involving the Hebrew language (9:11; 16:16), and the Hebrew spelling of Nero with the additional "Nun" has now been found in the Dead Sea Scrolls (see DISCOVERIES IN THE JUDAEAN DESERT II, p. 101, plate 29, line 1). That John expected his hearer-readers to think of Nero is supported by the fact that he uses the myth of the returning Nero elsewhere in Revelation (13:3; 17:9–11), and by the ancient interpretation as Nero, documented in the reading 616 in some manuscripts (Nero spelled in the normal Greek manner without the extra "nun" = 50).

163

Nero had once persecuted the church, the first Roman emperor to do so. The view that he was not really dead but would return from the East to wreak havoc on the empire was in the air. John sees a new persecution looming on the horizon, and pictures the advent of the new Roman oppressors as the "return of Nero." He did not intend this in any literal sense; he wanted to make a statement to those who saw commitment to Roman ideology as harmless and quite compatible with Christian commitment. His picture-language warns, "Beware, it is Nero all over again," just as one might say of a new dictatorial anti-Semitism that many might see as innocuous, "Beware, it's Hitler all over again." The whole passage calls responsible interpreters of the Bible not to "decoding" a "puzzle" but to alertness in discerning the nature and consequences of one's commitments.

REFLECTION
Interpreting Revelation's Satan Language

"Satan" has become in English a proper name for what was originally in the Hebrew Scriptures a generic word for "adversary." The word is often used in this generic sense in the Old Testament, especially in its specific use in the courtroom: "accuser," either as hostile witness or as prosecuting attorney (e.g., I Kings 11:14, 23, 25; Pss. 38:20; 71:13; 109:4, 20, 29). In three late (post-exilic) passages, the "accuser" takes on a particular identity as one of the angels in the heavenly court, the divine prosecuting attorney who presses God's case or does God's work of probing the integrity of human beings (I Chron. 21:1; Job 1:6–12; Zech. 3:1). In none of these instances, nor anyplace else in the Old Testament, is there a Satan as the personification of evil. In I Chronicles 21:1 the "satan" does what God himself did in the earlier version of II Samuel 24:1.

It was during the intertestamental period, especially under the influence of Iranian dualistic religion and its evil god Ahriman, counterpart to the supreme god of light Ahura-mazda, that the figure of Satan emerged in Jewish tradition as the personification of evil and the transcendent opponent of God. Jewish monotheism prohibited Satan from becoming a second god, but he became the leader of all evil spirits, with his own kingdom of darkness opposing the kingdom of God. Various versions of the origin of Satan as one of the fallen angels developed (I Enoch 6:1—16:4; II Enoch 29). The full-blown myth of the origin of Satan and evil in the rebellion of the angels, popularized in Milton's classic *Paradise Lost,* did not develop until later, but its beginnings, though later than the Old Testament, are already found in the intertestamental apocalyptic literature. Satan, also called Satanail, Beliar or Belial (as in the Dead Sea Scrolls), and Mastema, now becomes what he is when the New Testament opens: the one who tempts humanity to discord, violence, and immorality (Test. Gad. 4:7; Test. Benj. 7:1; Test. Reub. 4:7; Test. Sim. 5:3; Test. Asher 3:2; Jub. 11:5; II Enoch 31:6). Although the idea of Satan had not developed when Genesis 1—3 was written, in the later retelling of the story in Jewish apocalyptic the original sin of humanity was provoked by "the devil," "Satanail," now identified with the serpent (II Enoch 31:1–8). As Satan was thought of as the cause of human sin and misery, the binding and destruction of Satan became a standard part of the hoped-for eschatological drama (1QH 3:35; 6:29; Test. Levi 18:12; Test. Judah 25:3).

Early Christianity adopted this mythology as its way of expressing its conviction that evil, while not an eternal counterpart of God, was more than the accumulation of individual human sins. This supra-individual power of evil which has the world and humanity in its grasp is called by various names in the New Testament, including "the devil" (32 times), "Satan" (33 times), "Belial" or "Beliar" (II Cor. 6:15), and "Beelzebul" (7 times).

Revelation's talk of Satan and the devil is thus not peculiar but belongs to the mainstream of Jewish and early Christian apocalyptic thought. John is at one with the Gospels, Paul, and the whole New Testament in using language about Satan and the devil as a way of expressing his understanding of evil. John usually calls him "Satan" (2:9, 13, 24; 3:9; 12:9; 20:2,7) or "the devil" (2:10; 12:9, 12; 20:2,10). Echoing the sinister overtones of "Satan's" origin as the accuser in court, John refers to him as "the accuser" (12:10), a designation powerfully appropriate in the situation of the Asian Christians who found themselves accused before the Roman courts. John follows Jewish tradition—but not the Scripture—in identifying Satan with the serpent of the "fall" story in Genesis 3 (12:9, 14, 15; 20:2). More importantly, in 12:1—13:18; 16:13, and 20:2 he identifies both these figures with the primordial dragon, the chaos monster (Levia-

165

than, Rahab, Tannin) subdued by Yahweh at the creation (cf. Job 7:12; 9:13; 26:12–13; Pss. 74:13–14; 89:9–10; Isa. 27:1; 30:7; 51:9–10). All these "super-personal forces of evil" are not speculative abstractions for John and his church but are met in their embodiments in the social structures of John's situation and in the institutionalized evil of the Roman Empire, as well as within the religious conflicts of his own community (2:9, 13, 24; 12:1–13, 18).

Although John shows no interest in taking over the mythical picture of the origin of Satan and evil (12:7–12 does not refer to a pre-creation fall of the angels), he does adapt the traditional eschatological scenario for the destruction of the devil and all his influence. The decisive battle has already been fought and won in the Christ event (3:21; 5:1–10; 12:7–10). Though defeated in the transcendent world of the heavenly court and only awaiting his execution, the devil still has power on earth and, knowing that his days are numbered, is still wreaking havoc, especially through his agents the beast and false prophet (12: 13—13:18). Yet his doom is sure. At the end of the final plagues, the devil will be bound for a thousand years while the earth enjoys an era of eschatological fulfillment (20:1–6); then he will be released for one last deceitful effort, after which he is thrown into the lake of fire, the second death (20:7–10).

Such is Revelation's picture of Satan as the power of evil. It is no speculative metaphysical theory intended to satisfy intellectual curiosity about the origin of evil; it is a segment of the apocalyptic story with which John tries to offer encouragement to faithful Christians suffering absurd evil.

Such language has its dangers and its values. Among its chief dangers is a prosaic literalism, all the more dangerous because it supposes it is merely "taking the Bible for what it says," an encouragement to dwell in the story-world of another culture and century and adopt its pictures as objectifying representations of the way things are. Comparative study of religious literature that brings to light the elaborate mythical stories of Satan, Beliar, and Mastema lets us see how restrained is John's usage and prohibits us from adopting it as an objectifying revelation from heaven of the way things are in the supernatural world. This can degenerate into a modern form of gnostic speculation, studying and constructing theories about Satan as curiosity-titillating bits of occult science masquerading as Bible

166

study. It can result in a the-devil-made-me-do-it denial of responsibility for one's own actions. It can result in resignation in the face of concrete social and political manifestations of evil when we might take some effective measures against them. Including "Satan" in one's religious symbol system can even play into the hands of institutionalized evil, diverting attention from the real problem. In view of such real dangers, should not modern, intellectually honest Christians simply reject talk of "Satan" as an unfortunate vestige of a superstitious age?

Not necessarily. Satan language and imagery, like the language and imagery of apocalypticism generally, can be the vehicle of profound theological truths and may be the necessary vehicle for some essential Christian insights and affirmations. Not only fundamentalists but responsible liberal theologians of the social gospel era, the major theologians of the neo-orthodox era, and many contemporary Christian theologians with a deep social conscience have found the New Testament's imagery for the demonic power of evil to be valuable when taken seriously but not literally. "Satan" as a symbolic way of thinking of the super-personal power of evil is a valuable dimension of biblical theology. The power of evil is bigger than individual sins. John consistently speaks in political and national terms when he talks of the power of Satan (13:7; 18:3, 23; 20:3, 8). Satan is not merely the individualistic tempter to petty sins; he is the deceiver of the nations (20:7–8). We might now label this as "systemic evil," or picture it more in accord with our own times as a vast impersonal computer-like network of evil in which our lives are enmeshed and which influences us quite apart from our wills. A valuable dimension of this imagery is that it pictures the vastness of the reservoir of evil by which we are threatened and from which we cannot deliver ourselves. "Cosmic" is not too big a word; "dragon" is not too bizarre an image.

Paul Minear has emphasized another valuable aspect of such language. "To treat human enemies as ultimate enemies constitutes deception of the first order" (*New Testament Apocalyptic*, p. 108). One of the major functions of the prophetic revelation of the power of Satan behind the scenes was to disclose to the Asian Christians their real enemy. It was not the Jews and Romans harassing and even imprisoning and killing them but the power of evil of which they too were the victims.

The Truth About Salvation and Judgment (14:1–20)

In the preceding, John has unmasked the powers that lurk behind and in the historical threats to his churches. "Salvation" seemed to call for worshiping the beast. "Judgment" seemed to be what was meted out in the Roman courts for those who refused to acknowledge the cultural values as supreme. In 12:1—13:18 John has let us see how things presently *are*. In 14:1–20 he turns to the other side of the coin of this disclosure/exposé—he will let us see how things *finally* are. First there is a picture of the salvation of those sealed with the mark of the Lamb (14:1–6), then a picture of the judgment of those who bear the mark of the beast (14:7–20).

Real salvation: the Lamb, his mark, his followers (14:1–5). In a scene that recalls 7:1–8 and anticipates 21:1—22:6, John lets us see an advance picture of the redeemed church. It is in the holy city on Mount Zion, in the presence of God the true Creator and the true Lamb that conquers. The true nature of the church is disclosed. It is a "purchased" community. "Purchased," translated "redeemed" (14:3, 4), is the same word translated "ransom" in 5:9 and "buy" in 13:17. Those who could not buy because they did not have the beast's mark are themselves bought by the blood of the Lamb and bear his mark. The redeemed community is a worshiping, celebrating community that learns the new song of the new age. They are pictured as the "first fruits," like Christ in his resurrection (I Cor. 15:20–23), the first sheaf of grain harvested from the fields and presented to God in gratitude for the pledge of the full harvest to come (cf. Exod. 34:22; Lev. 23:15–22; Num. 28:26; Deut. 16:9–12). Unlike the false prophet, no lie is found in their mouths and they are blameless. Neither of these statements is a moralistic description of the church's piety; their refusal to lie means their resistance to the idolatrous propaganda of the false prophet, the master of the lie; "blameless" is the character of a sacrifice, as their martyr's deaths were understood to be (cf. 6:9–11).

Since the picture of the Lamb's followers who "have not defiled themselves with women" (14:4–5) is subject to misunderstanding, it requires special comment. We should not take offense at the word "defile"; in John's usage it does not suggest that women or sex is "dirty." It is used as we in the nuclear age speak of objects that have been exposed to powerful radiation as "contaminated." John stands in the Hebrew tradition that

168

regarded sex, fertility, and everything associated with them as potent with the mysterious power of life (cf. the regulations for the ritual containment of the power of menstrual blood that "defiles," Lev. 15:19–31). Because these forces are so powerful, they must be ritually insulated from normal life. The same was true of the Scriptures, which were said to "defile the hands." This meant that persons engaged in special occupations or missions such as the priesthood or God's army were, during the time of their service, expected to refrain from sex, not from moralistic reasons but to insulate the sacred service from other powers (Deut. 20:1–9; 23:9–10; I Sam. 21:5). Since John pictures the church as the army of God—the very word "thousands" here conjures up military units (cf. on 7:1–8)—and as priests (1:6; 5:10), it is therefore pictured as a community of chaste "virgins." The term "virgins" is used as in Philo, *De Cher* 49–50, in a metaphorical sense for God's people, male and female. Another of John's images for the church is that of the ideal prophetic community (see on 11:1–13). Since in early Christianity prophets lived a somewhat ascetic lifestyle, leaving home and family and traveling wherever needed in the service of Christ, here the whole church is presented as "virgins" that "follow the Lamb wherever he goes." "Virgin" also connotes the pure bride of Christ, in contrast to the harlotry with which idolatry was equated (21:2 vs. 17:1). All these converging and overlapping symbols that characterize the nature of the church are suggested by John's evocative language.

Real judgment: God the Creator and Judge (14:6–20). In this section the reality of God's judgment appears in contrast to the sham judgment delivered when Christians were condemned in the Roman courts. As 14:1–5 anticipates the eschatological salvation of the new Jerusalem, 14:6–20 anticipates the coming fall of Babylon and God's judgment on those who bear the mark of the beast.

The action is carried by a series of angels who make proleptic announcements of God's judgment. The first (14:6–7) emphasizes that the true judgment will be held by the one God, the Creator—in contrast to the forces of chaos that seem to hold judgment in 13:1–18. The judgment of God is called *euaggelion* ("gospel," "good news"), a word used in the emperor cult of the words and deeds of the Caesar. While Babylon/Rome seems to prevail on earth, John lets his hearer-readers hear a second angel announce that Babylon is already fallen (14:8; cf.

169

17:1—18:24). The third angel describes the terrors in store for those who bear the mark of the beast (14:9–12)—terrors so revolting that we must comment further on their interpretation below.

After a voice resounds from heaven pronouncing blessing on those who die in the Lord (14:13)—John has the martyrs particularly in mind—a figure "like a son of man" puts the sickle to the grain harvest of the earth (14:14–16). We do not have to decide whether or not this figure is Jesus. John's evocative language conjures up associations of Daniel 7, of Jesus' words about the coming judgment in the Gospel tradition, and of the vision of Christ in 1:12–16. The grain harvest of the one like a "son of man" is followed by the grape harvest executed by other angels. The clusters are thrown into the winepress of God's wrath, and blood flows in unimaginable depth and extent (14:17–20).

Two points in these visions of judgment need further comment. First, the punishment of those who worship the beast is described as their being "tormented with fire and sulphur in the presence of the holy angels and in the presence of the Lamb" day and night without rest "for ever." Anyone who tries to imagine this infinitely-worse-than-Auschwitz picture as somehow objectively real must ask whether God or John does not here overdo it. Such a picture calls in question both justice and the character of God. (For general principles in interpreting such language, see the "Reflection: Interpreting Revelation's Violent Imagery.") Here, we might only note that such language does not function to give an objective picture of what shall in fact happen to God's enemies, the outsiders. To even ask whether Revelation "teaches" eternal torment for the damned is to misconstrue the book as a source of doctrines, to mistake its pictures for propositions. John's language does not deliver a doctrine about the fate of outsiders; it functions to warn insiders, who ponder the question "Is it such a terrible thing to participate in the Roman worship?" John regards this worship as making a this-worldly substitute for the one Creator and Lord and answers, "More terrible than you can imagine!" Christians who refused such participation were risking death and must ask, "Is there anything worse than death?" John's answer: "The judgment of God that lies beyond death, the second death, the lake of fire" (20:14). As objectifying language about what shall happen to our enemies, it is cruel beyond imagination; as confessional language, intended not to describe the fate

170

of outsiders but to encourage insiders to remain faithful, it functions precisely like the language of Jesus in the Gospels (Matt.
10:28; 25:30, 46).

A second issue in interpreting all of 14:6–20 is whether
these visions express unqualified judgment in a negative sense
or whether they also somehow represent God's redemptive
work, not only through the blood of Christ but through the
blood of the martyrs. The whole series can be interpreted as
unrelieved judgment, so that both the grain harvest and the
winepress are images for the destiny of the wicked, as in John's
prototype Joel 3:13 (so e.g., A. Y. Collins, *Apocalypse*, pp. 102–
103). A second view sees some images of salvation mixed with
images of judgment, so that the grain harvest is the ingathering
of the saved, as in the parables of Jesus, while the winepress is
a picture of God's wrath upon the condemned (so e.g., D'Aragon, "The Apocalypse"). A third view sees the whole drama in
terms of ultimate salvation, a rebirth of images that transforms
traditional pictures of judgment into pictures of salvation. G. B.
Caird has made a powerful argument in this direction, interpreting the blood of the winepress as the blood of the martyrs
(*Revelation*, pp. 188–95).

All these options tend to interpret John's imagery too much
as steno symbols that can be "decoded" into univocal statements. An approach that perceives his imagery as tensive symbols need not attempt to resolve this issue into consistent
propositional language. On the one hand, the whole section
must be interpreted as an overwhelming impressionistic picture of God's judgment. Anything less than that takes the imagery with insufficient seriousness. On the other hand, there are
images and hints, even in this judgment section, that suggest
salvation. Already in 14:4 the redeemed church has been described as the "first fruits" of the harvest, which suggests—but
does not compel—that one see the grain harvest of 14:14–16 as
the ingathering of the rest of humanity into the security of
God's kingdom. The whole judgment section 14:6–20 stands
under the rubric of the "good news" of the Creator (14:6–7). As
the grain of 14:14–16 suggests being gathered into God's kingdom, as in Jesus' parables, so the "vine" of 14:18 suggests Israel,
the People of God (Isa. 5:1–7; Jer. 2:21; Ezek. 19:10–14; John
15:1–7). That the winepress was trodden "outside the city" suggests both the place of the shedding of Jesus' blood at the crucifixion, an element of the story of the cross that had already

become traditional, and the suffering of Christians with Christ (cf. Heb. 13:11–13). The rebirth of images of 19:13–15 (see commentary there) shows that Christ's conquering cannot finally be by brute force, that his judgment must finally be the expression of his love. Such reflections do not take the edge off the terrors of the judgment of the holy God; they may make it possible to take them seriously by readers who also affirm the ultimately redemptive purpose of God expressed elsewhere in the Bible, including elsewhere in Revelation.

Revelation 15:1—16:21
The Seven Last Plagues

Chapters 15 and 16 are one unit; preaching and teaching from any text in this unit should consider the function of the unit as a whole. The seven last plagues are announced in 15:1, and the last plague is referred to in 16:21. Although the action proceeds by pouring out the "bowls/plagues" on the earth, God in his wrath/justice is the theologically operative image. When the last plague occurs, this time there is no "canceled conclusion." The "It is over" of 16:17 (NEB) is final. This series concludes with the fall of Babylon/Rome, which is the end of history; the next scene will introduce the eschaton itself.

The Victory Celebration in the Heavenly Worship (15:1–8)

The seven last plagues of God's wrath are announced in the first verse, but before proceeding with their description, John places them in a double interpretive framework. The extremely violent pictures are interpreted as an exodus scene in which biblical memory is transfigured and as a liturgical scene in which Christian worship is transfigured. (See also the "Reflection: Interpreting Revelation's Violent Imagery.")

An exodus scene—biblical memory transfigured. A "sea" appears in John's vision, the same heavenly sea as 4:6. Beside the sea stands the congregation of those who have conquered, the victorious martyr church of 7:1–8 and 14:1–5 (identified by their rejecting the mark of the beast and by their harps). As the congregation is the 144,000 of the new Israel, so the sea is the sea of the transcendent world before God's throne and also the Red Sea of biblical memory. As Israel once stood on the banks of the Red Sea and celebrated God's liberating act of the exodus, the church will stand on the shore of the heavenly sea and sing the song of Moses and the Lamb.

John has often used the exodus story as a model for God's eschatological deliverance from the oppressive "Egypt" of his own day. This section (15:1—16:21) represents John's most thorough use of this motif in Revelation. "Egypt" is Rome; "Pharaoh" is the Caesar; the eschatological woes are plagues (16:2 sores ‖ Exod. 9:10–11; 16:3–4 sea and rivers become blood ‖ Exod. 7:17–21; 16:10 darkness ‖ Exod. 10:22; 16:12 drying up the waters ‖ Exod. 14:21–22; 16:13 frogs ‖ Exod. 8:3; 16:18, 21 thunder, fire, hail ‖ Exod. 9:24); the flood of troubles through which the church must pass is the Red Sea; the triumph song is the song of Moses (and the Lamb). Even the smoke of Sinai (15:8) and the tabernacle containing the law of God's justice appears (15:5; RSV's "temple" is literally "tent" or "sanctuary" throughout this scene). As the Red Sea (Exod. 14:21) and the Jordan (Josh. 4:23) were "dried up" as part of God's liberating activity of the exodus, here the Euphrates is dried up to facilitate the final events (16:12).

As at the Red Sea, there are only two groups pictured in this section: those who have the mark of the beast because they participate in the idolatrous worship of Rome and those who have conquered/been martyred because they live according to the call of discipleship set forth in John's revelation. Such language knows no nuances. It is entirely the language of win/lose, victory/defeat, insider/outsider, us/them. This means that the description of the terrors of eschatological judgment to follow is presented as confession of praise for what happens to "us," not objective descriptions of what happens to "them." And yet the martyrs' song of 15:4 does not rejoice over the defeated enemy, as does Exodus 15, but is focused entirely on the *one* God, to whom all nations will come and *worship.* The violence of chapter 16 must be seen in the light of this introductory scene.

A worship scene—Christian worship transfigured. At the Red Sea, God's people celebrated after the fact; in Revelation, the final victory is not yet realized (on earth) but is already accomplished and celebrated in heaven, the ultimately real

173

world, and can thus already be celebrated in this world, where the worship of the earthly church participates in the worship of the heavenly sanctuary. The juxtaposition of songs of celebration with scenes of terrible judgment is thus not gleeful gloating, but neither is it merely a promise of future celebration. The message is not that "now is the time of trouble, but someday we will be able to celebrate." Rather, Christian worship anticipates the eschatological victory and celebrates it in the present. Christian worship, especially its eucharistic dimension, points "backward" to the past and understands the present in its light (the "new exodus"), points "forward" to the future victory and celebrates its reality in the present, and points "upward" to the transcendent reality of God's world, participating in the worship of the heavenly sanctuary that unites past, future, and present.

We thus perceive the importance of John's presenting this last series of plagues within the context of a worship setting. The language throughout is the language of worship and praise. The whole vision of 15:1—16:21, like all appropriate worship, is theocentric. The action proceeds as a heavenly liturgy, a stately liturgical picture of the glory of God: In response to a voice from within the heavenly sanctuary, a solemn procession of angels robed in priestly attire carry "bowls" from the tabernacle, the repository of God's law, and pour them out on the earth. In Greek ears the word translated "bowl" (*phiale,* literally "vial") connotes specifically a bowl used in offerings. The Greek Old Testament uses this word for the vessels of the tabernacle (RSV "pots") used to carry ashes from the altar (Exod. 27:3). John uses the same word in 5:8 as part of the equipment for the heavenly sanctuary. The altar itself occurs in 16:7 and recalls the heavenly altar on which the martyrs were sacrificed in 6:9–10. As the bowls are poured out on the earth to set the last plagues in motion, one gets the picture that the earthly plagues are a result of the heavenly worship in which the prayers of earthly Christians play a part (cf. 5:8; 8:3–5). As the troubled church on earth prays "Thy kingdom come" and "Come, Lord Jesus!" (22:20; cf. 22:17 and Matt. 6:10; I Cor. 16:22), its prayers are effective in the heavenly world and help to inaugurate the eschatological events of the establishment of God's kingdom. But before the final triumph, and as a part of it, the eschatological woes must be described once again, this time in their ultimate intensification.

174

The Seven Bowls of the Wrath of God (16:1–21)

The final series of eschatological woes is not a chronological continuation of the preceding ones. It refers to the same period but presents it from a different perspective. It is a vision of cosmic catastrophe in which the preceding visions are paralleled but intensified. Not merely a fourth or third, as in the first two septets, but *all* the world is struck by the blow against the sun and by the darkness, and everything in the sea dies. Not just the earth but the cosmos itself (heavens, sun, dry land, sea, rivers) is struck (16:1–8). Human rebellion against God has infected the creation itself (cf. Gen. 3:17; Isa. 24:5–6). As it is to be redeemed (21:1—22:6; cf. Rom. 8:18–23), so it passes through the judgment.

Like the plagues inflicted on Egypt in the mighty act of God's liberation of his people in the exodus, the terror of the eschatological plagues is pictured by John as a manifestation of the righteous judgment of God. No matter how severe the scenes may appear, John's point is that they are *just*. The establishment of God's reign as the goal of history is a matter of justice. The present world is not just, but no injustice happens at the eschaton. John inserts into the vivid images of terror interpretive heavenly voices that speak of God's justice (16:5, 7). When the plagues are called expressions of the "wrath of God" (introduced for the first time in 14:10, 19, and then repeatedly in this section: 15:1, 7; 16:1, 19; cf. 19:15), the expression is to be understood forensically, not emotionally.

The focus narrows from the cosmos to the representative of the world's rebellion against the creator, Rome, leading up to the climactic chapters 17—18, the fall of "Babylon." The first four plagues are cosmic, but already the fifth plague refers specifically to the throne of the beast and its kingdom, Rome (16:10).

Like the parallel sixth trumpet (9:13–21), the pouring out of the sixth bowl reveals a demonic army released to cross the Euphrates and attack the Roman civilization. This was the great phobia of the Romans, the Parthian threat writ mythologically large. Just as God dried up the Jordan to allow his people to attack the idolatrous Canaanites (Josh. 3:1—4:18), so God will dry up the Euphrates to allow the dreaded "kings of the East" to destroy the arrogant Roman civilization. We are presented with another mind-wrenching rebirth of imagery, in which not

175

only the "Parthians" but the demonic powers behind them—
dragon, beast, and false prophet—are used by God in his eschatological judgment. The kaleidoscope turns slightly, and the
imagery shifts to that of the "last battle." In the traditional
image the kings/nations of the earth are gathered against the
holy city, but are defeated by God. John can use this image in
the traditional way (see e.g., 20:7-9), but here he transmutes it
into an image of judgment: The call goes forth to assemble for
battle on the great Day of the Lord, but the place of the battle
and the object of their attack is not clear. It is certainly not
Jerusalem; is Rome itself the object of their wrath? Before we
can be sure what John intends to picture here, a discussion of
the "battle of Armageddon" (16:14-16) is necessary.

The "battle of Armageddon." Popular, uncritical interpretations of Revelation have often supposed that it predicts some
great battle at Megiddo, in northern Israel, as part of the final
events of history. These assumptions are wrong. That John is
writing "prophecy" does not mean that he is predicting historical events of the long-range future; it means that he is presenting an inspired interpretation of contemporary events for the
Christians of his own time (cf. Introduction). Revelation 16:
14-16 does not predict any historical event beyond John's own
generation. Nor is there any "battle" described. John uses the
traditional military imagery, but in his own theology the decisive victory was already won at the cross and resurrection of
Jesus (see above on 5:1-14; 12:7-12). Revelation thus contains
no descriptions of eschatological battles (cf. 19:11-21; 20:7-10).

The popular identification of "Armageddon" with Megiddo
in Israel is likewise questionable. John specifies that he is giving
the name in Hebrew, which must therefore be significant. Since
the first part of the word ("har-") corresponds to the word for
"mountain" in Hebrew, the name would mean "Mountain of
Mageddon." Since there is no such place in the Hebrew Scriptures or Palestinian geography, the hearer-readers' mind is
teased into activity—precisely what John's evocative language
calls for. By a slight adjustment in spelling, the name can be
seen as referring to biblical Megiddo, a fortress-city in northern
Israel where some battles important for biblical history were
fought (Judg. 4:4—5:31, cf. 5:19; II Kings 23:28-29). There is,
however, as modern visitors to Megiddo are surprised to learn,
no mountain at Megiddo! Like many ancient cities, the town
itself is built atop a small artificial tell. The Bible speaks of the

176

"waters" and "plain" of Megiddo (Judg. 5:19; II Chron. 35:22), but never of a "mountain of Megiddo." If John's hearer-readers had enough knowledge of Palestinian geography, they might have associated Megiddo with the nearest mountain, Mount Carmel, where Elijah defeated the idolatrous prophets of Baal (I Kings 18:20–46). This would indeed fit John's view that the prophetic Christian community stands in the tradition of Elijah in resisting Roman idolatry (cf. on 11:4–13). If, as is likely, John was originally from Palestine, he might have made this connection, but could hardly have expected it from his readers.

Another possibility argued by some scholars also calls for slightly adjusting the spelling of the mysterious "Mageddon" so that in Hebrew it would read "Assembly," and "Armageddon" would mean "Mount of Assembly" (e.g., Rissi, *Time and History*, pp. 84–85; Eller, pp. 150–51). This not only fits the context ("assemble," 16:14) but associates this text with the passage about the "mountain of assembly" in Isaiah 14:12–15, a text that portrays the "king of Babylon" in mythological terms. John could thus readily adopt imagery from this text for his eschatological pictures of the fall of "Babylon" and the defeat of its "king." Since the Babylonian king is ironically called the "bright morning star" ("O Day Star," Isa. 14:12), a title John uses for Jesus (22:16), this would be another instance of the beast's parody of the Lamb.

Probing of John's meaning of the "battle of Armageddon" thus reveals that we should not be concerned to locate it on a map or give it a date. It is not a prediction of some historical battle to be located on the map and calendar but one of his pictures of the penultimate eschatological events, the climax of the eschatological woes that John saw himself and his churches as already experiencing. The meaning of the "battle" and its outcome is John's concern, not its location in time or space. In this context the meaning seems to be that at the climax of God's eschatological judgments he will allow the "evil trinity" to gather the kings of the East, including the feared Parthians from beyond the Euphrates, for a final onslaught against rebellious Rome, something that John pictures as happening in his immediate future. In the concluding visions of this section, John pulls back from actually describing their destruction of Rome. No battle is described, no Parthians ever reach Rome. This is because he considers the final destruction of this symbol of worldly evil to be God's own work, in principle already accom-

plished in the Christ event, and because he has a detailed account of the "fall of Babylon" to present as the climax of the
eschatological woes in the next section, 17:1—18:24.

After the "seventh bowl" is poured out (16:17–21), the
shout goes forth that it is finally over (cf. NEB), the "great city"
splits and the cities of the nations fall amid the terror of the
appearance of God. The seventh and last scene points to the
appearance of God, who has not forgotten the injustice of the
arrogant human city, "great Babylon" (16:19), and now appears
as her judge. John saves the details for 20:1—22:6.

In the midst of these graphic scenes of the eschatological
future already breaking in, a voice is heard, the direct voice of
Christ speaking through his prophet: "Lo, I am coming like a
thief! Blessed is he who is awake, keeping his garments that he
may not go naked and be seen exposed!" (16:15). This is not, as
has sometimes been supposed, a misplaced verse more at home
among the messages of 2:1—3:21 (cf. 3:3). It is John's way of
reminding his hearer-readers that the visions are not to provide
speculative information about the future but are a challenge
from the living Christ for them to orient their lives in the
present toward the coming eschatological reality.

Revelation 17:1—18:24
The Fall of Babylon and the Lament

Chapters 17 and 18 are one unit concentrated on the theme
of the fall of "Babylon." Chapter 17 identifies Babylon and
announces her fall; chapter 18 is a lament for the destroyed city.
This section, though not structured as one of the series of numbered visions, is not an "interlude" or an "appendix" but a
major section of John's composition (cf. Introduction). His description of the angel that introduces the vision as "one of the
angels who had the seven bowls" (17:1) relates the fall of Babylon to the preceding "seven last plagues" as the climax to which
they were leading. When the angel that introduces the vision
of the new Jerusalem is later described in exactly the same
words (21:9), the fall of Babylon is represented as the parody
and mirror image of the Holy City. As the new Jerusalem is
John's most extensive picture of salvation, so Babylon is his most

178

extensive picture of judgment. John has deliberately structured his composition in order to place this detailed description of Babylon and its judgment immediately before his pictures of the parousia and the descent of the new Jerusalem.

Rome Is Babylon (17:1–18)

The angel takes John into the wilderness (17:3) to behold the city—not because it is located there but because the "wilderness" is the place of refuge for the People of God, from which perspective they can see the city for what it is (cf. 12:6, 14, the only other instances of "wilderness" in Rev.). John sees the city in the form of a woman—an alluring prostitute (17:1, 18). Picturing a city as a woman was common in the prophetic Jewish tradition in which John lives and from which he draws: Jerusalem was pictured as virgin (Isa. 37:22; Lam. 2:13), faithful wife and mother (Isa. 66:7–14), a married woman who became unfaithful (Ezek. 16); Nineveh and Tyre as harlot (Nahum 3:1–7; Isa. 23).

The Identification of the City

There can be no doubt that the harlot city of John's vision is Rome, "the great city which has dominion over the kings of the earth" (17:18). He refrains from saying so explicitly, not to hide his meaning from the Roman police, for his image is too transparent to conceal its meaning from even the most obtuse Roman. He wants rather to involve the imaginations of his hearer-readers in evocative symbolic language that resonates with several levels of meaning at once. His images are not one-to-one allegories that may be neatly "decoded"—they overlap and fade into each other with more than one meaning at the same time (cf. 17:9–10). For many Romans, the Great Mother goddess common in the ancient Near East had become the goddess Roma, giver of all blessings, just as she had previously become Athena for the Greeks. Archaeology has documented the presence of temples to the goddess Roma in Ephesus, Smyrna, and Pergamum (cf. 2:1, 8, 12), but all the churches to whom John wrote recognized the reversal of imagery his revelation asserts: Roma is not great mother but whore! (Christians who talked like this were not likely to be thought patriotic.)

179

Yet it is clear that John intends to picture Rome at a variety of levels: the goddess, the city of Rome, the Roman Empire astride the Mediterranean, the Caesars and the Caesar cult and the mythology associated with them, Nero and the legends associated with him (cf. on chaps. 12—13 above). The woman is "seated upon many waters," 17:1 (or: "enthroned above the ocean," NEB; or "built near many rivers," TEV; no one translation catches all the nuances). This description was originally applied to Babylon (Jer. 51:13) and was meant literally: Babylon is a city on the Euphrates, with many canals. Rome, however, is not literally a city of many waters or a seaport. The description is not a matter of geography but theology and Scripture: Rome is Babylon, enthroned upon her multinational commercial empire that spans the seas (17:15), but also sitting upon Leviathan, the sea monster representing the powers of chaos, doomed finally to destruction by the Creator. It is Rome with whom the "kings of the earth" have "committed fornication," in scriptural parlance, "engaged in idolatry." This refers not only to participation in the idolatrous worship of Roman gods, including the Caesar, but accepting Rome as the point of orientation for life in this world, that is, making Rome herself a god. It is Rome who has persecuted the People of God—John and his hearer-readers think especially of the cruelty under Nero in 64 C.E.—and is "drunk with the blood of the saints and . . . martyrs of Jesus" (17:6). Rome dresses well and drinks expensive wine, but her clothes are harlot's finery and her wine is made from the blood of God's people.

The beast on which the woman is seated is Rome, as in 13:1–8. Its seven heads represent both the "seven hills" that had been for generations the trademark of Rome and the "seven kings," the full line of Roman emperors (17:9–10). As another parody of the name God's people wear on their foreheads, harlot Rome has a name of mystery emblazoned on her forehead: "Babylon the Great" (17:5). In the biblical and Pauline tradition in which John stands, "mystery" does not mean "puzzle" but insight revealed through God's prophets (1:20; 10:7; Rom. 11:25; I Cor. 15:51; Eph. 3:3–5; Col. 1:26–27). In Jewish tradition, "Babylon" came to mean "Rome" after Rome destroyed Jerusalem in 66–70 C.E., as Babylon had done in 586 B.C.E. (cf. II Esdr. 3:1–3; I Peter 5:13).

Rome, the Beast, and the Christians

180

The most specific portrayal of Rome and her relation to John's hearer-readers is given in the description of the beast on which the woman is seated (17:8–12), which calls for particular attention. The beast image evokes several layers of meaning at once: the resurgence of the power of chaos held in check at creation but finally to be destroyed at the eschaton; the beastly empires of Daniel's vision, in contrast to the humane kingdom of the "son of man" (Dan. 7:1–14). From more recent times it evokes the persecuting imperial power, as represented in the advocates of the Caesar cult, the Caesars themselves, particularly Nero and the legends about his "return" from death at the head of an army from the East (see on 13:1–8).

John considers the phases of the "career" of the beast important enough to repeat them twice in 17:8: it "was," "is not," and "is to come." On the one hand, this cryptic description shows that the beast is a parody of the true God who "is, was, and is to come" (1:4, 8; 4:8). On the other hand, this description also serves to "locate" the reader with reference to the activity of the beast. It once "was": it is a reality that has already appeared in the past. Imperial persecution was first manifest in Nero, 64 C.E. At the moment it "is not": there is no full-scale persecution of Christians by Rome under way as John writes. John believes this has lulled many Christians into a false sense of security and an accommodation to Rome and what she stands for. But the beast is to ascend from the abyss—John sees the return of the beast as imminent and is trying to prepare his congregations for the great persecution to come. But it goes to perdition. When it appears, it is already on the way out. John is afraid his fellow Christians will surrender to an enemy already defeated. His revelation is to remove the cover (the literal meaning of *apocalypse*) and let them see the reality of things.

This same pastoral function is also the goal of the somewhat complex symbolism of 17:10–11, which interprets the situation of his churches in relation to their place in the series of Roman emperors ("kings," RSV). These and the dates of their reigns are as follows:

Julius Caesar	d. 44 B.C.E.
Augustus (Octavian)	31 B.C.E.–14 C.E.
Tiberius	14–37
Gaius (Caligula)	37–41
Claudius	41–54
Nero	54–68

Galba	68–69
Otho	69
Vitellius	69
Vespasian	69–79
Titus	79–81
Domitian	81–96
Nerva	96–98
Trajan	98–117
Hadrian	117–138

John says that the first five emperors have "fallen," have died. At the time of the writing of Revelation, he and his fellow Christians live in the time of the sixth emperor, who "is." There will be another emperor, the seventh, who will remain only a little while. Then comes the last emperor, the eighth, who is also one of the seven. This eighth emperor will rule for only a short time and will share his rule with ten kings—a motif derived entirely from John's appropriation of the imagery of Daniel 7.

This text has been important for interpreters rightly interested in locating the date of the writing of Revelation as precisely as possible. At first glance, the task seems to be simple enough: John writes in the reign of the sixth emperor (17:10). But three problems immediately emerge: (1) It is not clear with which emperor we should start counting. Is it with the first emperor? Either Julius Caesar or Augustus could be considered first, and we do not know which John would consider the first emperor. Is it with the first emperor to persecute Christians? In this case, we would begin with Nero. Is it with the first emperor to rule after Jesus' death-resurrection, who was also the first to insist on the idolization of himself with a statue (Caligula)? Interpreters have argued for each of those options. (2) We do not know which emperors to count. All of them? Only those who had "fallen" in the sense of suffering violent deaths? Only those who had been declared divine by the Senate? Are Galba, Otho, and Vitellius, who held power only briefly in the confusion after Nero's death, to be counted? By juggling different combinations of these two possibilities, various scholars have identified every emperor from Nero to Trajan as the emperor under whom John is writing. A few scholars have even decided the passage must be the interpolation of a later editor, because they assume that its purpose is to reveal the identity of the emperor under whom

John is writing, which is so different from John's practice elsewhere. (3) But the third problem is decisive: Did John intend
the number "seven" literally at all? Based on his practice elsewhere, it seems more likely that it is a symbolic number standing for the whole line of Roman emperors, whatever their
actual number (just as the "seven" churches of chapters 2—3
represent the churches of Asia—and the world).

John is writing a *pastoral letter* to address the immediate
problem of his reader-hearers, not a *puzzle* for later readers.
John was not concerned that his original hearer-readers learn
from this passage who the reigning emperor was—they knew
that already—but rather *what* he was, what he represented. He
was afraid that his fellow Christians might not recognize that
imperial power was ultimately demonic, that the current lull in
persecution was only the calm before the approaching storm.
When the "eighth" emperor appeared he would be both another parody of Jesus Christ (the true "eighth") and another
incarnation of the beastly power that had appeared in Nero.
The present distress under Domitian was only the leading edge
of the great persecution to come; when the beast appeared
again, though appearing to be powerful, it would last only a
little while, since it was already destined to go to perdition. All
this John wanted to disclose in his evocative revelation of how
things ultimately are to Christians who had to decide how to
evaluate rival claims to ultimate allegiance made by the god
represented in Rome and the God represented in Jesus Christ.
He may have chosen a deliberately imprecise means of expression in order to allow his hearer-readers to become participants
in the disclosure of the true nature of the Roman threat. John's
mode of communication calls for a discerning response, not a
simplistic identification of Rome or any other government with
the Satanic beast.

Is *Roman/Human Culture Utterly Depraved?*

Despite John's picturing the imperial persecuting power in
such dark colors, two aspects of his text should cause contemporary interpreters to hesitate to see him condemning Rome in a
wholesale fashion.

1. John writes in the time of the Domitian whose administration had exiled him to Patmos and killed Antipas (1:9; 2:13),
but John does not consider Domitian to be "the beast." He
understands that it is with the transcendent powers of evil

183

("Satan," "the dragon,") that the church struggles, but he hesitates to label his own contemporaries, actual historical personages, with Satanic labels (cf. "Reflection: Interpreting Revelation's Satan Language"). Contemporary interpreters are most true to him when they follow his restraint.

2. The lament over the fall of Babylon which immediately follows expresses two of John's views: that Satanic power has been expressed through Rome's arrogant oppression of the peoples of the world and persecution of Christians *and* that human culture is valuable, is finally the object of God's redemptive love (21:14–16)! Its perversion and requisite judgment is something to be genuinely lamented. The woman presented in chapter 17 is presented from only one side. It is a side which must be seen—the perversion of culture into arrogant, idolatrous human empire. It is arrogant human empire as such that is here condemned, not just its embodiment in Rome in John's time. But John knows there are other dimensions to human government and culture and presents these in other passages. Teaching and preaching on this passage (and the "anti-Rome" passages in Revelation in general) can let people see the seductive, demonic evil of human achievement. *Other* passages in the Bible, including some in Revelation, can point out the positive values in culture and politics.

The Self-destructive Power of Evil

John calls these bizarre pictures of evil before his hearer-readers' imaginations to disclose the powers behind the earthly thrones and to disclose that they are already doomed (17:8, 10, 11). He gives two pictures of the end of evil. They are not predictions of some future historical event but revelations of the nature of God's final victory. They are thus not to be fitted together into some chronological scheme; taken at this level they are in fact inconsistent with each other (cf. Introduction, and the discussion below on John's use of a variety of pictures for the eschatological victory of God).

In 17:12–14 the beast who appears at the end is directly defeated by the Lamb, along with the "ten kings" who are his cohorts in the last days. This is John's pictorial, not historical, affirmation that evil, however it is imagined, will finally be defeated by the power of God already manifest in the victory of the Lamb who by his cross has conquered (5:1–14). Evil is doomed because it is already defeated by God's act in Christ.

184

In 17:15–18 evil as symbolized by Babylon/Rome is defeated in a self-destructive battle. John's imagery takes a new turn here (though cf. on 9:1–12). After repeatedly picturing Rome as an embodiment of the beast, he now gives us a picture in which the beast and its allies, the ten kings, turn on Rome and destroy it. Evil is not only judged and destroyed by God; evil is self-destructive. At one level, John's hearer-readers would think of Nero returning from the underworld to lead the Parthian hordes against Rome as the instrument of God's eschatological wrath. At another level, the picture drawn from biblical imagery does not refer to particular historical nations at all but portrays the biblical God who is able to use even the powers of evil as his instruments of final judgment. Just as God once put it into the heart of pagan rulers to judge his people Israel and even destroy faithless Jerusalem, so at the eschaton God is the sovereign (even if unacknowledged) power behind the presumed thrones of this world, even of the power-behind-the-power-behind-the-thrones. When evil turns on itself and the powers fall, it is the purpose of God announced in his words spoken by the prophets that are being fulfilled (17:17).

The Fall of Babylon Celebrated/Lamented (18:1–24)

In interpreting this chapter, one of the most poignant compositions in Revelation, attention to context, sources, model, and form are all very important.

Literary and historical context. This is the last scene we see before the eschaton proper; it is the final climactic scene of the eschatological woes that precede the final coming of the kingdom of God. John has been building toward the scene of the destruction of "Babylon"; now it is here. These words celebrating/lamenting the fall of Rome are not uttered in the easy wisdom of hindsight but with prophetic insight, while Rome is at the height of her splendor and power.

Source and model. The dirge over the fall of Babylon is composed by John with materials drawn from various biblical laments, taunt-songs, and dirges over the destroyed cities of the enemies of God's people (cf. Isa. 13:21; 23:1–16; 34:11–14; 47:7–9; Jer. 50:39; 51:37; Zeph. 2:14–15). By making his lament a pastiche of quotations and allusions from biblical laments, John underscores his conviction, affirmed in the preceding chapter, that the eschatological destruction of evil represented by the fall of Babylon is the fulfillment of the words of the

185

prophets expressing the purpose of God in history; therefore it is an affirmation of the faithfulness of God. Since John draws his language from the Bible the charge of malicious vengeance sometimes leveled against him is mitigated. The command to repay Babylon "double" is not a call for vindictive injustice but an echo of the language of the Scripture (Jer. 16:18; Isa. 40:2), language directed against God's own people as well as the pagan enemy.

Form. Instead of letting us see the ultimate destruction of Babylon directly, the devastation of the evil city occurs "off-stage"—the hearer-readers perceive it only indirectly, as it is described by heavenly voices and by earthlings who lament Babylon's fall: the interpretive voice of an angel (vv. 2–3); a voice from heaven (vv. 4–8); the kings of the earth (vv. 9–10); the merchants of the earth (vv. 11–17a); those whose livelihood depend on the sea (vv. 17b–19); an angel again (vv. 21–24), forming a bracket with the angelic voice of verses 2–3. This indirect mode of communication, of which John is a master, has two advantages: (1) the hearer-readers cannot be passive but must in their imaginations construct the scene themselves from the spectators' laments, and (2) it gives them the freedom to choose whether to identify with the speakers in the drama. John does not tell his congregations how they should respond. On the one hand, the dirges of those who lament Babylon's fall can be taken as occasions for celebration. This need not be vindictive gloating but can be celebration that the justice of God finally triumphs. Indirect communication also opens the way for venting feelings of resentment and anger against enemies (in this case Rome/Babylon), as did the laments and dirges of the Old Testament on which it is based. The indirect mode of presentation also leaves the way open for Revelation's hearer-readers to join in the lamentation for a real loss of the values inherent in the great city. The hearer-reader may take the lamentations ironically and celebrate what is lamented by the speakers on the visionary stage, and/or they may actually join with them in lamenting what was good in human culture but which has now been perverted and consequently subjected to the judgment of God.

186   *What Is Wrong with "Babylon"?*

The reasons for Rome's judgment become crystal clear in the interpretative voices from heaven, and also indirectly from the lamentations of those earth-dwellers who admired Rome and hated to see her go. Adela Yarbro Collins has provided a helpful summary ("Revelation 18," p. 203):

1. **"The idolatrous and blasphemous worship offered and encouraged by Rome, especially the emperor cult."** This has headed John's list of charges throughout (cf. especially 13:1–18) and is what he means by describing Babylon as a "harlot" and charging her with "fornication," that is, idolatry, a breach of the first commandment (18:3).

2. **"The violence perpetrated by Rome, especially against Jews and Christians."** Christians who resisted the emperor cult were subject to violence or death. Yet since Babylon is condemned not only for "the blood of prophets and saints," but "of all who have been slain on earth" (18:24), we begin to see that John's announcement of judgment upon Rome/Babylon is more than the natural response of the persecuted Christian against those who enforced emperor worship. Rule-by-violence is itself condemned; "Babylon" is charged with executing Christians (John would have the Neronic persecution and the resurgence of persecution in his own time especially in view) and with killing the prophets (so that not only Rome, but faithless Jerusalem can also be "Babylon") and is responsible for "all who have been slain on earth" (18:24). Ruthless use of violence by every empire is here included in "Babylon."

3. **"Rome's blasphemous self-glorification."** She "glorified herself" (18:7) rather than God; as "Eternal Rome" she considers herself the absolute and eternal ruler, and says "A queen I sit . . . mourning I shall never see." Her hubris is an affront and challenge to God the only sovereign. *Strenos* and *streniao* of 18:3, 7, 9, rendered by various forms of "wantonness" and "luxury" in many translations, might better be rendered as "hubris" or "arrogance" (so Sweet, p. 268).

4. **"Roman wealth."** No one can fail to notice the massive use of economic and commercial language in this lament (18:3; 11–19, 23). The use of actual violence against Christians was still rare in John's time. Economic pressure was far more prevalent (cf. on 13:18). They faced external economic pressures to participate in the pagan culture and to share its values, just as they faced internal pressures of longing for the dainties and the good life of Roman prosperity, from which too strict commitment to the Christian faith might exclude them. Once again, however, Babylon is condemned for more than exerting economic pres-

187

sure on Christians that might contribute to their loss of faith; Rome's economic policies of living in luxury at the expense of the poor is condemned as such, quite apart from its direct religious consequences.

Yet not everything about the "Great City" was evil. There is some genuine pathos in the lament that the sound of music, skilled fashioners of civilization, the voice of bride and bridegroom are to vanish (18:21–23) and be replaced by a dead and haunted city (18:2). John himself has some admiration for the great city (17:6–7), even in its perverted state. "She has fallen, to be sure, but the poet walks among her ruins feeling the weight of the loss and singing God's victory with a heavy heart" (Craddock, p. 277). All that is good and valuable will be redeemed and will be present in the Holy City (21:1—22:6, cf. especially 21:24–26).

What Are Christians to Do?

Here as elsewhere, the indicative of John's description contains an implicit imperative of Christian action. More revolutionary-minded modern Christians may be surprised or disappointed that John does not call for his hearer-readers to overthrow Rome and establish a more just rule. There are good reasons for the absence of such a call to violent action: (1) it was not a real possibility in John's situation, where his hearer-readers were relatively powerless over against Rome's might; (2) John had witnessed the catastrophe—perhaps at first hand—of the Zealot attempt at liberation of Palestine which brought on the disastrous war of 66–73; (3) his theology that the ultimate power of the universe is the power of God manifest and effective in the self-sacrificing power of the Lamb (see on 5:1–14) prohibited him from advocating violence; (4) his apocalyptic theology of the imminent end of history made such action not only unnecessary and futile but a challenge to God's own claim to destroy "Babylon" and establish justice. Modern Christians cannot share all of these presuppositions with John and thus may be more inclined to use force in the effort to replace tyrannical governments with a more just political structure. Yet such efforts must be viewed in the light of the message of the Bible as a whole, including the apocalyptic theology of Revelation.

188 However, not even John offers a license for passive acceptance of injustice and listless waiting for God to establish eschatological justice. Christians find themselves addressed by two, but

only two, commands in this chapter (18:6–7 are directed to the eschatological agents of God's judgment, not to Christians):

1. "Come out of her, my people." At one level, John and his readers may have thought of actual Christians living in Rome who are advised to depart before the coming judgment strikes. Yet the major thrust of this command cannot be literal—it is heard by John's hearer-readers in the churches of Asia, not by Roman Christians. The call to "come out" is not a matter of geographical relocation but of inner reorientation; such will then become effective in the ways Christians live their lives in Ephesus and in the other towns of Asia addressed by John; it will become effective also in the way readers of every time and place resist the values of the "Great City" and orient themselves to the coming justice of God in the Holy City.

2. "Rejoice." The Christians of John's churches are called to join in the rejoicing of heaven that the heavenly court has already reversed the judgment of this world's systems. This courtroom language had a particular meaning for Christians condemned in the Roman courts of John's day; it can be good news also to Christians of every age who see their own commitments rejected in the value system of the culture but vindicated in the decisions of the heavenly court. The church does not have to postpone its celebration until the new Jerusalem. Amid the injustice of this world, and without resignation to it, the church joins with the saints, apostles, and prophets of all the ages in celebrating in its worship the victory of God's justice, already pronounced in the divine throneroom, in the sure hope that it will be realized ultimately throughout all creation.

PART THREE

God Redeems the "Holy City"

REVELATION 19:1—22:21

Each of the three major divisions of Revelation begins with a transcendent scene of the glory of God and/or Christ, from which proceeds a sevenfold vision. In Part One the inaugural vision of the glory of Christ (1:9–20) results in the seven messages to the churches (2:1—3:21). Part Two is introduced by the vision of the throneroom of God and the Lamb (4:1—5:14), which opens into the sevenfold visions of the last plagues, culminating in the fall of Babylon (6:1—18:24). In Part Three the final septet of visions portraying the parousia, last battle, binding of Satan, millennium, defeat of Gog and Magog, last judgment, and new Jerusalem (19:11—22:21) is likewise preceded by a vision of the heavenly glory of God (19:1-11).

This opening scene is parallel to that of the second major division (4:1—5:14). Both begin with "after this," both picture the worship of the twenty-four elders, both refer to the heavenly voice and the throne. Although this is a new and final act of the eschatological drama, continuity with the preceding is maintained by evoking once again the preceding lament over the fall of Babylon. In contrast to the dirge over the dead and silent city which had been usurped by the false rule of the beast, there is the song of praise to God, the true ruler of all, who has judged and avenged the injustice practiced by the oppressive imperial city of earth.

191

Revelation 19:1–10
Hallelujah Choruses Praise God's Victory

God is praised by acclamations of "Hallelujah" and "Salvation and glory and power belong to our God" (19:1). "Hallelujah," found only in this passage in the New Testament, is an English transliteration of the word often found in the Psalms translated "Praise the LORD." "Salvation to our God," rather than being a descriptive statement, is an acclamation of praise, like "Hail to thee" or like the "thine is the kingdom and the power and the glory" which concludes the Lord's Prayer (Matt. 6:13, note). It is the language of confession and worship, not the language of description. The hallelujah choruses of the heavenly worship are sung by the "great crowd" (v. 1), reminiscent of the triumphant church of faithful martyrs already in heaven (cf. 7:9–10), by the twenty-four elders, and by the four living creatures (see commentary on 4:4–8). Then the boundaries that separate heavenly and earthly worship grow thin, and a voice from the throne invites/commands all God's servants, including the hearer-readers of Revelation in the worship services of the Asian churches, to join in praise to God (v. 5; cf. 5:11–14; 8:3–5).

"Salvation to our God" is a victory acclamation. God is praised because he has defeated and judged the arrogance of earthly empire and has taken his power and begun to reign *de facto* as king. God had never abdicated his kingship, nor had he been dethroned despite the pretensions of earthly claims to sovereignty. Yet usurpers had falsely operated in this world as though they were its rightful lords. The eschatological events now beginning only disclose what had always been the case: God alone is the true sovereign of the world. The community of heaven and earth celebrates that this is now becoming effective and manifest, that God's eternal kingship has now become actual and concrete in the judgment of Babylon, and he has "begun to reign" (ingressive aorist, as in the similar scene of 11:17). The jubilation over the judgment of "Babylon" (19:2) is thus not gloating but the celebration that God has reversed Rome's judgments against the Christians in a higher court and has made it manifest that he is the true judge. It is important to John that God's justice finally prevails and that it be *seen* to prevail.

Even with all the language of judgment, the scene never ceases to be a worship scene. The smoke of Babylon that ascends "forever" is only a grisly contrast to the incense of the heavenly worship (5:8; 8:3–4). Worship celebrates the "mighty acts of God," not our pious feelings. The voices in the heavenly sanctuary celebrate the (in the perspective of the vision) past judgment of God on Babylon; they also announce the festive celebration to come: the marriage feast of the Lamb. Like the Hebrew Scriptures (Hos. 2:14–20; Isa. 62:5; Jer. 2:2), the Gospels (Mark 2:19; John 3:29), and the Pauline tradition in which John stands (II Cor. 11:2; Eph. 5:25–32), John pictures God/Christ as the bridegroom and the People of God, Israel/Church, as the bride. In a related image the redeemed community are the wedding guests (Matt. 22:1–14; 25:1–13). The present is thought of as the time of courtship, promise, and engagement. The Bridegroom, "absent" for now, will return to join the bride and the guests in a festive wedding celebration. It is a happy image of reunion, intimacy, community, and festivity. The blessing pronounced in verse 9 is, like all beatitudes, an indicative statement for those already invited and who have accepted the invitation, as implied by the perfect participle translated "invited." It also functions indirectly as an invitation to those not yet decided, an invitation underscored by the angel's somewhat abrupt announcement that "these are true words of God." Although this invitation is taken up in a profoundly ironic sense in the next vision (19:17), true closure is made in the final vision (21:1), with the description of the redeemed community as the Bride prepared for her Husband. The first announcement of the wedding feast in 19:7 is an invitation to the hearer-reader, sealed by God himself, to share in the eschatological wedding party at the consummation of the ages.

Worship is the dominating note of the concluding scene of this vision. In an astounding scene, John, who has proclaimed such strict warnings against worshiping anything or anyone except the one God, himself bows in worship before the angel/Spirit who communicates the revelation (19:10). The purpose of this little charade becomes immediately clear, as the angel denies that he belongs to the category of deity and places himself in the same category as John: a servant of God, a vehicle of revelation. We know that in some of the churches in Asia angelic beings were exalted, dangerously confused with Christ, and worshiped (Col. 2:18; cf. II Cor. 11:14). John was not in danger of confusing God and Christ with angelic beings, but his churches in which charismatic phenomena were alive might have developed too high a view of the spirit/angel phenomena they experienced (cf. Gal. 1:8–9).

John includes this scene so that his hearer-readers could overhear the rebuke reminding him and them that the Spirit that inspires prophecy is "the testimony of Jesus" (v. 10). The Greek genitive "of Jesus" here has three senses which are inseparable: (1) Prophecy is bound indissolubly to the testimony the earthly Jesus gave as he faced the Roman authorities (subjective genitive), (2) to the testimony from the risen Jesus identified as the Word of God (1:2, 9; 19:9) (genitive of origin), and (3) to the message of the church centered on the crucified earthly Jesus (objective genitive). As God identifies himself as the one revealed in Jesus, so Jesus is the Word of God (19:13). "Jesus" stands on the divine side of reality as the definitive revelation of God, the "human face of God." God-who-reveals-himself-through-Christ, and no one else, is to be worshiped.

Revelation 19:11—22:5
Seven Visions of the End

With 19:11 the prelude to the end is over and the absolutely final events of history are portrayed in seven scenes: the return of Christ, the last battle, the binding of Satan, the thousand-year reign, the defeat of Gog and Magog, the last judgment, and the descent of the new Jerusalem. Just as the first two major parts of the book have a sevenfold structure, so has the major division which delineates the final events. "Then I saw . . ." is the usual structural marker (19:11, 17; 20:1, 4, 11; 21:1), missing only at 20:7, where it is clear that a new scene begins. Unlike the first two parts of the book, where the narrative is structured more diachronically, John does not number the last visions, thereby avoiding the false idea that he is giving a strictly chronological progression of the eschatological events. The order of scenes is only loosely chronological, with overlapping and synchronous

194

imagery. There is no reason to suppose, with R. H. Charles'
classic commentary, that an original clear chronology has been
damaged by an obtuse redactor, so that the "original" order
must be restored by the modern interpreter (II, 144–54). Nor
should we strain the text and ourselves to discover a consistent
pattern of thought developed in this series of pictures of the
End (as in Rissi, *Future*, pp. 29–38). Rather, with "kaleidoscopic
changes of metaphor" (Caird, p. 243), each picture is intended
to say something about the character of the End as such, not
merely describe one "part" of the final drama. Here is no calen-
darization of the End, but a tour through an eschatological art
gallery in which the theme of God's victory at the end of history
is treated in seven different pictures, each complete in itself
with its own message and with little concern for chronology.

Parousia (19:11–16)

John's standpoint seems to be again on the earth, as it was prior
to being called up into heaven at 4:1. He sees heaven opened,
but instead of being called into heaven, he sees a mighty warrior on a white horse descending to earth. Some motifs familiar
to Jewish tradition are evoked by John's language. Wisdom of
Solomon, describing God's judgment on Egypt at the exodus,
speaks of "thy [God's] all-powerful word [that] leaped from
heaven, from the royal throne, into the midst of the land that
was doomed, a stern warrior carrying the sharp sword of thy
authentic command" (18:15).

Likewise, the "white horse" reminds the hearer-reader of
the first apocalyptic horseman of 6:2, the two images thus brack-
eting the intervening depiction of the last plagues, but the rider
on the white horse of 19:11–16 is not to be identified with that
of 6:1–2 (see commentary there). Here, there can be no doubt
that the figure is Jesus: he has the same flaming eyes as in the
vision of Christ in 1:14, the same sword of the word of God
proceeds from his mouth (1:16; 2:12), he is named by the same
names as in his messages to the churches ("Faithful and True,"
3:14; cf. 1:5), he bears the name of the definitive self-revelation
of God, "Word of God."

The figure might well be called "Jesus the Conqueror." In
a picture without parallel in the New Testament's portrayals of
the parousia (Mark 13; Luke 17; 21; I Thess. 4; II Thess. 1; I Cor.
15), Jesus rides a white war horse at the head of the armies of
heaven. He is the designated Messiah who will rule the nations

195

with a rod of iron (Ps. 2:9); he wears the bloody garments of the warrior god of Isaiah 63:1–3; on his head are the many diadems of his rightful sovereignty over the world; he properly bears the title claimed by the Caesars, "King of kings and Lord of lords."

This militaristic imagery has seemed to some Christians to be too alien to be applied to Jesus of Nazareth, the Prince of Peace (Isa. 9:6; cf. Matt. 21:1–9). Yet, though not all of his interpreters have remembered, John has not forgotten the definitive picture of the nature of Christ's conquest already given in 5:1–14. The death by which he conquers is his own, the once-for-all offering of his life on the cross. John uses all of the traditional messianic imagery, but he consistently asks the hearer-reader to interpret the Lion as the Lamb, as he himself does, even in this bloody scene. This conqueror destroys his enemies, not with a literal sword, but with the sword of his mouth; his only weapon is his word, the Word of God which he himself is (19:13). The word for "rule" (*poimainei*, 19:15), also means "shepherd," evoking both Psalm 23 and Revelation 7:17, "the Lamb will be their shepherd," which uses exactly the same word. The conquering rider arrives wearing a garment dipped in blood. Before the "last battle" ever begins, his garments are already bloody with his sacrifice of himself (1:5; 5:9). In contrast to the divine warrior of Isaiah 63:1–3, the source for this imagery, this blood is not the blood of his enemies but his own martyr blood in union with the martyr blood of his followers who, like him, have suffered/testified at the hands of Rome. This is the meaning of the fact that he treads (Greek *patei* is here present tense, not future as in the RSV) the winepress of God's wrath (see commentary on 14:17–20). This view that the eschatological Divine Warrior is red with his own blood rather than that of his enemies, while championed by the Church Fathers, has been challenged by some modern scholars and pronounced "absurd" by one (Müller, p. 327). Yet it is not absurd for one who can define "conquering" as "dying" and "Lion" as "Lamb" (5:1–7). It is analogous to the idea that Christians wash their garments and make them white in the blood of the Lamb (7:14). John's theology as a whole calls for this interpretation. He uses the ancient *form* of portraying the ultimate victory of God as winning a great battle in which those who have resisted God are slaughtered. But he fills this with new *content*. This is simply what has happened in the Christian confession as such, that the Christ, the triumphant military king, is Jesus, the crucified man of Nazareth, who was crucified not as preliminary to his victory but as his victory.

The "armies of heaven" (19:14) may be simply the angelic hosts that were expected in both Jewish and Christian apocalyptic tradition (Test. Levi 3:3; 1QM 12:1–5; 19:1; Matt. 25:31; Mark 13:27; II Thess. 1:7–8), but the image may also properly evoke the triumphant church in heaven. These are also "conquerors," but like their leader their conquest is that they have been faithful unto death (2:10; 3:21). They can be pictured as in heaven and thus returning with Jesus at the parousia, not because they have been earlier "raptured" (in contrast to modern dispensationalist theory), taken to heaven to escape the eschatological trouble, but because they have been taken to heaven in the same manner as their Leader—through death. They are thus identical with the martyr church previously pictured as already triumphant in heaven (7:9–17; 14:4; 17:14), and wear the same white linen garment that signals the faithful martyr church (19:14; cf. 6:11; 7:14; 19:8; 22:14). In John's paradoxical imagery their garments are white because they have washed them in the blood of the Lamb, and his are red because he has died for all, even those he "conquers" in the eschatological "battle." Unlike some portrayals of the eschatological battle (e.g., the War Scroll of the Qumran community), in Revelation the saints do not participate in the final battle. The victory belongs to God/Christ alone, and was already achieved in the Christ event that spans incarnation and crucifixion.

This is the One we meet at the end of history. We should note that the second coming does not in fact play a large role in John's eschatology. It is only one of several pictures, described much more briefly than the new Jerusalem. And yet it is an important symbolic way of picturing the goal of history. John's first response to the implied question "What will the End be like?" is to give us a picture of the return of Christ. As God's definitive revelation was not in an abstract principle, a law, a book, or a thing, but a *person,* so at the End we meet not something but Someone. As the Bible's pictures of ultimate beginnings are personal (not a Big Bang but "In the beginning God . . ."), so also its pictures of the End are neither bang nor whimper but the God revealed in Christ. Though pictured in transcendent apocalyptic imagery, John intends to say that at the End of all things we meet not a stranger or newcomer but One we know. It is return and reunion, wedding celebration

197

after a long engagement, not the arrival of an alien. At the End of history we confront no utterly unknown mystery, no abyss of nothingness, no figure of apocalyptic fantasy. We are awaited by the One who has already made himself known in the life and death of Jesus of Nazareth, and has made everything different by his appearing. The theological symbol of the second coming means that the ultimate future makes effective and manifest to all the reality that has already appeared in history in the person of Jesus, at present visible only through eyes of faith.

The idea of a second coming of Christ is one aspect of a set of tensive symbolic pictures which are not to be rationalized or harmonized. John is at one with New Testament theology in general in holding several pictures of the advent of Christ together without forcing them into a false conceptual consistency.

1. Christ came as the revelation of God and never left. Christ remains in the world, is present not only to and with his church but in the lives of those who do not recognize him (Matt. 1:23; 18:20; 25:31–46; 28:20). All the indications of the Holy Spirit's presence in the church and the world, identified as the continuing presence of Christ, belong to this way of thinking (Mark 13:11; John 14:15–17, 25–26; 15:26; 16:7–15; Rom. 8:9–10). John affirms this view in Revelation (1:13, 20; 2:1).

2. Alongside this view, often in the same author and document, is the view that Christ has in fact departed, but that he makes himself present from time to time; he "comes" again in judgment and grace, within the events of history and the experience of the church and individuals (John 14:1–3). This view is conditional: Christ comes in judgment if the church or individual does not repent. Christ comes in grace to make himself known in the church's worship (Luke 24:35). John affirms this view in Revelation (2:5, 16; 3:3, 20).

3. Not as an alternative to the first two views, but also not reducible to them, is the view that Christ is absent in heaven but will return unconditionally at the end of history to bring this age to fulfillment and establish God's new order. John affirms this view in the text before us. The future "coming" of Jesus at the end of history is not reducible to the repeated conditional "comings" within history. John uses all these pictures and does not attempt to harmonize them. He knows that his visions do not and cannot reveal how things ultimately are, that his pictures are at least one remove from claiming to capture the

divine mystery (cf. the Introduction and commentary on 10:4 above). Like the God of the exodus whom he represents, the returning Messiah not only has names that reveal his character and function (Faithful and True, Word of God, King of kings), he also has a name known only to himself (19:12).

Last Battle (19:17–21)

The picture of the parousia merges with that of the last battle. This is an image with a long and venerable history. From the mythical pictures of ancient Near East religion, Israel adopted and adapted the image of the primeval battle between the deity and the chaos monster. Though provisionally defeated by the act of creation, the struggle goes on, and the power of chaos erupts in the historical troubles of the People of God. But God is the warrior leader of his people, who is pictured as leading them in battle against their historical enemies, who will one day win the decisive battle against the chaos monster, thus bringing the reign of evil to an end once for all. In apocalyptic literature God's salvation of Israel from historical enemies, the wartime longing for the return to the good life, and the joyous celebration of victory when the conflict is finally over are all projected onto a cosmic, eschatological screen, where God defeats the ultimate enemy in a final battle (Ezek. 38—39; II Esdr. 12; II Bar. 70—74; 1QM 18). John's Christianized version of this apocalyptic picture is presented in 19:17-21.

Christ and his heavenly army are on the one side, opposed on the other side by two combined groups. (1) Opposed to Christ are rebellious human beings—not just the "high and mighty," but also the little people, even slaves (19:18; cf. the same motif in 6:15; 13:16). Revelation's protest is more than the sociological reality of oppressed people resenting their oppressors. Though John and his community belong to the marginal, relatively powerless victims of injustice at the hands of the powerful, the conflict he pictures is not between haves and have-nots, first and second versus third world, oppressors versus oppressed but between rebellious humanity and its Creator and Lord. (2) The primary opposition is not the historical, finite, this-worldly human community but the transpersonal powers of evil that have inspired and deceived them, as symbolized by the beast and false prophet. Both groups are "defeated" by Jesus the Conqueror, but in different ways.

199

No battle is described; there could be none in John's theology. The decisive battle was won long ago. The End only makes that victory effective and manifest. Without a struggle, in a manner reminiscent of the messianic king of Isaiah 11:1–5, the transcendent powers of evil are taken and cast into the transcendent place of destruction, the lake of fire (19:20). The historically rebellious human community, the "kings of the earth" and the "peoples" that follow them, "great and small," are "killed" with the "sword" and receive the awful judgment reserved for those who have rebelled against God. They too participate in the final great supper of God. The motif of the invitation to the messianic banquet, the wedding feast of the Lamb (19:9), is taken up again in 19:17, this time in a grisly ironic tone. John offers his hearer-readers an invitation to an eschatological meal, and lets us choose whether it is to be the wedding celebration of the Lamb or the slaughter-meal of the vanquished. As in the eschatological reversal of Zephaniah 1:7–9 (and using the language and imagery of Ezek. 39:4, 17–20), those who supposed they were to be guests turn out to be the menu (19:21). It is a fearfully revolting picture. Yet this is not the only, or final, picture that we see of them (cf. the commentary on 20:3, 8; 21:24–26; 22:2, as well as the "Reflection: Universal Salvation and Paradoxical Language"). John's imagery gives us compelling pictures that communicate both terror of rejecting the Creator and celebration that follows from receiving his grace, but the impossibility of fitting them into one conceptual picture makes clear that both God's judgment and God's grace are more than we can imagine.

Satan Bound (20:1–3)

If we can free our own imaginations from the chains of literalism, what a dramatic picture we see in this chaining of the dragon! An angel with lasso and key swoops down from heaven and without a struggle Satan, whose time has come (12:12; cf. Matt. 8:29), is bound and cast into the abyss. The threefold verbs of 20:3, "threw," "shut," and "sealed," have the same ring of finality as our "signed, sealed, and delivered."

In the preceding visions we have seen Satan's agents disposed of, as the beast and false prophet disappear into the lake of fire (19:20). The symbols of rebellious, self-deifying human empire and those who promote its worship are gone forever. But the dragon, Satan, the personification of the ultimate power of evil, is still at large. Will he again find a way to deceive humanity and begin the cycle all over again? Some sour voice is present at the celebration of every victory: "Yes, but what about . . . ?" So long as the power of evil is free at all, these cynical voices always have a point and an audience. John addresses the question of the ultimate destruction of evil with a dual visionary response. In one picture, evil is overpowered and imprisoned while the world still endures (20:1–3); in the other, evil is finally destroyed and the threat is removed forever (20: 10).

This scene of the binding of Satan deserves its own treatment in preaching and teaching, since it is not merely the prelude to the millennium but a separate vision with its own picture of the End. Like other visions in this series, it begins with its own introductory formula, "I saw." The repetition of this formula at 20:4 brackets 20:1–3 as a unit. The scene attains closure in 20:3 with the release of Satan, although this is not narrated until 20:7. The theme with which it deals is a discrete motif in apocalyptic tradition, independent of millennial ideas.

John here takes up a motif rich with traditional connotations. Iranian religion, which forms the ultimate background of many apocalyptic images, also has the picture of the evil serpent Azi-Dahaka being chained up at the End. The later apocalyptic sections of the Old Testament had already adopted this motif, as Isaiah 24:22 illustrates: the power of evil represented by the host of heaven and kings of the earth "will be gathered together as prisoners in a pit; they will be shut up in a prison." As in Revelation, this is a temporary holding station before their final judgment. This motif of the eschatological "binding" or "imprisonment" of the powers of evil was developed in later apocalyptic thought, Jewish and Christian, in a variety of ways: I Enoch 10:4–10; 18:12—19:1; 21:1–6; Testament of Levi 18:12; cf. Mark 3:26–27; 5:3; II Peter 2:4; Jude 6.

John will give us an impressionistic picture of what a devil-free world might look like in his next picture (20:4–6). Here, he singles out "deceiving the nations" as the work of Satan in this world. The devil's work is not merely tempting individuals to sin. (See the "Reflection: Interpreting Revelation's Satan Language.") "The nations" is in John's language the same as "the Gentiles," "the pagans," the "heathen." They are destined to be "healed" and considered as people of God (see 21:3; 22:2). Just as individuals are part of God's good creation, and therefore not inherently evil or rebellious but have been victimized by the evil structures in which their lives are enmeshed, so the nations themselves are not only the perpetrators of evil but its victims. With the "binding of Satan" this deceitful activity is brought to an end, and not only individual persons but, above all, national and social structures get to breathe the free air of an undemonized existence.

The picture of the eschatological binding of Satan is more than a picture of hope for the future. It says something about the present: there is no ultimate dualism. The power of evil, deadly real though it be, is temporary and finally operates by permission of the one God. The victory of God already accomplished in the Christ event, though real, is presently hidden. This hidden reality, already apparent to the eyes of faith, but only to them, will finally become manifest to all.

All of this is described in the indicative mode. But, as always in biblical theology, the indicative contains a veiled imperative. John's readers in the cities of Asia are indirectly asked whether their lives have been oriented to the apparent reality of the "Great City," open to empirical observation, or to the true reality of the "Holy City," to be revealed to all in the future but now revealed through the prophet to the church in "what the Spirit says to the churches" (2:7).

The Millennium (20:4–6)

John calls before our imaginations a scene in which the Christ, God's anointed king, will finally reign on earth, and his people with him. Although Christian faith offered Christian believers the sure hope for eternal life as an element of Christian faith, it was not personal survival beyond the grave but the social and historical hope for Christ's reign on this earth that was at the center of the early Christian vision. After Satan is bound (20:1–3), martyred Christians are raised from the dead and with Christ reign on earth as priests and kings for a thousand years, the "millennium." Although the millennium has attracted much attention from interpreters, it is not a quantitatively large item in John's eschatological repertoire, occurring only in this brief passage in his entire composition (and found nowhere else in the New Testament). He devotes much more space, for instance, to the series of eschatological plagues of Part Two (6:1—18:24). In John's "chronology," he uses 6:1—18:24 for three and a half years, and three verses for a thousand years! It is an abuse of John's own structure to make "the millennium"

202

the interpretative key to his whole revelation. Like the picture of the second coming, which also receives relatively little space, the picture of the millennium is only one of John's ways of thinking about the End.

Yet, it is *one* way. We will focus the eyes of our imagination on this one scene in John's gallery of eschatological pictures. The scene is on this earth. The new heaven and new earth appear in another scene, 21:1—22:5, but this scene takes place on this earth as the end and fulfillment of this world's history. This is another way John has of affirming this world as God's good creation, which shall not be kept forever in a state of bondage to alien powers but shall finally come into its own (cf. Matt. 5:5–6; 6:10; Rom. 8:19–23). And yet in contrast to pictures of the eschatologically renewed earth in traditional Jewish apocalypticism, John's description of the millennial earth is very restrained. There is nothing like the picture from II Baruch 29: "The earth will also yield fruits ten thousandfold. And on one vine will be a thousand branches, and one branch shall produce a thousand clusters, and one cluster will produce a thousand grapes, and one grape will produce a cor [40 gallons] of wine." Rather, all of John's attention is focused on the *persons* who experience millennial fulfillment.

Without explanation, "thrones" come into focus. Figures are seated on the thrones, but John does not immediately identify them. The next phrase can be translated "judgment was given *to* them" (i.e., they were given the authority to be judges, as RSV, NEB, and most English translations interpret) or "judgment was given *for* them" (i.e., the case was decided in their favor, as in Daniel 7:9, on which the imagery of this passage is dependent). Since, as we shall see, John is intent on calling only one group before our imagination, we should not picture those seated on the thrones as any different from faithful Christians themselves. This is in accord with traditional apocalyptic imagery in which the People of God will participate in the eschatological reign as kings and judges (Matt. 19:28; Luke 22:30; I Cor. 6:2–3; and cf. previously in Rev. 1:6; 5:10). These eschatological kings and judges are identified as those who have been beheaded because of the testimony of Jesus and the word of God, using the same formula that has become standard for faithful Christian witness in John's churches (1:2, 9; 6:9; 12:11, 17; 19: 10). The only persons we see in this scene are the faithful martyrs who are raised from the dead to participate with Christ in

203

the eschatological rule during the thousand-year reign, who are further described as blessed, reigning as priests (20:6). These are specifically identified as those who had not worshiped the beast or its image and had not received its mark, those who had not participated in the emperor cult. The scene is thus intensely focused to portray only one picture: the eschatological reign of the martyr church.

Does this mean that John expects all faithful Christians to be martyred? Since an affirmative response to this question has seemed extreme to some, it has been suggested that the sentence structure of 20:4 means that John saw two groups participating in the millennium: martyrs *and* Christians who resisted the idolatry of the Caesar cult, but were not killed. It is probably better to see John as not interested in offering a speculative answer to the question as to whether or not all faithful Christians will be beheaded in the persecution he believed to be approaching. Rather, as in the analogous images of the church in 7:1–17 and 11:4–13, the imagery represents one group, not one group of martyrs and another group of non-martyrs. The church as a whole is pictured as a church of martyrs. Whether or not John literally expected every faithful Christian to be martyred, he saw faithfulness even to death as the essence of the Christian life in his situation and pictures the triumphant church as having been faithful.

True to what he has proclaimed all along (1:6; 5:9–10; 11:4), John here pictures the period of eschatological victory in which the faithful People of God will find their fulfillment as "priests" and "kings." As the "new Israel," the church assumes the role of the People of God as a "royal priesthood" (Exod. 19:6). Their characterization as "priests" and "kings" is a description of their nature, not of functions they are to exercise during the millennium. His portrayal of Christians as "priests" and "kings" is non-inferential language which makes it useless to ask "to whom" they shall be priests or "over whom" they shall rule (see below).

John intends to portray the nature of the fulfilled Christian life itself as *priestly* existence. As the true People of God, the church of priests is a worshiping community elected by God that lives in the presence of God, treading holy ground not permitted to others. As he uses the martyr image to express the nature of the church as a whole, so he uses the priest image to characterize the meaning of belonging to the People of God as

204

such. To be a priest is an essential aspect of what it means to be a member of the People of God. There is, however, a secondary connotation evoked by this image. The People of God exists in the world not for its own sake but for the sake of the world. This was the case for Israel (Isa. 42:1–4; 42:6; 49:1–6; 51:4; 60:3), and this is how it is for "Israel" as it continues in the church. The church as the true Israel mediates between God and the world. The priestly nature of the church symbolizes that it is not self-centered, that it exists for others, and it represents hope for the human community as such.

John intends to portray the nature of the fulfilled Christian life itself as *royal* existence. As the true People of God, the church of kings is not indulging itself in lording it over others (there are no "others" in this picture!), but is experiencing the liberty of having finally been set free from the powers that have enslaved and robbed human life of its inherent freedom (cf. Rom. 8:18–25, where Paul develops a similar point). The picture thus functions to encourage John's hearer-readers to faithfulness, to announce the vindication of those already martyred, and to affirm the goodness of this creation as the setting of the martyrs' triumph. Satisfying curiosity about the program of the eschaton is not its function.

Later interpreters, who misunderstood John's pictorial language as objectifying, propositional, and chronological (see Introduction, "In Apocalyptic Language and Imagery") developed the terms "pre-millennial" (Christ returns to earth before the millennium), "post-millennial" (the parousia occurs only after the triumph of the kingdom of God on earth for a millennial period), and "a-millennial" (there will be no literal millennium, either before or after Christ's return). If John himself is forced into this scheme, he should be labeled "pre-millennial," since the parousia occurs in 19:11–16 and the "millennium" not until 20:4–6. If forced into this scheme, the interpretation offered in this commentary is "a-millennial." Yet both labels would indicate a major misunderstanding of the nature of John's eschatological language. To understand the millennium only as a segment in a chronological series of events that may be plotted on a calendar or chart is to miss the theological message communicated by its own pictorial medium. If one understands this language in an objectifying sense, one must for instance attempt to identify the subjects over whom Christians "reign" and for whom they are "priests" during the thousand-

205

year period. As a possible answer to this question, "the nations" can be brought in from other scenes (19:15; 21:24, 26). If one attempts to attain a consistent picture by combining references from these different scenes, one could (falsely) infer that during the millennium the pagan nations continue to exist alongside the faithful church, which will rule over them and/or evangelize them, converting them from their previous hostility (19:15) to become proper citizens of the new Jerusalem (21:26). By this means, a picture of what happens during the millennium is constructed; it makes "logical" sense within our inferential system and it maintains the "logical consistency" of the interpreter's reconstructed calendar for the End. But such a calendar is not pictured by John at all, and one "reconstructs" it only at the cost of effectively losing the message communicated by John's pictorial language. This is analogous to objectifying the protological pictures of Genesis 1—4, with the result that instead of focusing on the meaning of the story of Cain in 4:17–26 one feels constrained to raise such questions as where Cain obtained his wife. In interpreting each of John's pictures of the End, preaching and teaching attuned to the medium of the text will not use it to obtain supposed increments of information about the eschatological events which may then be added together to present John's "teaching about the End," whether "pre-", "post-", or "a-" millennial. Rather, remembering that no one picture of the End can do justice to the eschatological message John proclaims, the message of *this* picture will be allowed to impress itself on the imagination of the interpreter. Effective preaching and teaching will then attempt to facilitate the grasping of John's visionary picture by the imaginations of modern hearer-readers in all its symbolic power.

For the modern interpreter to "get the picture," it is helpful to understand that the idea of a millennial period at the end of history was not original with John, but was a part of the tradition he inherited. The distinctive elements John wants to emphasize become apparent as we compare and contrast his picture with those of his tradition. The idea of a millennial period (of whatever length) resulted from the combination of two different kinds of eschatology. Prophetic eschatology tended to picture a this-worldly fulfillment of God's purpose. At the end of history, the world's evil would be overcome and life would come into its own as it was intended to be in God's good creation (Isa. 65:17–25; Ezek. 34:25–31). Prophetic eschatology understood salvation in continuity with this world and its history; this world would be the setting for eschatological bliss.

In contrast, apocalyptic eschatology saw this world as already too overwhelmed with evil for redemption to occur from within it. The present world must pass away to make way for eschatological fulfillment in the setting of new heavens and a new earth (Isa. 65:17; 66:22; I Enoch 91:15–16; II Peter 3:12–13). In this frame of reference, the Messiah is no this-worldly royal figure empowered by God but is a transcendent figure who brings salvation from the other world. In apocalyptic eschatology, the final kingdom of God does not grow out of this world but breaks into it from the beyond. By John's time, these two views had already been combined into a scheme in which a this-worldly messiah brought this-worldly salvation during a transitional kingdom, which was then superseded by eternal apocalyptic salvation in the new world. The "two ages" were bridged by an intermediate period resulting in the scheme "this age" ‖ "the days of the Messiah" ‖ "the age to come." The intermediate period of the Messiah's rule was ascribed various lengths: forty years (Apoc. Elijah); four hundred years (II Esdr. 7:28); a thousand years (II Enoch 32—33), with rabbis interpreting selected texts to yield varying numbers of years for the "millennium" (365, 365,000, 7,000; cf. Beasley-Murray, p. 288). John adopts the picture of an intermediate period partly because he stands in this tradition, but also because he is influenced here as elsewhere by the story line of Ezekiel (cf. above, on 7:1–8): The "first resurrection" and millennial period (20:4–6) corresponds to Ezekiel 37, the defeat of Gog and Magog (20:7–10) to Ezekiel 38—39, and the coming of the Holy City (21:1—22:5) to Ezekiel 40—48. In addition John inherits from his Jewish background the tradition that only the just are raised (Isa. 26:19; Ps. Sol. 3:13–14; I Enoch 83–90) and the tradition that all the dead, good and bad alike, are raised (Ezek. 37; Dan. 12:2–3; Test. Benj. 10:8; As. Mos. 41:2–3; II Esdr. 7:37; II Bar. 50—51; I Enoch 46:6; 58:3–5). By adopting the scheme of an intermediate eschatological period, he is given a conceptual means of affirming both traditions. It was the Jewish tradition that provided the elements for John's picture, but the Christian tradition in which he stood, particularly the Pauline stream, could speak of Christians reigning and judging as part of the eschatological scenario (I Cor. 4:8; 6:2–3).

207

John emphasizes that those who are resurrected to share in the millennium participate in the "first resurrection." This is often taken in contrast to a "second resurrection" to follow. While it is true that in another picture (20:12) all the dead come to life and stand before God in judgment, there is no reference to this as a "second resurrection." By announcing that this resurrection which happens in the eschatological future is the first resurrection, John may not have a subsequent "second" resurrection in mind but may be addressing claims, made by prophet-theologians of the Johannine and Pauline traditions in his own churches, that the resurrection has already happened (cf. John 11:1–44, esp. vv. 25–26; Eph. 2:1–7; Col. 2:12; 3:1; contrast II Tim. 2:18). Over against this hyper-realized eschatology, John emphasizes that there is no resurrection presently experienced—the *first* resurrection will occur at the eschaton (cf. Phil. 3:7–16).

The Defeat of Gog and Magog: Satan's Last Stand (20:7–10)

John has already announced to his hearer-readers that after Satan has been bound for the thousand years he "must" be released for a little while (20:3). The question occurs to every reader of this text, "Once Satan is bound and the earth enjoys a millennium of undemonized celebration, why 'must' he be released again?" One explanation is certainly wrong: to take this language as objectifying, as though in the objective world God were subject to some external constraints. The matter was understood precisely in this manner in some apocalyptic traditions. Second Esdras, for example, presents a God who would like to save more of his creation but is not able to do so, because it would violate the rigid theological system which the author perceives as more ultimate than God. This conceptual trap still ensnares some modern theologies in which God "can" act only in certain ways because the theological system demands it. But in biblical theology, God is always sovereign over every theological system. In the "Little Apocalypse" of Mark 13, for example, God adjusts the apocalyptic timetable for the sake of the elect (13:20). According to one interpretation of 10:4, John specifically affirms the same. In any case, the "must" of 20:3 is not any "law of history" external to God, but as in 1:1; 11:5; 13:10; 22:6, it reflects the phrase in Daniel 2:28 and is always equivalent to "God's will."

In John's composition, Satan "must" be released for a combination of traditional, literary, and theological reasons. John has yet another picture of the final defeat of Satan that he wants to incorporate by relating it to the traditional picture of the defeat of Gog and Magog. The loose "chronological" structure he has composed called for a scene in which Satan was bound (20:1–3) in order to incorporate that traditional picture. The same compositional constraints required that Satan "had to" remain bound during the millennium. Since John has identified the resurrection and millennial period with the "resurrection" scene of Ezekiel 37, and will identify the new Jerusalem with the picture of the restored Holy City in Ezekiel 40—48, the intervening description of Gog/Magog in Ezekiel 38—39 required that John insert a picture of their destruction between his pictures of the millennium in 20:4—6 and the new Jerusalem in 21:1—22:5, since, as we have said above, he is following Ezekiel's story line. And since John sees Gog and Magog as operating under the sway of the ultimate power of evil, symbolized by Satan, it is "necessary" that Satan be released in order to deceive the nations and gather them for the "last battle."

Ezekiel 38—39 had painted a graphic picture of "Gog, prince of Magog," whom God would raise up in the last days as the ultimate representative of evil and then destroy as a demonstration of his own sovereignty and glory. The scene in Ezekiel is entirely theocentric—"Gog" is there little more than a stage prop, like Pharaoh in the exodus story, a foil for God's eschatological power (38:16, 23; 39:7, 13). By John's time, Jewish tradition had long since transformed "Gog of Magog" into "Gog and Magog" and made them into the ultimate enemies of God's people to be destroyed in the eschatological battle. The Jerusalem Targum to Numbers 11:27 says "At the end of the days Gog, Magog, and their host will come against Jerusalem." The Septuagint of Amos 7:1 inserts "Gog" into the vision of the eschatological locust plague as though it were self-evident. For John, too, evil as embodied in historical individuals and nations is not the ultimate enemy. By "Gog and Magog" we should not think of historical nations that have had a continuing existence during the preceding scene of the millennium, nor of nations of our own time "predicted" by biblical prophecy. John is preparing to present before our imaginations a picture of the ultimate destruction of evil and needs for this scene antagonists to God who are larger than life. Evil must be magnified to its fullest before being destroyed forever. In order to participate in this mythical scene, the devil "must" be released to engage in his characteristic activity of "deceiving the nations."

As in 11:17–19 and 19:17–21, the "last battle" is no battle at all. There is no other victory than that long since won by God the Victor in the cross of Christ. We have only the paradigmatic scene in which all the forces of evil, with Satan at their head, surround the embattled "camp" of the People of God. It is not an objectifying prediction of something that will literally occur in some particular geographical spot but a picture of the essential nature of the embattled church. "Camp" is interchangeable with "city" in this text as an indication of the pilgrim existence of God's people in this world. "Here we have no continuing city" (Heb. 13:14). Without any struggle, fire comes from heaven and destroys the enemies of God's people, and the devil disappears into the lake of fire forever. This is another affirmation of the apocalyptist's view that, while we must responsibly resist evil, "deliver us from evil" is a prayer that finally must be answered from God's side.

The Last Judgment (20:11–15)

Revelation 20:11–15 is the *only* judgment scene John knows, and *everyone* is there. Here is a good test for our interpretative procedure of dealing with each visionary scene individually as one way of picturing the eschatological victory of God, without feeling any more compulsion than John himself does to fit the scenes together into a super-picture, a consistent, comprehensive eschatological program. This scene is not part of a series of judgments which could be reconstructed by combining pictures of eschatological judgment drawn from other parts of the Bible (e.g., Isa. 2:12–22; 13; Dan. 7:9–14; 12:2; Wis. Sol. 3:1–9; Matt. 19:28; 25:31–46; John 5:28–29; 12:31; Rom. 14:10; I Cor. 6:2; 15; II Cor. 5:10; II Peter 3:7; Jude 6), as done, for example, in modern dispensationalist interpretation. (The Scofield Reference Bible lists *seven* judgments in its eschatological scheme.)

Nor is this scene to be fitted into an eschatological chronology constructed from Revelation itself. One could infer from 20:5 that, since faithful Christians have been raised to reign with Christ at the beginning of the millennium, those who are restored to life and stand before God in 20:12 "must" be only non-Christians. From this, one could then conclude that they are all condemned, since they are not Christian believers (or since they are judged by works, and no one is justified before

God by works [Rom. 3:27–28; Gal. 2:16; 3:10; Eph. 2:8]); or that
they are all saved, since God eventually saves all, believers and
unbelievers; or that the good are saved and the bad are condemned, on the same logic as Romans 2:6–11. Yet such speculative constructions would misconstrue John's language as
objectifying and would make his thinking much more systematic, linear, and consistent than he intends. The picture of resurrected martyrs in 20:5 functions to say "the martyr church shall
reign with Christ at the eschaton," not to provide information
with which to construct an eschatological scenario. Here as
elsewhere, John is not hesitant to present us with one picture
at a time, whether or not they are "consistent." In the picture
of the last judgment in 20:11–15, it is "the dead, great and
small" (20:12), "all" of them (20:13), those in the book of life and
those not (20:12, 15), who stand before the great white throne
of judgment.

This throne has been a continuing motif in Revelation, a
symbol with political connotations representing the true source
of power and authority in the world over against the false claims
to the throne by the dragon and the beast (13:2). It is from the
throne that judgment proceeds, in this world and in the eschatological vision. The Christians of John's churches had faced
or were to face the Roman courts, where they would be condemned if they were faithful to their Christian confession. In
John's vision he sees the decision appealed to a higher court. Yet
we are not presented with a merely self-serving picture in
which Christians are acquitted and Roman oppressors are condemned. The "great and the small" are there, and judgment is
without partiality.

As in the initial throneroom scene of 4:1, the figure seated
on the throne is not identified. In traditional Jewish imagery the
last judge is of course God, though in some later apocalyptic
traditions the heavenly "Son of Man" was authorized by God to
judge as his representative. By failing to specify the figure here,
John is enabled to continue to be spared the necessity of distinguishing between God and Christ; "God or Christ" is not a
possibility in his thought. We have seen elsewhere in his imagery and theology how these "two" figures fade into each other.
The Lamb is never an independent figure, but always Lamb-as-
representative-of-God; God is never a figure defined apart from   211
Christ, but always God-who-defines-himself-by-Christ. Thus
John does not and can not have a "severe" judgmental God who

is ameliorated by a "compassionate" Christ. He refuses to parcel out the roles of judge and savior between God and the Lamb. But even our discussion has already become more cerebral than John's powerful imagery, in which the universe would flee from the awful presence of the Judge if there were anyplace else to go.

Judgment functions on the basis of books that are opened in the heavenly courtroom. The plural is important. In accord with traditional apocalyptic imagery, books are opened in which the deeds of human beings stand recorded, and people are judged by what they have done. This picture makes human freedom and human responsibility as serious as it can get. What we do matters, and matters ultimately. Yet in this same scene another book is opened, the book of grace, the Lamb's book of life. Names are written there before the creation of the world, purely as a matter of God's grace (13:8; 17:8). *This* picture takes grace with absolute seriousness. Those who are saved from the eternal "second death" are saved only by God's grace—not by their deeds but by God's. In these two books are pictured the paradox of works and grace, a paradox not unfamiliar in the Pauline tradition (Eph. 2:8–10; Phil. 2:12–13). We are ultimately responsible for what we do, for it has eternal consequences—we are judged by works. God is ultimately responsible for our salvation, it is his deed that saves, not ours—we are saved by grace. Propositional language will always sound paradoxical on such ultimate issues; John's pictorial language makes both statements in one picture.

Although one element of the picture testifies to the absolute grace of God, like all judgment scenes this picture as a whole functions to warn of the great separation that is to take place at the end of history. Now, in this ambiguous world, good and evil are mixed up, no decision is untainted, we deal in shades of gray rather than black and white. But at the great judgment day, the omniscient and omnipotent One will make the great separation. It is futile to attempt to escape the conclusion that John has some scenes of damnation for the unfaithful. The "second death," the place of torment beyond the "first" physical death, awaits not only the transcendent powers of evil (dragon, beast, false prophet, death [I Cor. 15:28!], and hades) but unfaithful human beings as well. This scene concludes with the somber note, uncelebrated but unrestrained, that ". . . if any one's name was not found written in the book of life, he was

212

thrown into the lake of fire" (20:15). John's listing of the types of such people (21:8, 27) shows that this is no hypothetical, idle threat. Yet this scene as a whole must be placed alongside scenes of the universal salvation of God (see the "Reflection: Universal Salvation and Paradoxical Language"), which place its message in the proper perspective without neutralizing it.

Further evidence that "being tormented in the lake of fire" cannot be literal is seen in that it happens not just to mortal beings but to a transcendent power, the "last enemy" (I Cor. 15:26). At the last judgment, Death and Hades are thrown into the lake of fire. It is the death of Death. Here is much more than a self-serving claim to individual survival beyond the grave. It is the promise that the power of death that enslaves us even during our average threescore years and ten (Ps. 90:10) will finally be destroyed. In this world, all life lives by devouring other life. The eschatological vision pictures the Giver of life as finally destroying not only death but predatory life (cf. Isa. 11:1–9).

The New Jerusalem (21:1—22:5)

John knows that human language is incapable of expressing, just as human imagination is incapable of perceiving, the reality of things in the eternal world as they truly are. But rather than being paralyzed by the finitude of human existence, he is set free to portray the End in a variety of this-worldly pictures used metaphorically to allow the character of the eternal world to break through. Thus we have seen the victorious return of a Mighty Conqueror, the last battle, the binding of Satan, the thousand-year celebration of Christ with his followers on an undemonized earth, the last judgment, the defeat of the mythological enemies Gog and Magog, and destruction of their Satanic leader. Just as the culmination of John's pictures of God's penultimate judgment in Part Two was the fall of the "Great City" "Babylon," the climax and fulfillment of John's series of eschatological pictures is the vision of the "Holy City," new Jerusalem. This is John's last depiction of the End, by far the largest and most detailed of his collection of eschatological pictures, that to which he has been building. Its importance in his theology is signaled by its final position, the detail with which it is drawn, and the repeated anticipations of its imagery in the preceding visions.

213

The idea of a heavenly Jerusalem that will become the

ultimate home of the People of God is not original with John. Like other Christian authors before and beside him (Gal. 4:24–31; Phil. 3:20; Heb. 11:10; 12:22; 13:14), John found this idea already present in the apocalyptic tradition that came to him. This tradition included even such details as the "descent" of the Holy City to earth on the Last Day (i.e., its establishment by God rather than by human effort [cf. Pss. 46; 48; Isa. 2:1–4; 65:17–25; Sib. Or. 5:420-25; I Enoch 90:29], the imagery of God's throne [Ps. 47:8; I Enoch 24:4–5], seeing the face of God [II Esdr. 7:98], the tree of life [Test. Levi 18:11; I Enoch 25:5], gold and jeweled construction [Exod. 25:5–14, 17–29; Isa. 54: 11–14; Ezek. 28:11–17; Tobit 13:16–18], golden streets, and gates of pearl [Isa. 60:11–14; Tob. 13:16–18; Sanh. 100ᵃ]). All these and more are repeatedly found in the Old Testament and on the palette of Jewish apocalyptic tradition in which John stands and from which he draws the colors for his own grand portrayal of the new Jerusalem. The list of jewels in the wall foundations of 21:19–20, for example, are related to Exodus 28:17–21; 39:10–14 and also to Ezekiel 28:13 (as found in the LXX, not the Hebrew text, which has only nine items). Since a similar description is found in both Josephus and Philo, it is clear that John is following a tradition of interpreting the stones of the breastplate of the High Priest in this symbolic manner. A scroll from Qumran (4QpIsᵈ) gives an allegorical interpretation of Isaiah 54:11–17 in which the new Jerusalem is the community itself. The gates are "the heads of the tribes of Israel," the sapphire foundations are the founding of the community, the pinnacles of rubies are the twelve leaders of the community; in II Esdras 10:27–28 the seer talks with a woman who is also a city that has come down from heaven. In II Baruch 4:3–6, the new Jerusalem was always pre-existent in heaven; in a rabbinic tradition (Baba B. 75a), the gates of the new Jerusalem are cut out of precious stones and of pearls thirty by forty-five feet wide.

Not only are there massive elements of Jewish tradition in John's picture of the new Jerusalem, it also reflects much of the Hellenistic/Roman aspirations for the ideal city, as well as Herodotus' description of the actual Babylon, and Rome's proud claim to be the Eternal City, as found on Roman coins and inscriptions from John's time. In John's view, the new Jerusalem is the fulfillment of all human dreams for the community and security of life in an ideal city. Cities constructed by human beings, even on the magnificent scale of "Babylon"/Rome, are at best only fragmentary realizations of the divine reality, at worst idolatrous expressions of human pride.

Such observations on the religious and cultural antecedents of John's thought are of historical interest in that they help us gain an insight into the nature of the prophetic experience and writings. Parallels from related religious literature help us to see as well that though John had visionary experiences, his portrayal of the new Jerusalem is not a reporter's description of what he "actually saw." It is his literary composition as the means of expressing, in symbolic theological terms, the meaning of his revelation of the nature of God's goal for this world. Once again, the thrust of John's message is seen in the choices he makes and in the arrangement, modifications, and additions he gives to these traditional elements, not in the elements themselves. What is this theological meaning?

"In the End, God . . ."

John has already given remarkable expression to the Christian conviction that at the End we meet not an event but a Person (see on 19:11–16 above). All Revelation's statements about the "End" are really statements about God; eschatology is an aspect of the doctrine of God. Shining through the varied pictures of "what it will be like" is the conviction which John shares with Paul that at the end of the historical road God will be "all in all" (*panta en pasin,* RSV "everything to everyone," I Cor. 15:28). For John, God is not finally one "item" in the new Jerusalem; God is himself the eschatological reality who embraces all things. In 21:3 a voice interprets the descending city as "God's dwelling with humanity," and declares that "God himself will be with them" (cf. the closing lines of Ezekiel's description of the restored Jerusalem, "The name of the city henceforth shall be 'the Lord is there' " [48:35]). In the only two instances in which the voice of God directly addresses the hearer-readers (21:6, cf. 1:8), God declares "I am the Alpha and the Omega, the beginning and the end." God does not merely bring the End, God *is* the End. As a perfect cube (21:15–16), the golden city as a whole is a holy of holies in which the divine presence is directly, intimately available (I Kings 6:20; II Chron. 3:8–9). Thus in contrast to all pious expectation and the pattern of Ezekiel 40—48 which John is following, there is no temple in this city—because God-as-defined-by-the-Lamb is himself the temple, the "place" of the divine-human encounter (21:22).

215

The jasper wall that surrounds the city is not just another jewel, but the glory of God himself (cf. 4:3, where "jasper" represents God's glory, and Zech. 2:4–5 on which John is drawing); indeed the city as a whole shines with the divine jasper-glory (21:11). Moses, on the most intimate terms with God (Exod. 34:29–35), never saw God's face, only his "backside" (Exod. 33:17–23); but in the new Jerusalem God's people will see his face (22:4; cf. I Cor. 13:12), and God himself will address them as "my son." "Son" in biblical parlance is not interchangeable with "child" and should not be sacrificed to contemporary concerns for "inclusive language," as legitimate as those concerns may be in some respects. "Son" does not connote childish dependence but the freedom of adult personhood (John 8:31–36; Rom. 8:15–17; Gal. 4:1–7) and has echoes of the christological title "Son of God." What awaits the believer and the world at the End of all things? John's first and last word is "God."

Via Negativa

If to speak of the ultimate future, and therefore the meaning of the present, means to speak of God, how can one speak of God? John has no philosophical interest at all in this abstract question. Since he knows that all our language of God and ultimate things is metaphorical and fragmentary, he is liberated to speak freely his divinely given insights into ultimate reality. Yet he does make some use of that philosophical tradition which claims that, while we cannot say what the transcendent world of God *is*, we can to some extent truly represent it by saying what it is *not*. John thus sprinkles his "description" of the new Jerusalem with affirmations of what will *not* be there.

No sea (21:1). There may be a personal, existential element here. It was in fact the sea that separated John and his beloved communities of anxious Christians. But for the sea, he would be there personally to speak his word of encouragement he must now communicate in writing, and be with them during the great ordeal they must endure. The new world coming will mean the removal of all present barriers to human relationships. Yet "sea" has a deeper meaning in John's theology than this aspect of his personal circumstance. Throughout Revelation, "sea" has represented the chaotic power of un-creation, anti-creation, the abyss-mal depth from which the dragon arises to torment the earth, the very opposite of the creator God (cf.

216

commentary on 13:1 and 4:6 above). Driven back at creation and held at bay during aeons of history, in the new creation "sea" will vanish forever. Evil, even as a potential disturber of creation, will have been irrevocably overcome.

No tears, death, sorrow, crying, pain (21:4). Although philosophical arguments for the character-building value of these built-in afflictions of the human condition can be made, John is not writing philosophy. He is the prophetic mediator of the word of that One who declares that the "former things" (with this one phrase he sums up all the world's misery of all the ages) have "passed away," because he makes all things new. Here the Almighty himself promises that all that now robs life from being fulfilled, joyful, vibrant *life* will be absent from the transcendent reality to which he is leading history.

No cowardly, faithless, polluted, murderers, fornicators, sorcerers, idolaters, or liars (21:8). The new Jerusalem will be a city where right and justice prevail, not as abstract virtues, but as the will of God. To paint his picture of a city freed from the sins that infect the present world, John uses a "vice catalog" which has some similarity to those used by other New Testament authors as a means of inculcating Christian ethics, particularly those authors in the Pauline tradition in which John and his churches stand (Rom. 1:28–32; 13:13; I Cor. 5:9–11; 6:9–10; II Cor. 12:20; Gal. 5:19–21; Eph. 4:31; 5:3–5; Col. 3:5, 8–9; I Tim. 1:9–10; 6:4–5; II Tim. 3:2–5; Titus 3:3; I Peter 4:3; Mark 7:21–23; Luke 18:11; cf. Rev. 9:21; 22:15). Yet he does more than pass on a traditional list; he gives it the nuance appropriate to his situation. His beginning with cowards and ending with "liars" is no general statement against cowardice and falsehood but has in view the failures of Christians under the pressure of persecution and the threat of it: lack of courage before the Roman courts, lack of truthfulness in making the declaration of their Christian faith regardless of the consequences. The other terms on this list are likewise not general broadsides against human sinfulness but are sins that in John's eyes were particularly associated with participation in the emperor cult and yielding to the pressures of pagan society. His declaration that these people will not be in the city of eschatological salvation functions as an exhortation to faithful witness in the present. John does not say, however, that anyone who has ever been guilty of these failings is prohibited from participation in the Holy City, only that no

217

one will bring these sinful practices with him or her into the Holy City. The list serves to characterize life in the city of God, not a limitation on who will finally be there.

No temple (21:22). From 19:1 on, throughout all of Part Three of his composition, John in general adopts the narrative line of Ezekiel 37—48 as the model for his own presentation. Although John gets many of the details for his new Jerusalem from the description of the restored Jerusalem in Ezekiel 40—48, there is a fundamental difference in that as a priest Ezekiel was very concerned for the priestly principle of separating the holy from the profane. Thus in his vision of the restored Jerusalem, the temple dominated the new city, with a wall dividing the temple from the rest of the city, effectively distinguishing the holy and the profane. Ezekiel 44:5 has directions for marking out who may enter and who may not, and in 44:7 condemns Israel for allowing foreigners into the sanctuary. Priests are to teach the people the difference between the holy and the common; Zadokites are praised because they have done this, and Levites are condemned because they have not (44:10, 15, 23).

Like Ezekiel his source, John too is concerned to portray the new Jerusalem as a holy city (see below). Yet John's Christian understanding of God leads him to a different vision of the ultimate city. For him the city has no temple because the city as a whole is holy. God is directly present to all throughout its streets, not only in some designated holy place. All of life is holy and God is present in the midst of the everyday, not only at special places and times, and all the people of God are "priests."

No sun, moon, night, closed gates (21:23, 25; 22:5). God is transcendent, unbearable, glorious Light. God's presence in the city at once banishes night and all its anxieties and makes all other forms of light irrelevant.

No curse (22:3). At the beginning of things, humanity was perverted by its original rebellion against the Creator, wanting to be its own god (Gen. 3:1–6; Isa. 24:4–6; cf. Rom. 5:12–21). When sin entered the good creation, the world itself felt the blow, and a curse was pronounced on the very earth (Gen. 3:17), so that all historical human existence has been lived out in a fallen world (Gen. 3:17, cf. Rom. 8:18–25). John's vision of the new Jerusalem pictures a purified and redeemed humanity and a fallen world delivered from the bondage of evil by the God whose grace transforms pious individual souls as well as all of creation, "far as the curse is found."

218

The City of God

A city. In view of the role "Babylon" has played in John's experience and theology, we might be surprised that John's last vision of the ultimate destiny of humanity is not the idyllic Elysian fields of the Greeks, the happy hunting grounds of the native American, not even the romanticized country life of those who consider the city the concentration of all human evil, but—a city! Early Christianity quickly became an urban religion, a faith that had to do with establishing justice in the gates and witnessing to the faith in the marketplace amid the complexities of social, economic, political life. John does not write to individual Christians who have withdrawn from public life, or to groups of Christians in retreat centers, but to churches in seven large cities.

A city is the realization of human community, the concrete living out of interdependence as the essential nature of human life. In the individualistic ideal, each person is independent, self-reliant, doing everything for himself or herself. In a city the tasks of life are divided up, each one does a part, and the beauty of life is not a solo but a symphony. As community, a city is not streets and buildings but people. Beneath John's imagery of pillars, gates, walls, and foundations is his conviction that God's final dwelling place is in and with his people. There is thus no contradiction in the promise of 3:12, that the faithful Christian shall become a pillar in the temple of God in the new Jerusalem, and the statement of 21:22, that there will be no temple in the holy city, for the city as a whole is the community of believers, the temple in which God dwells (cf. 13:6; in I Cor. 3:16–17, the "you" is plural, referring not to the individual as in 6:19 but to the body of believers). The very "walls" and "gates" are marked with the representative names of God's people (21:12–14). The city has "twelves" built into it throughout (21:15–17)—all its dimensions are multiples of the "twelve" that connotes the People of God: twelve tribes of Israel, twelve apostles of the church. (Biblical translations, such as Today's English Version, that translate this into modern dimensions miss this symbolism.)

A particular city, "Jerusalem." As John writes, the earthly Jerusalem that had been the scene of the story of God's dealing with humanity lay in ruins. The divine Author does not break off the earthly story and begin afresh. The last chapter is the continuation and climax of the old story that began in Eden and passed through Ur and Egypt, then settled down and went wrong in Jerusalem from David through Jesus. Yet God cannot forget Jerusalem, graven on the palms of his hands (Isa. 49:16); its story continues.

A renewed city. Even though the first earth and the first heaven have passed away, the scene continues very much as a this-worldly scene. This is due in part to the fact that the other world can be spoken of only in language and images that derive from this world. More importantly, it is an affirmation of the significance of this world and history, even after the new heaven and new earth arrive. The vision of God in chapter 4 is fulfilled: God is the creator. Yet the one who does not quench a smoking wick or break a bruised reed (Isa. 42:3; Matt. 12:20) does not junk the cosmos and start anew—he renews the old and brings it to fulfillment.

The advent of the heavenly city does not abolish all human efforts to build a decent earthly *civil*ization but fulfills them. God does not make "all new things," but "all things new" (21:5). The end of history is not a return to its beginning, a "getting back to the Garden" as in the romantic Woodstock song of the sixties. One could indeed picture the whole biblical drama as a fall from the original paradise of Eden, represented by human construction of cities (the first one was built by Cain, the first murderer, Gen. 4:17!), and thus picture salvation as finally getting rid of human civilization and a return to the undefiled Garden. This is specifically what John does *not* do. Elements of the Garden are indeed in the new Jerusalem (tree of life, 22:2; cf. Gen. 2:9; river of life, 22:1; cf. Gen. 2:10), but this represents a recovery of the original goodness of creation by the redemption of the historical process rather than its elimination. Thus the kings of earth bring the glory and honor of the nations into the city (21:24, 26). Like apocalyptic thought in general, John affirms this world and its value and thus pictures eternal salvation as the salvation of the world and of history itself. Salvation does not, according to John, offer escape from the tragedy of historical existence. Like Dante's *Divine Comedy*, John envisioned transcendent salvation as a world in which all that is human is taken up and transformed, a world in which nothing human is lost. Salvation is beyond but not without this world. Concretely, this means that the "religious" deeds of humanity are by no means all that is preserved in the eternal city. This "secular" city-without-a-temple is in continuity with and ulti-

220

mately redeems and makes worthwhile every effort in our little this-worldly lives to have a decent city: all our striving for a just and fulfilling human society. The Bride-City is clothed in the "righteous deeds of the saints" (19:8): not only the expressions of piety but actions in behalf of justice. Every ditch dug, every brick laid, every vote cast, every committee decision that has contributed to the decency of human life is preserved, and built into the eternal city. And yet the city is not a human achievement, rising Babel-like from the earth, culminating human efforts. Without in the least minimizing human responsibility (John has throughout affirmed the eternal consequences of human actions), he pictures the new Jerusalem as "coming down from heaven from God" (21:2). As important as "works" are for John, participation in the heavenly city is finally a matter of grace freely given (21:6).

A big, inclusive city. The temptation of a suspect, marginal minority is to envision some great reversal in which only the faithful few are saved while the overt enemy and nominal friends receive the just reward for their unfaithfulness. One signal of the divine inspiration of John's revelation is that he has not succumbed to this understandable temptation. Throughout, he has pictured the number of the redeemed as uncountable (7:9–17). His new Jerusalem is no tiny village of the "faithful few"; it is a vast city twelve thousand furlongs (1,500 miles) cubed (21:16).

Against everything that we might have expected, he has modified his tradition in order to portray a radically inclusive city. In 21:3 John quotes Ezekiel 37:27, "My dwelling place shall be with them; and I will be their God, and they shall be my people," but the last word is modified to the plural, *"peoples"* (cf. RSV margin; the plural is read by the best Greek texts). The new Jerusalem is not populated by the "chosen people" only; the peoples of the earth, the very nations and even their kings (21:24!) that had opposed God's rule and oppressed the church, are here pictured as redeemed citizens of the Holy City. Again, Ezekiel 47:12 pictures the restored Jerusalem as having trees whose leaves will be used for healing. John modifies this from individualistic terms to those of geopolitics: The tree of life will be in the new Jerusalem for the healing *of the nations* (22:2). The nations of earth shall walk in the light of the glorious city, and bring their glory and honor into it (21:24–26). Ezekiel's city had twelve gates which served as exits for going out into the

221

land (Ezek. 48:30–35). The earthly Jerusalem had had a temple with a wall that separated men from women and Jews from Gentiles (cf. Acts 21:27–29; Eph. 2:14–16). The new Jerusalem has no temple, and its only wall is pierced by twelve gates that are always open and have only one-way traffic—outside to inside (21:24, 26, 27). The twelve gates had had astrological connotations in previous apocalyptic tradition (cf. e.g., I Enoch 33–36), and were related to the jewels of the breastplate of the High Priest, which also had developed astrological associations in both Philo and Josephus. John lists the twelve gates in a peculiar order (East, North, South, West), the exact reverse of their use in astrological calculations. Instead of sectarian separateness or astrological determinism, John makes the eternally open gates a powerful symbol of the radical inclusiveness of the city in which the hope of Isaiah 19:24–25 is finally fulfilled. "All" are there, because of the power and grace of the One who "makes *all* things new" (21:5)—the "all" is added by John to his Old Testament source (Isa. 43:19).

A beloved, beautiful, bridal city. In step with his tradition from the Old Testament and apocalyptic literature, John pictures the eschatological city as a woman, indeed as a bride (cf. Isa. 49:14–23; 54; Zech. 9:9–10; II Esdr. 10:25–59). This happy image for the People of God speaks of celebration, festivity, fulfillment, the most intimate of relationships—union (John 3:29–30; II Cor. 11:2; Eph. 5:25–32). "Bride" also speaks of beauty, and the city is pictured as the eternal affirmation of all that is beautiful. The beauty of this world (gold, precious stones, pearls, dazzling light) becomes the vehicle of expressing the beauty of the Eternal City, and yet it must be transformed: *transparent* gold (21:18), *crystallizing* jasper (21:11). Eternity is no odorless, colorless, tasteless void; it is (in contrast to the dead, silent streets of earthly Babylon, 18:22) a living city of light and color.

A Holy City. "Holiness" is not primarily moral correctness, but *otherness*. That God is "holy" means first that God is creator and not creature, that God is wholly other, that God is God (Rev. 4:8; 6:10). The holiness God demands of his people is more than compliance with a list of pious acts; God demands a different, distinctive life oriented to his will for them, rather than "being conformed to this world" (Rom. 12:1–2; II Cor. 6:16–18). The church is the community of the holy, the saints—the same

222

word in John's Greek (5:8; 8:3; 11:18; 13:7, 10; 16:6; 17:6; 18:20, 24; 19:8; 20:6, 9; 22:11).

In this world the struggle to do God's will is always the struggle of the holy with the profane. "Holiness" always designates separation, over-againstness. The idea of holiness requires the contrast between "inside" and "outside," "sacred" and "profane." Like "win," which functions only in relation to "lose," "holy" functions only in contrast to "unholy." Thus John's picture of the new Jerusalem as God's eternal affirmation of the holy life to which his people are called also includes a list of those who are "outside"—the Holy City stands in contrast to those who are in the lake of fire (21:8, 27). The inside/outside aspect of holiness still exists even in the new Jerusalem. Paradoxically, alongside the inclusive idea expressed above that all are insiders, there is still a wall that separates insiders from outsiders. The primary meaning of the wall is to connote the idea of a city as such, a secure community. But since there are no enemies from which to be defended, the wall also serves to *mark off* the holy community from "outsiders" (21:8, 27; 22:15). Yet the wall is pierced by gates that are forever open. Both senses are paradoxically present: There are no outsiders; there are outsiders—but the gates are forever open.

Just as John takes the word "win" from one language game and transforms it so that "everybody wins" (with no "losers" implied), so he takes "holiness" and expands it to include all reality. In the transcendent city of God, unqualified holiness, the nature of God himself, will prevail—the city will be a holy city (21:2, 10). This is the meaning of picturing the city as a perfect cube—though it has no temple, the whole city is a holy of holies, encased in gold like the most holy place of the temple (I Kings 6:14–22). The city is holy in a priestly sense; the redeemed People of God are priests.

An active city. In John's vision the eternal city is not an eternal rest but a place of ceaseless activity. John offers no mythical details to satisfy our curiosity about "what we shall do in heaven." He fills in the content of eternal life with God with only two pictures: "His servants shall worship/serve him" (22:3) and "they shall reign for ever and ever" (22:5). The height and depth of the meaning of life in this world, grateful worship/service to the Creator, freed from the tyranny of the enslaving powers of historical existence, is raised to the power of infinity

223

and made into the picture of the destiny of all God's people. "Lived happily ever after" pales in comparison.

The imperative. John lets his picture speak for itself. His language throughout this vision is indicative: "This is how it will be." And yet as always the indicatives of biblical theology contain an implicit imperative, the gift becomes an assignment. If this is where the world, under the sovereign grace of God, is finally going, then every thought, move, deed in some other direction is out of step with reality and is finally wasted. The picture does not attempt to answer speculative questions about the future; it is offered as an orientation for life in the present.

Revelation 22:6–20a
The Vision Ends

The section 22:6–21 is no "epilogue"; it has an important function in the reading forth of the revelation in worship (cf. 1:3). The heavenly vision has ended on the majestic strains of the "Hallelujah Chorus" (22:5). With these words John provides the worshipers with a needed transition back to the world of the here and now, back to the familiar church setting of Asia. There is nothing new in this section except for the formula of 22:18–19, often found at the conclusion of ancient documents in a day prior to copyright laws (Deut. 4:2; I Enoch 104:10; Ps. Aristeas 311). It is nonetheless a powerful summary of the themes John has repeatedly emphasized throughout his visions.

"Worship God." In a scene which repeats 19:10, John again illustrates by his own example that one can righteously oppose the external idolatry as found in the imperial cult and still fall victim to the tendency within the church to idolize the means of revelation. John warns his parishioners against a false fascination with spiritual phenomena. Revelation that is theocentric throughout concludes with the command to worship only God.

"I am coming soon." The God who is worshiped is the one who has so defined himself in Jesus that their words are interchangeable (22:13; cf. 21:6). This One is himself the eschaton, the one to whom the believer and the whole creation move, the

224

Beginning and the End. In closing, John reinforces the urgency of the message by declaring that the End will come soon (22:6, 10, 12, 20). Unlike the pseudonymous Daniel and apocalyptic literature in general, the book is not to be sealed as though its message is for future generations—it is specifically for John's own generation. (See the "Reflection: Interpreting the 'Near End' in Revelation.")

Revelation. John closes on the same note with which he opened (1:1–2), with the claim that what he communicates is the prophetic word of God mediated through Christ and the revelatory angel (22:6). Like the prophets of Israel and the church, John speaks in his own voice ("I John," 22:8). Yet this voice of John modulates into the voice of Jesus ("I Jesus," 22:16), which mediates the voice of God. As the prophetic word of God, John's words are "trustworthy and true," as is Christ, the personal Word of God (19:11–13). They are therefore just as sacred as Scripture itself and require the same care in transmission—nothing may be added or subtracted from them (22:18–19; cf. Deut. 4:2; 12:32).

A call for faithful response. John's revelation has throughout been a call to action. Revelation offers words of prophecy to be "kept," in the sense of "keeping" the Sabbath, that is, living according to the will of the one God who will reward each person according to his or her works (22:12; cf. 20:11–15). He ends with the severe reminder of the either/or call to decision by picturing again the two groups into which humanity is divided by its choice of whom to worship/obey (22:14–15). This non-speculative call for personal responsibility becomes an open invitation in which John rings the changes on the word "come!"—a word which played an important role in the early church's eucharistic worship (22:17–20; cf. I Cor. 16:22). The voice of the prophetic Spirit that animates the church is heard in the worship as the bride/church prays "Come!" The hearers are to join in the prayer and say "Come!" These prayers are part of the eschatological event and set it in motion, as the prayers of the saints are effectively heard in the heavenly worship (5:8; 8:3) and are echoed in the voices of the living creatures before God's throne who inaugurate the prelude to the End (6:1, 3, 5, 7). The exalted Christ responds with his solemn word of threat and promise, his last words before his actual appearance as history's Judge and Redeemer, "Surely I am coming soon" (22:20).

225

Revelation 22:20*b*–21
The Letter Ends

Revelation ends as it began, a letter from an exiled pastor-prophet to be read forth in the worship services of the Asian churches. The divine splendor of the vision is gone, and they are back in this world, meeting together in their little congregations. Like Paul's letters, this letter is designed to be read in the liturgy, probably just prior to the celebration of the Eucharist. With wonderfully tensive ambiguity, John joins his worshiping congregations in the liturgical prayer that had already become traditional, words that can be a prayer for Christ to come in power at the End and establish the justice of the kingdom of God, and/or words that can be a prayer for the presence of Christ at the eucharistic worship of the church: "Come, Lord Jesus!"

The last word of the "book" is a word of the grace of God to "all." This is the reading of the best Greek texts; some manuscripts added "the saints," finding the word of universal grace too much to bear and limiting the pronouncement of God's grace to the church. Whatever may have been John's original ending, the ambiguity of this final word is symbolic of the provocative tension of the Revelation as a whole, guarding us from both the despair of limited hope and the complacency of cheap grace.

REFLECTION
Universal Salvation and Paradoxical Language

"Salvation" here means eschatological restoration to fellowship with God and the blessedness of eternal life in God's presence. "Universal salvation" here means the view that all human beings will finally be redeemed by God's unconditional grace manifest in Jesus Christ, not merely that there will be a univer-

226

sal opportunity or that a selection from all nations shall finally
be saved. "Limited salvation" here means the view that only
those who prior to their death are converted to Christ as Lord
will finally be saved.

None of this terminology, of course, is found in Revelation.
Neither "universal" nor "limited" is found in John's vocabulary.
He never uses the verb "save" or the noun "savior," and only
uses the word "salvation" three times, never as the destiny of
human beings but each time as an acclamation to God (7:10;
12:10; 19:1). John deals in pictures, not theological concepts,
and offers us word pictures of both universal and limited salvation. (See the commentary on each text.)

Some texts in Revelation which portray or imply universal
salvation are 1:7; 4:3; 5:13; 15:4; 21:5; 21:22—22:3. Some texts
in Revelation which portray or imply limited salvation are
14:9–10; 20:11–15. Each group of texts belongs to a significant
stream of biblical theology. One stream maintains that ultimate
salvation is limited (some passages which indicate that are Isa.
26:20–21; 27:12–13; 51:22–23; 66:15–16, 24; Matt. 25:31–46;
John 3:16, 36; II Thess. 1:6–10). Another stream tends toward
or explicitly affirms inclusive, universal salvation (some passages
which belong to that stream are Gen. 12:1–3; Ps. 86:9; Isa. 2:2–4;
19:24–25; 25:6–10a; 40:5; 43:25; 44:2–5; 45:22–23; 49:6; 51:4–6;
52:7–10; 66:18–23; Ezek. 16:49–63; Matt. 20:1–16; John 3:17;
12:32; Rom. 5:15–21; 11:32–36; I Cor. 15:20–28; Eph. 1:3–22;
3:20; Phil. 2:6–11; Col. 1:15–20; 2:15; I Tim. 2:3–4; 4:10; Titus
2:11).

How shall we understand these data from Revelation?
There are three options:

1. The first option is that John's real view is universal salvation. Texts that seem to imply limited, conditional salvation are
actually to be understood in the light of the universalistic texts.

2. The second option is that John's real view is limited salvation. Texts that seem to imply universal salvation are actually
to be understood in the light of the limited texts. As representative of the fear found in many "evangelical" writings that God
will save everyone, we may take the commentary on Revelation
by R. H. Mounce. He takes the universal salvation passages
"figuratively" but the hell passages literally (cf. pp. 277, 282,
287–89, 304, 387). His justifying dictum, "A moral universe
requires that evil be punished" (p. 304), does not consider the
questions of (a) God's forgiveness, (b) whether a "moral uni-

227

verse" can allow an eternal punishment for a finite sin, and (c) whether there is a "moral universe" external and superior to the sovereignty of the one God, who wills to save all (I Tim. 2:4).

3. The third option is that John has no *one* consistent view. Neither group of texts can be subordinated to the other. This is the view affirmed here. Although inconsistency is often a defect, the mark of a muddled thinker who is not the master of his sources or traditions, that is not the case here. John was a profound thinker, a dialectical theologian who intends to present both sets of pictures, and does so using paradoxical language. Revelation intends to present pictures in which the one sovereign and gracious God is finally victorious and restores all his creation to its intended blessedness, redeeming all his creatures (pictures in which all are saved unconditionally because of God's decision to accept them). He also intends to present pictures which portray human beings as responsible for their decisions, pictures of how inexpressibly terrible it is to reject one's creator and live one's life in allegiance to false gods (pictures in which the faithful are saved and unbelievers are damned because they did not decide to accept God). By offering pictures of both unconditional/universal and conditional/limited salvation and thus affirming both poles of the dialectic, John, in accord with biblical theology in general, guards against the dangers inherent in a superficial "consistency" obtained by affirming only one side of the issue. The interpreter's task is not to seek ways to reconcile the tension in the text; the task is to find the thrust of Revelation's message precisely in this tension. His juxtaposition of contrasting pictures of "how it finally will be" is a confession that all our knowledge of ultimate truths, even revealed knowledge, is broken and fragmentary. John knows the danger of claiming to know too much, even as one who has had a tour of heaven (cf. Paul, in whose tradition he stands: I Cor. 13:12; II Cor. 12:1–5). John knows that for Christians the question of universal or limited salvation is not an abstract speculative question, addressing the question "How many?" It is rather faith's confession of the meaning of the act of God in Christ; the God whose victory does not depend on ours, who loves us when we do not love him or ourselves, who forgives us when we do not forgive him or ourselves, who believes in us when we do not believe in him or ourselves, who saves us when we do not believe we need saving or are worth saving.

Confession of the saving act of this God generates more than one set of meaningful pictures. By affirming both sets of pictures together, John's soteriology gives us the following guidelines for expressing the doctrine of eschatological salvation. With regard to the doctrine of universal salvation, we consider four possibilities for misunderstanding:

1. The doctrine of universal salvation should not be held in an undialectical way that relativizes the ultimate revelation-salvation event of Jesus Christ. "Universal salvation" can be affirmed in a way that makes Jesus Christ only one of many paths to God. John does not do this. There are not many gods but one God, and this God is the God definitively revealed in Jesus for all peoples whether they know and acknowledge it or not. For John, creation is not saved by being converted to the Christian religion. God saves humanity. But for John, the God who saves humanity is the God who has definitively acted to reveal himself as the savior of all in the eschatological event of Jesus Christ.

2. The doctrine of universal salvation should not be held in such a way that it permits the relaxation of human responsibility. "Universal salvation" can be affirmed in such a way that salvation becomes a fate rather than a gift, robbing human beings of their ability and responsibility to decide and the church of its evangelistic mission. John's dialectic avoids this. He also has pictures in which we are responsible for our own destiny.

3. The doctrine of universal salvation should not be held in such a way that it minimizes God's judgment on human sin. An undialectical affirmation of universal salvation has difficulty doing justice to the stern side of God's justice and portraying the awfulness of rebellion against God. Alongside pictures of universal salvation, John offers pictures of the terror of God's judgment. Finding universal salvation in Revelation is a matter of exegesis, not of the sentimentality of interpreters not tough-minded enough to accept John's pictures of judgment and damnation.

4. The doctrine of universal salvation should not be held in such a way that it minimizes the importance of faith and the urgency of evangelism. As affirmed by John and the New Testament generally, the implication of the doctrine of universal salvation is not that there is nothing for the church to do since the whole creation will be saved anyway. Rather, the good news

229

of the one God who brings final salvation to all demands to be lived out and shared in the present, and the pictures of God's judgment against unbelievers and the necessity of human decision for God prevent the universalistic pictures from cutting the nerve of action and mission. All of this means that the doctrine of universal salvation cannot be held in isolation from a doctrine of judgment. Pictures of heaven, including pictures of a heaven for everyone, require pictures of limited salvation, pictures of hell.

There is, however, a corresponding list of dangers in affirming a doctrine of conditional, limited salvation:

1. Limited-salvation pictures of judgment and damnation should not be affirmed in such a way that God is pictured as vindictive or frustrated. The logic of some nondialectical affirmations of God's judgment and final damnation of sinners leads to the inescapable picture of a deity who punishes beyond measure (eternally for finite sins), a vindictive god whose lust for revenge is never satisfied as the smoke from the torture of his enemies ascends for all eternity (Rev. 14:9–10). This is not the God revealed in Jesus Christ portrayed in Revelation. Likewise, John's method of dialectical pictures avoids the picture of a frustrated God who wanted to save his whole creation but was able to salvage only a small fraction of it. Revelation delivers us from a picture of a deity who wants to save but must finally throw up his cosmic hands to most of a rebellious creation and say "All right! Have it your way." This too is unworthy of the Lord God Almighty praised in Revelation (19:6).

2. Limited-salvation pictures of judgment and damnation should not be "explained" by reducing them to purely remedial terms. Sometimes biblical pictures of hell are interpreted as only a purifying, redemptive stage on the way to universal salvation. This is closer to a biblical picture of God than the vindictive monster described above, but it still suffers from the claim to explain ultimate truth without remainder.

3. Limited-salvation pictures of judgment and damnation should not be affirmed in such a way that a doctrine of conditional salvation is *necessary*. The urgency and necessity of evangelism and the believer's response in faith can be made into an axiom to which all other Christian truth must be subject. A doctrine of limited salvation can be affirmed because it is necessary in order to maintain the coherence of one's theological system or the meaning of one's own salvation. "If all are going

to be saved anyway, what is the use of evangelism and faith?" It is an impoverished understanding of evangelism and faith that makes these human acts as important as the act of God in Christ. This can lead to a heretical (synergistic) understanding of salvation in which it does not matter that God has sent Christ for the world's salvation unless the Christian evangelist and believer also do their "parts," thus placing the acts of Christian preaching and belief on the same plane with God's act in Christ. John's dialectical affirmation of both sets of pictures avoids this arrogance. Likewise, it is a petty, insecure understanding of salvation that derives its meaning and value from the reassurance that most will be damned (like being disappointed to learn that everyone received an invitation to a party one thought was only for the chosen few).

There is, however, also a danger in using John's method of juxtaposing paradoxical pictures. Paradox is not a cure-all for every difficult theological problem. Paradox affirms what must be affirmed in order to communicate the truth of the gospel, whether it can all be made logically consistent or not, but it is not an excuse for fuzzy thinking, a cop-out on rigorous theologizing. In John's method, one begins with faith in God's saving act in the Israel-Christ event and thinks to the paradoxical pictures in which it must be expressed, rather than using paradox or picture-language as an excuse for not thinking. (For further information see Bibliography, l.c.)

BIBLIOGRAPHY

1. For further study

a. Christian Prophecy

AUNE, DAVID E. *Prophecy in Early Christianity and the Ancient Mediterranean World* (Grand Rapids: Wm. B. Eerdmans Publishing Co., 1983).

BORING, M. EUGENE. *Sayings of the Risen Jesus: Christian Prophecy in the Synoptic Tradition* (Cambridge/London/New York: Cambridge University Press, 1982).

HILL, DAVID. *New Testament Prophecy* (Atlanta: John Knox Press, 1979).

b. Eschatology and Apocalyptic

COLLINS, JOHN J. *The Apocalyptic Imagination: An Introduction to the Jewish Matrix of Christianity* (New York: Crossroad Publishing Co., 1984).

MINEAR, PAUL S. *New Testament Apocalyptic.* INTERPRETING BIBLICAL TEXTS SERIES (Nashville: Abingdon Press, 1981).

ROBINSON, JOHN A. T. *In the End God.* RELIGIOUS PERSPECTIVES, Vol. 20 (New York/Evanston/London: Harper & Row, 1968), esp. chaps. 10–12.

RUSSELL, D. S. *The Method and Message of Jewish Apocalyptic, 200 BC–AD 100.* THE OLD TESTAMENT LIBRARY (Philadelphia: The Westminster Press, 1964).

c. Universal Salvation

AULEN, GUSTAF. *Christus Victor: An Historical Study of the Three Main Types of the Idea of the Atonement.* Trans. by A. G. Hebert (London: SPCK, 1970).

BORING, M. EUGENE. "The Language of Universal Salvation in Paul," *Journal of Biblical Literature* 1105:269–91 (1986).

BRAATEN, CARL. *The Flaming Center: A Theology of the Christian Mission* (Philadelphia: Fortress Press, 1977), pp. 93–120.

DEAK, ESTEBAN. *Apokatastasis* (Toronto: Deak, 1979).

ELLER, VERNARD. *The Most Revealing Book of the Bible* (Grand Rapids: Wm. B. Eerdmans Publishing Co., 1974), pp. 181–205.

FERRÉ, NELS F. S. *The Christian Understanding of God* (New York: Harper & Brothers, 1951), chap. 9.

MOULE, C.F.D. *The Meaning of Hope.* FACET BOOKS BIBLICAL SERIES 5 (Philadelphia: Fortress Press, 1963).

RISSI, MATHIAS. *The Future of the World. An Exegetical Study of Revelation 19.11—22.15.* STUDIES IN BIBLICAL THEOLOGY, Second Series, 23 (London: SCM Press, Ltd., 1972).

———. "The Kerygma of Revelation," *Interpretation* 22:3–17 (1968).

———. *Time and History: A Study on the Revelation* (Richmond: John Knox Press, 1966).

ROBINSON, JOHN A.T. See 1.b.

233

d. Revelation

CAIRD, G. B. *A Commentary on the Revelation of St. John the Divine.* HARPER'S NEW TESTAMENT COMMENTARIES (New York/Evanston: Harper & Row, 1966).

CHARLES, R. H. *The Revelation of St. John.* 2 vols. THE INTERNATIONAL CRITICAL COMMENTARY (Edinburgh: T. & T. Clark, 1920).

COLLINS, ADELA YARBRO. *The Apocalypse.* NEW TESTAMENT MESSAGE, Vol. 22 (Wilmington, Del.: Michael Glazier, 1979).

———. *Crisis and Catharsis: The Power of the Apocalypse* (Philadelphia: The Westminster Press, 1984).

ELLER, VERNARD. See 1.c.

FIORENZA, ELISABETH SCHÜSSLER. *The Book of Revelation: Justice and Judgment* (Philadelphia: Fortress Press, 1985).

———. *Invitation to the Book of Revelation: A Commentary on the Apocalypse with Complete Text from The Jerusalem Bible* (Garden City: Image Books, 1981).

GLASSON, T. F., editor. *The Revelation of John.* THE CAMBRIDGE BIBLE COMMENTARY ON THE NEW ENGLISH BIBLE (Cambridge: The University Press, 1965).

MINEAR, PAUL S. *I Saw a New Earth: An Introduction to the Vision of the Apocalypse* (Washington/Cleveland: Corpus Books, 1968).

RISSI, MATHIAS. *The Future of the World.* See 1.c.

SWEET, J.P.M. *Revelation.* WESTMINSTER PELICAN COMMENTARIES (Philadelphia: The Westminster Press, 1979).

2. Literature cited

AHLSTROM, SIDNEY E. *The Religious History of the American People* (New Haven/London: Yale University Press, 1972).

AUNE, DAVID. "The Apocalypse of John and Greco-Roman Magic," *New Testament Studies* 33:484–89 (1987).

———. "The Influence of Roman Imperial Court Ceremonial on the Apocalypse of John," *Biblical Research* 18:5–26 (1983).

BARR, DAVID L. "The Apocalypse of John as Oral Enactment," *Interpretation* 40:243–56 (1986).

BEASLEY-MURRAY, G. R. *The Book of Revelation.* NEW CENTURY BIBLE (London: Marshall, Morgan & Scott Publishers, and Grand Rapids: Wm. B. Eerdmans Publishing Co., 1974).

BECKWITH, I. T. *The Apocalypse of John* (New York: The Macmillan Co., 1919).

BOUSSET, WILHELM. *Die Offenbarung Johannis* (Göttingen: Vandenhoeck & Ruprecht, 1906).

BOWMAN, JOHN W. "Revelation, Book of," in George A. Buttrick et al., editors, *The Interpreter's Dictionary of the Bible* (Nashville: Abingdon Press, 1962).

BRUCE, F. F. "The Revelation of John," in G.C.D. Howley, editor, *A New Testament Commentary* (London: Pickering & Inglis, 1969).

CAIRD, G. B. See 1.d.

CHARLES, R. H. See 1.d.

CHARLESWORTH, JAMES H. *The Old Testament Pseudepigrapha,* 2 vols. (Garden City, N.Y.: Doubleday & Co., 1983, 1985).

COLLINS, ADELA YARBRO. "Revelation 18: Taunt Song or Dirge," in Jan Lambrecht, editor, *L'Apocalypse johannique et l'apocalyptique dans le Nouveau Testament* (Gembloux: J. Duculot and Louvain: Louvain University Press, 1980).

COLLINS, JOHN J. "Introduction: Towards the Morphology of a Genre,"in John J. Collins, editor, *Apocalypse: The Morphology of a Genre* (Missoula, Mont.: Scholars Press, 1979).

———. "Sibylline Oracles," in Charlesworth, editor, *The Old Testament Pseudepigrapha*, Vol. 1.

CRADDOCK, FRED B. "Preaching the Book of Revelation," *Interpretation* 40:270–82 (1986).

D'ARAGON, JEAN-LOUIS. "The Apocalypse," in Brown, Fitzmyer, Murphy, editors, *The Jerome Biblical Commentary* (Englewood Cliffs, N.J.: Prentice-Hall, 1968).

DODD, C. H. *The Interpretation of the Fourth Gospel* (Cambridge: Cambridge University Press, 1963).

ELLUL, JACQUES. *Apocalypse* (New York: Seabury Press, 1977).

FIORENZA, ELISABETH SCHÜSSLER. See 1.d.

FUNK, ROBERT. "Myth and Literal Non-Literal," *Parables and Presence* (Philadelphia: Fortress Press, 1982).

HALSELL, GRACE. *Prophecy and Politics: Militant Evangelists on the Road to Nuclear War* (Westport, Conn.: Lawrence Hill & Co., 1986).

HANSON, PAUL D. *The Dawn of Apocalyptic* (Philadelphia: Fortress Press, 1975).

HENNECKE, EDGAR, and WILHELM SCHNEEMELCHER. *New Testament Apocrypha*, 2 vols., R. McL. Wilson, editor and translator (Philadelphia: The Westminster Press, 1963–1964).

JAMES, M. R. *The Apocryphal New Testament* (Oxford: Clarendon Press, 1924).

LINDSEY, HAL. *There Is a New World Coming* (Ventura, Calif.: Vision House, 1973).

LOHMEYER, ERNST. *Die Offenbarung Johannes* (Tübingen: J.C.B. Mohr, 1926).

MINEAR, PAUL S. *New Testament Apocalyptic*, 1.b. *I Saw a New Earth*, 1.d.

MOUNCE, ROBERT H. *The Book of Revelation* (Grand Rapids: Wm. B. Eerdmans Publishing Co., 1977).

MÜLLER, ULRICH B. *Die Offenbarung des Johannes* (Gütersloh: Gütersloher Verlagshaus Gerd Mohn and Würzburg: Echter-Verlag, 1984).

NAPIER, B. D. *Song of the Vineyard* (New York: Harper & Row, 1962).

OGDEN, SCHUBERT. *The Point of Christology* (New York: Harper & Row, 1982).

RISSI, MATHIAS. See 1.c.

ROWLEY, H. H. *The Relevance of Apocalyptic* (New York: Association Press, 1963).

RUSSELL, D. S. See 1.b

SAGAN, CARL. *Cosmos* (New York: Random House, 1980).

SATAKE, AKIRA. *Die Gemeindeordnung in der Johannesapokalpse* (Neukirchen: Neukirchener-Vluyn, 1966).

SCHELL, JONATHAN. *The Fate of the Earth* (New York: Alfred A. Knopf, 1982).

SCHERRER, STEVEN J. "Signs and Wonders in the Imperial Cult," *Journal of Biblical Literature* 103:599–610 (1984).

STRINGFELLOW, WILLIAM. *An Ethic for Christians and Other Aliens in a Strange Land* (Waco, Tex.: Word Books, 1973).

SWEET, J.P.M. See l.d.

THOMPSON, LEONARD J. "The Mythic Unity of the Apocalypse," in Kent H. Richards, editor, *Society of Biblical Literature 1985 Seminar Papers* (Atlanta: Scholars Press, 1985).

TILLICH, PAUL. *Dynamics of Faith* (New York: Harper & Brothers, 1957).

WHEELWRIGHT, PHILIP. *The Burning Fountain* (Bloomington: Indiana University Press, 1968).